GRAND PRIX'S WINNING COLOURS

A VISUAL HISTORY
70 YEARS OF THE FORMULA 1 WORLD CHAMPIONSHIP

MICK HILL

The History Press

For my sister Josie and son Christian.

Flag colours on decade title pages refer to:

RED	Race stopped
RED and YELLOW	Warns drivers that track is slippery (usually from oil)
BLUE	Driver is about to be lapped/overtaken
YELLOW	Danger, no overtaking
GREEN	Danger passed, resume racing
BLACK	Accompanied by car number, driver is disqualified from race
BLACK ORANGE DISC	Accompanied by car number, driver has mechanical issue, return to pits
CHEQUERED FLAG	End of race

First published 2021. The History Press, 97 St George's Place, Cheltenham, Gloucestershire, GL50 3QB www.thehistorypress.co.uk
© Mick Hill, 2021

British Library Cataloguing in Publication Data. A catalogue record for this book is available from the British Library.
ISBN 978 0 7509 9615 0
Typesetting and origination by The History Press. Printed in Turkey by IMAK.

CONTENTS

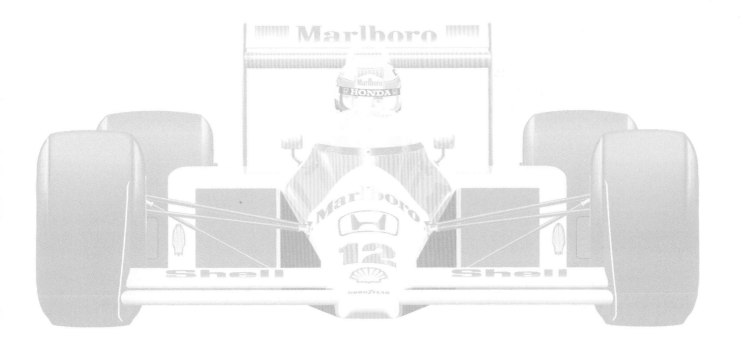

FOREWORD

It's hard to believe that seventy years have passed since the first World Championship race was held at Silverstone in 1950. There's no doubt that cars have come a long way since those early days. Today, the cars are much safer than they were then, with technology playing a greater part in not only the designs of the car but driver safety. The early cars were made from tubular steel frames then changed to the monocoque chassis of the '60s and later the carbon-fibre cars of today. As well as winning a Grand Prix in an alloy monocoque chassis back in 1976, I was fortunate to be the first driver to win a Grand Prix in an all carbon-fibre car and the first to walk away from a 140mph crash at Monza – something that I don't think I would have been able to do had the car not been made from carbon fibre, and proof that safety has come a long way. Sponsors have also played a major part in shaping the cars we see today, giving us many different colour schemes over the decades, from the famous black and gold JPS Lotuses and day-glow red and white McLarens of the '70s and '80s to the multicoloured cars of today.

It's with this in mind that Mick began his four-year journey to bring this book to life. Each of the cars has been painstakingly researched and drawn to represent the car as it raced in its heyday, with reference to the drivers, designers, tracks, record of pole positions, fastest laps, race wins and finishing positions. It's a complete insight to how the cars have looked and performed over the last seven decades. There are also a couple of cutaways giving an insight to what lies beneath the bodywork. One of the most important pieces of safety to a driver is his helmet; this is very personal to the driver, not only for his safety, but it is also seen as his calling card. There is a section in the book dedicated to the colour schemes of the winning drivers' helmets over the last seventy years, from the leather caps of the '50s to the carbon-fibre helmets of today. Sponsors too are always looking for other ways they can advertise their products and services. Not only was the car covered in the team's colours and logos, but many of the teams would hand out stickers on race weekends to the many fans. Reference to these can be found in the last section, which brings down the chequered flag on the first seven decades of Grand Prix's winning colours.

John Watson MBE
Racing commentator and five-time Grand Prix winner

INTRODUCTION

Formula 1 for me has been a kind of obsession, since going to the Race of Champions back in 1974 at Brands Hatch, standing in the pouring rain at Druids Bend with stars such as Niki Lauda, James Hunt, Graham Hill and Jacky Ickx thundering past. I knew then that I wanted to be associated with this sport.

Four months later at the British GP I was rubbing shoulders with most of the stars of the time, asking them to sign my illustrations of their cars. As a technical illustrator I have a fascination for machines and how they work and can think of nothing better than drawing these masterpieces of engineering. Over the years I've had the privilege of working with many of the teams and meeting many personalities, the most memorable being John Surtees, Keke Rosberg, Ayrton Senna, Michael Schumacher and Fernando Alonso. In the words of Bruce McLaren, it's not how long you're here but what you achieve while you're here. This book is based on his philosophy and my ambition of having a book with my name on the dust jacket. However, more importantly, it's about the best sport in the world.

It has taken over thirty years to happen and I would like to thank The History Press for allowing me to achieve this lifelong ambition. I have tried to steer away from a book packed with editorial mainly as I am an artist and not a writer, and there are plenty of such books out there. I wanted to make the book interesting, clear and precise. I hope you enjoy its contents as much as I have enjoyed researching and illustrating the winning cars and helmets that make up the first seventy years of the Formula 1 World Championships' winning colours.

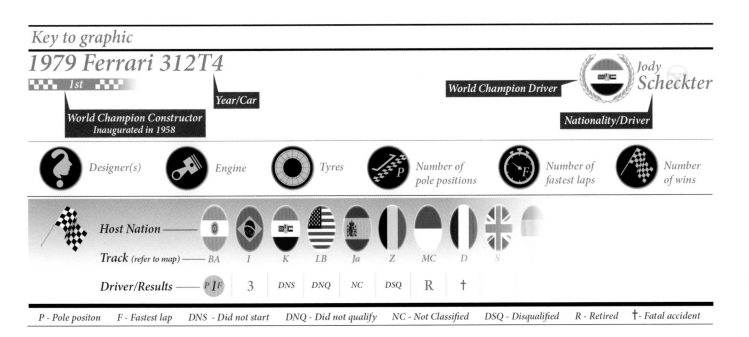

Key to graphic

1979 Ferrari 312T4

1st — **World Champion Constructor** Inaugurated in 1958 — **Year/Car** — **World Champion Driver** — **Nationality/Driver** — *Jody* **Scheckter**

Designer(s) | Engine | Tyres | Number of pole positions | Number of fastest laps | Number of wins

Host Nation

Track (refer to map) —— BA · I · K · LB · Ja · Z · MC · D · S

Driver/Results —— P 1 F · 3 · DNS · DNQ · NC · DSQ · R · †

P - Pole positon   F - Fastest lap   DNS - Did not start   DNQ - Did not qualify   NC - Not Classified   DSQ - Disqualified   R - Retired   † - Fatal accident

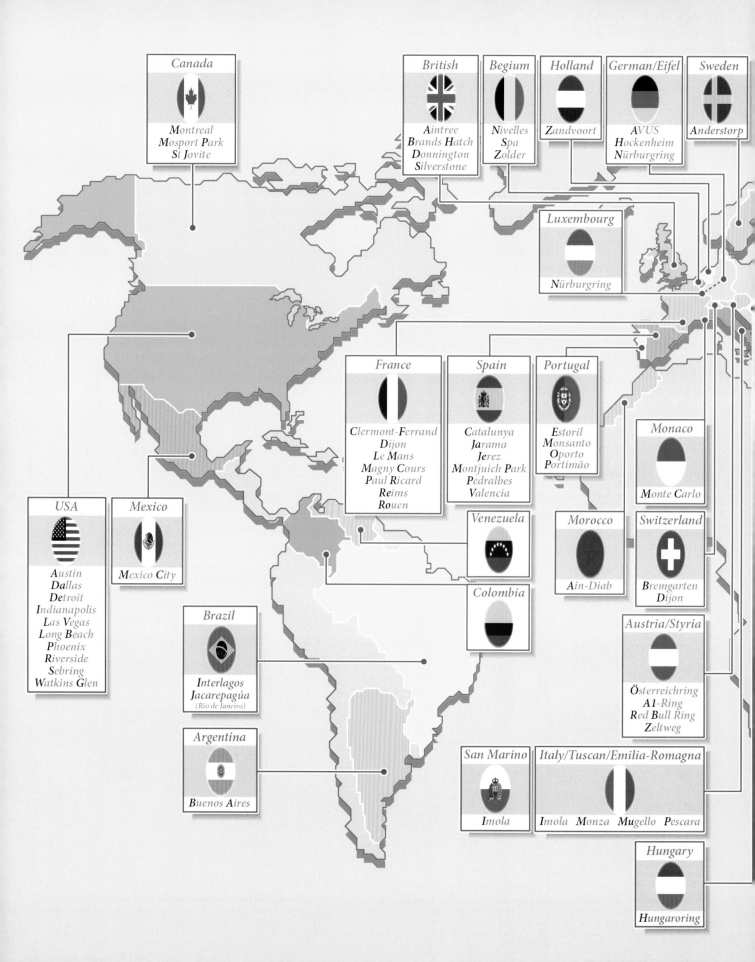

Canada
Montreal
Mosport Park
St Jovite

British
Aintree
Brands Hatch
Donnington
Silverstone

Begium
Nivelles
Spa
Zolder

Holland
Zandvoort

German/Eifel
AVUS
Hockenheim
Nürburgring

Sweden
Anderstorp

Luxembourg
Nürburgring

France
Clermont-Ferrand
Dijon
Le Mans
Magny Cours
Paul Ricard
Reims
Rouen

Spain
Catalunya
Jarama
Jerez
Montjuich Park
Pedralbes
Valencia

Portugal
Estoril
Monsanto
Oporto
Portimão

Monaco
Monte Carlo

USA
Austin
Dallas
Detroit
Indianapolis
Las Vegas
Long Beach
Phoenix
Riverside
Sebring
Watkins Glen

Mexico
Mexico City

Venezuela

Morocco
Ain-Diab

Switzerland
Bremgarten
Dijon

Colombia

Brazil
Interlagos
Jacarepagúa
(Rio de Janeiro)

Austria/Styria
Österreichring
A1-Ring
Red Bull Ring
Zeltweg

Argentina
Buenos Aires

San Marino
Imola

Italy/Tuscan/Emilia-Romagna
Imola   Monza   Mugello   Pescara

Hungary
Hungaroring

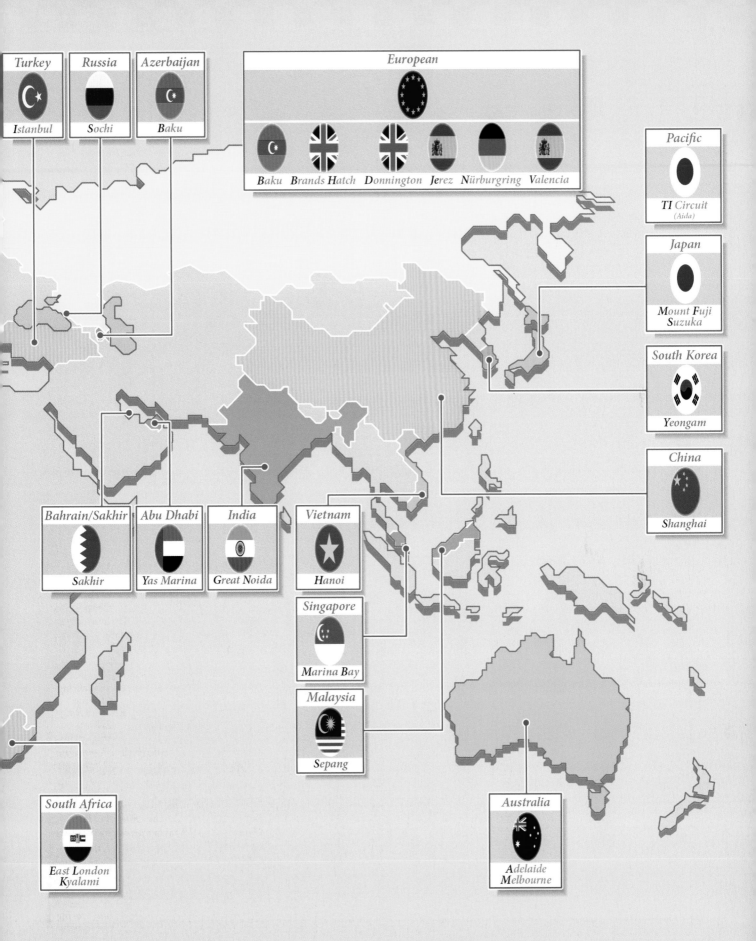

Turkey — Istanbul

Russia — Sochi

Azerbaijan — Baku

European — Baku, Brands Hatch, Donnington, Jerez, Nürburgring, Valencia

Pacific — TI Circuit (Aida)

Japan — Mount Fuji, Suzuka

South Korea — Yeongam

China — Shanghai

Bahrain/Sakhir — Sakhir

Abu Dhabi — Yas Marina

India — Great Noida

Vietnam — Hanoi

Singapore — Marina Bay

Malaysia — Sepang

South Africa — East London, Kyalami

Australia — Adelaide, Melbourne

1950-59

The Formula 1 Championship began in earnest in 1950 when F1 was put firmly on the map of great sports.

It was an era of bravery, sportsmanship and immense skill, with drivers battling it out wheel to wheel in front-engined cars with no seat belts or roll bars. They drove on the edge for every mile, inches from death on tracks with no safety barriers and a total lack of safety measures which, unfortunately, led to many fatalities.

Giuseppe Farina won the first championship race at the British Grand Prix held at Silverstone and was later crowned the inaugural World Champion. Juan Manuel Fangio would go on to win the World Championship driver's crown five times over the decade, a record that many thought would be a hard act to follow.

To gain superiority over their competitors, teams fought for technical advantages and at the end of the decade rear-engined cars started to make an entrance, which laid the foundation for the cars we see today.

1950-1959 Seasons race by race.

Year	Argentina	Monaco	Belgium	Morocco	Britain	Italy	Dutch	Portugal	France	Swiss	Germany	Spain	Italy	USA
1950		MC	S		S				Re	B			M	
1951			S		S				Re	B	N	P	M	
1952			S		S		Z		Ro	B	N		M	
1953	BA		S		S		Z		Re	B	N		M	
1954	BA		S		S				Re	B	N	P	M	
1955	BA	MC	S		A		Z						M	
1956	BA	MC	S		S				Re		N		M	
1957	BA	MC			A	P			Ro		N		M	
1958	BA	MC	S	A	S		Z	O	Re		N		M	
1959		MC			A		Z	M	Re		A		M	S

for track abbreviations refer to map on pages 6/7

1950 Alfa Romeo 158

Giuseppe **Farina** Juan Manuel **Fangio**

Gioacchino Colombo 1.5 s/c Alfa Romeo 158/50 8 Pirelli P 6 F 6 6

	S	MC	B	S	Re	M
Farina	P1F	R	1F	P4F	R	1
Fangio	R	P1F	PR	1	P1F	PRF *took Taruffi's car* R

1951 Alfa Romeo 159

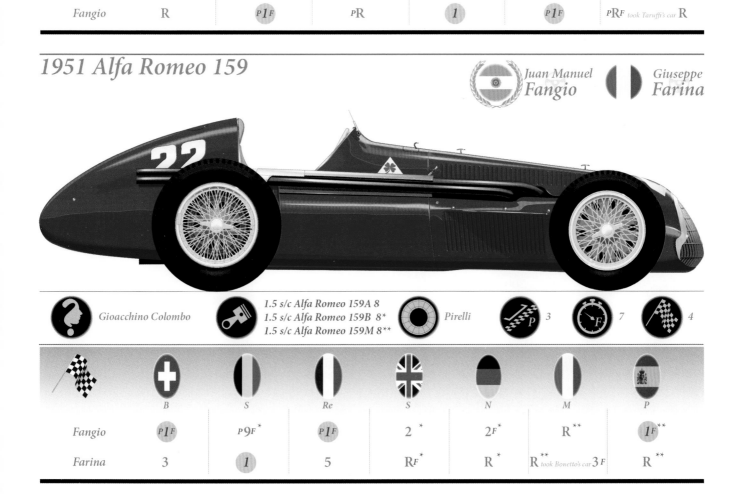

Juan Manuel **Fangio** Giuseppe **Farina**

Gioacchino Colombo 1.5 s/c Alfa Romeo 159A 8
1.5 s/c Alfa Romeo 159B 8*
1.5 s/c Alfa Romeo 159M 8** Pirelli P 3 F 7 4

	B	S	Re	S	N	M	P
Fangio	P1F	P9F*	P1F	2*	2F*	R**	1F**
Farina	3	1	5	RF*	R*	R** *took Bonetto's car* 3F	R**

1951 Ferrari 375

 Alberto **Ascari**  José Froilán **González**

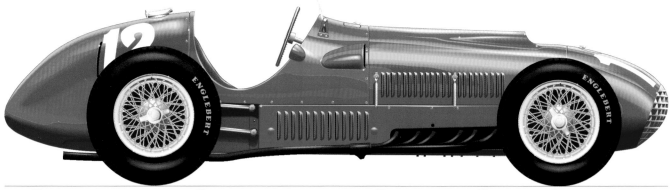

 Aurelio Lampredi   4.5 Ferrari V12   Pirelli Englebert*   P 3 F 0   3

	B	S	Re	S	N	M	P
Ascari	6	2	R* took González's car 2	R	P1	1	P4
González			2*	P1	3	2	2

1952 Ferrari 500 (F2)

 Alberto **Ascari**   Piero **Taruffi**

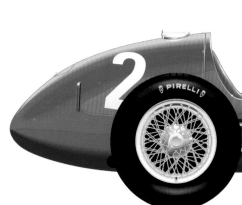 

 Aurelio Lampredi   2.0 Ferrari in-line 4   Pirelli Englebert*   P 5 F 7 7

	B	S	Ro	S	N	Z	M
Ascari		P1F	P1F	1F	P1F*	P1F	P1F
Taruffi	1F	R	3	2	4*		7

1953 Ferrari 500 (F2)

Alberto **Ascari** · Mike **Hawthorn** · Giuseppe **Farina**

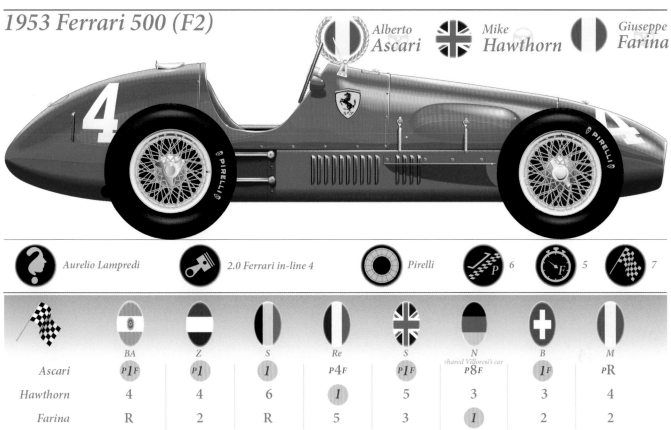

Aurelio Lampredi · 2.0 Ferrari in-line 4 · Pirelli · P 6 · F 5 · 7

	BA	Z	S	Re	S	N *shared Villoresi's car*	B	M
Ascari	P1F	P1	1	P4F	P1F	P8F	1F	PR
Hawthorn	4	4	6	1	5	3	3	4
Farina	R	2	R	5	3	1	2	2

1953 Maserati A6GCM 6

Juan Manuel **Fangio**

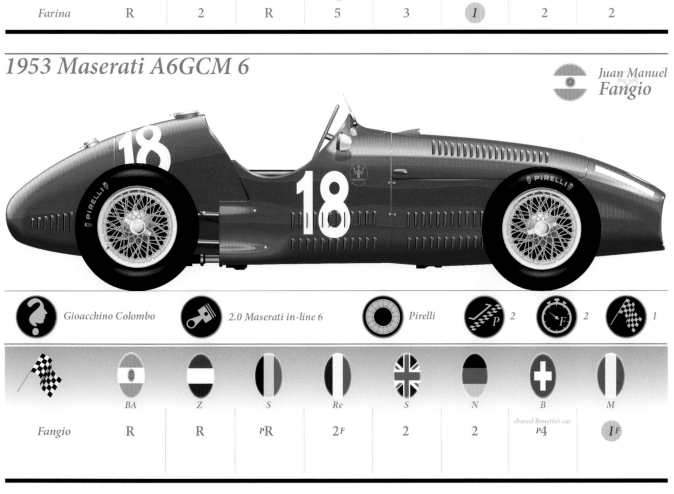

Gioacchino Colombo · 2.0 Maserati in-line 6 · Pirelli · P 2 · F 2 · 1

	BA	Z	S	Re	S	N	B *shared Bonetto's car*	M
Fangio	R	R	PR	2F	2	2	P4	1F

1954 Maserati 250F

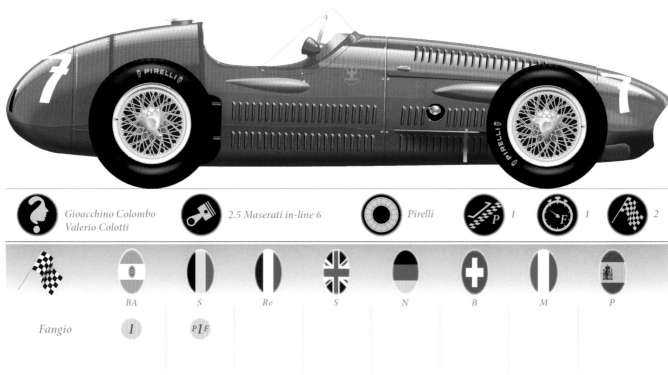

? Gioacchino Colombo Valerio Colotti	2.5 Maserati in-line 6	Pirelli	P 1	F 1	⚑ 2

	BA	S	Re	S	N	B	M	P
Fangio	1	P 1 F						

1954 Mercedes-Benz W196 Streamliner

? Rudolf Uhlenhaut	2.5 Mercedes-Benz W196 8	Continental	P 3	F 1	⚑ 2

	BA	S	Re	S	N	B	M	P
Fangio			P 1	P 4 F			P 1	

1954 Mercedes-Benz W196

 Rudolf Uhlenhaut	2.5 Mercedes-Benz W196 8	Continental	P 1	F 1	2

	BA	S	Re	S	N	B	M	P
Fangio					P1	1F		3

1954 Ferrari 625

José Froilán *González*

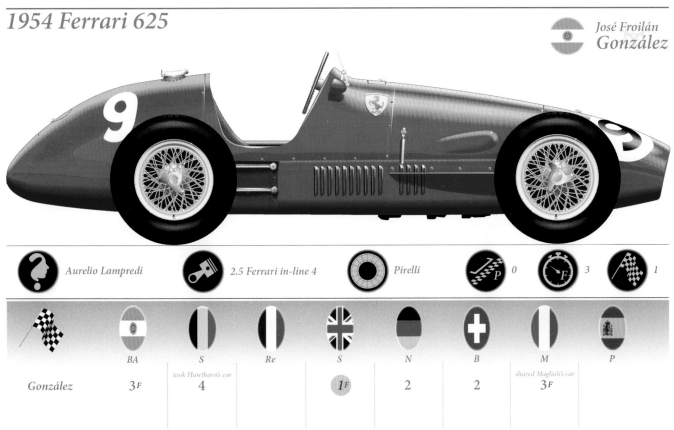

Aurelio Lampredi	2.5 Ferrari in-line 4	Pirelli	P 0	F 3	1

	BA	S	Re	S	N	B	M	P
González	3F	took Hawthorn's car 4		1F	2	2	shared Maglioli's car 3F	

1954 Ferrari 553

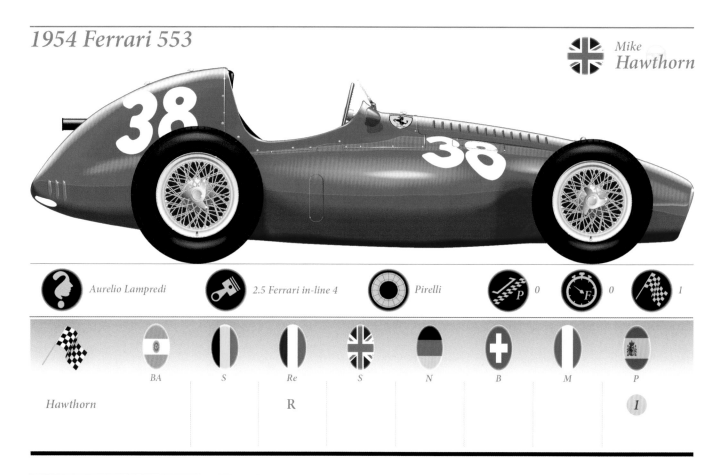

Mike **Hawthorn**

	Aurelio Lampredi		2.5 Ferrari in-line 4		Pirelli	P	0	F	0		1

	BA	S	Re	S	N	B	M	P
Hawthorn			R					1

1955 Mercedes-Benz W196

Juan Manuel **Fangio**   Stirling **Moss**

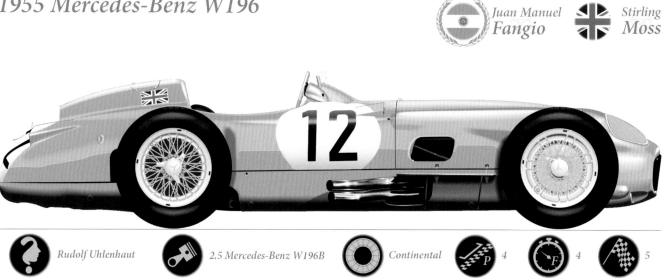

	Rudolf Uhlenhaut		2.5 Mercedes-Benz W196B		Continental	P	4	F	4		5

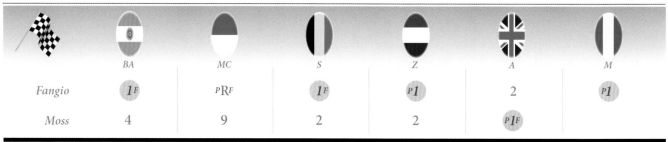

	BA	MC	S	Z	A	M
Fangio	1F	PRF	1F	P1	2	P1
Moss	4	9	2	2	P1F	

1955 Mercedes-Benz W196 Streamliner

Stirling
Moss

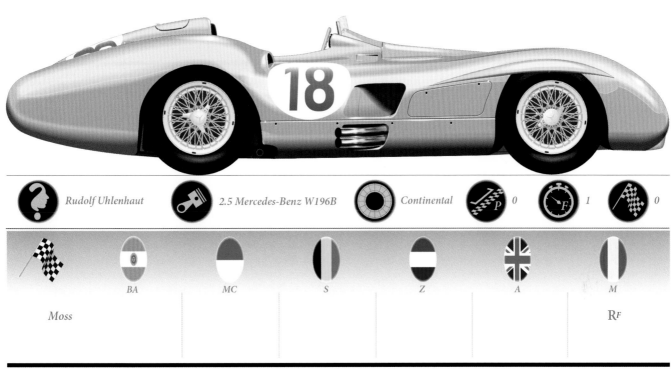

Rudolf Uhlenhaut	2.5 Mercedes-Benz W196B	Continental	P 0	F 1	0

	BA	MC	S	Z	A	M
Moss						R*F*

1955 Ferrari 625

Maurice
Trintignant

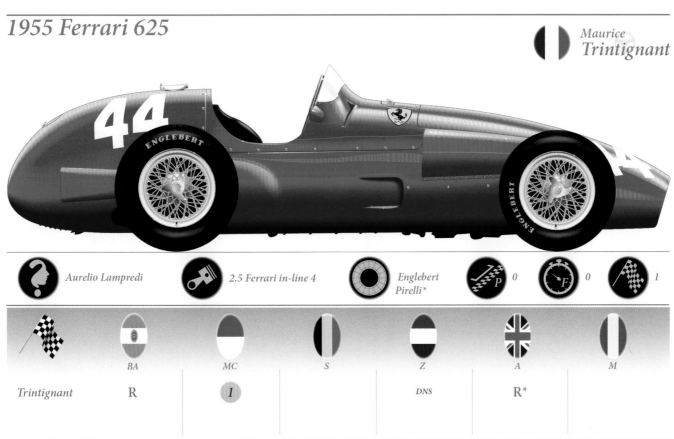

Aurelio Lampredi	2.5 Ferrari in-line 4	Englebert Pirelli*	P 0	F 0	1

	BA	MC	S	Z	A	M
Trintignant	R	*1*		DNS	R*	

1956 Lancia-Ferrari D50

Juan Manuel **Fangio** — Peter **Collins** — Luigi **Musso**

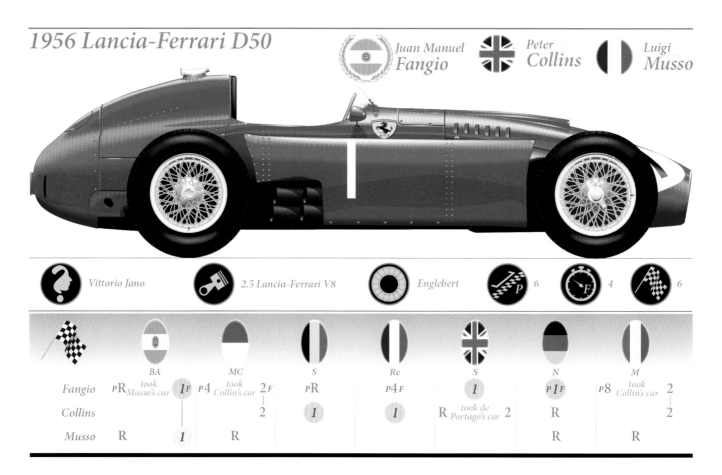

Vittorio Jano | 2.5 Lancia-Ferrari V8 | Englebert | P 6 | F 4 | 🏁 6

	BA	MC	S	Re	S	N	M
Fangio	PR *took Musso's car* 1F	P4 *took Collin's car* 2F	PR	P4F	1	P1F	P8 *took Collin's car* 2
Collins		2	1	1	R *took de Portago's car* 2	R	2
Musso	R 1	R				R	R

1956 Maserati 250F

Stirling **Moss**

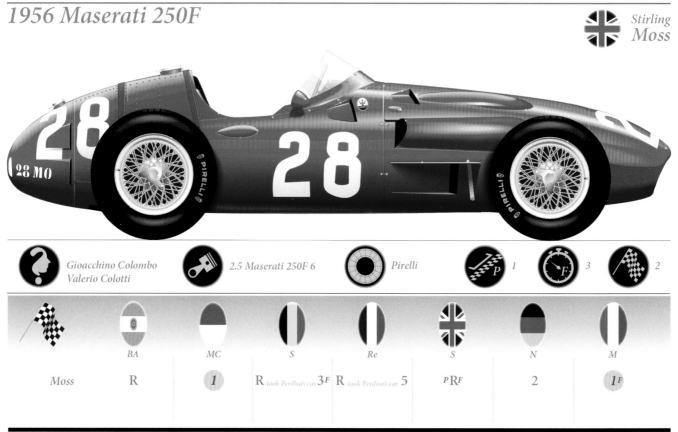

Gioacchino Colombo / Valerio Colotti | 2.5 Maserati 250F 6 | Pirelli | P 1 | F 3 | 🏁 2

	BA	MC	S	Re	S	N	M
Moss	R	1	R *took Perdisa's car* 3F	R *took Perdisa's car* 5	PRF	2	1F

1957 Maserati 250F

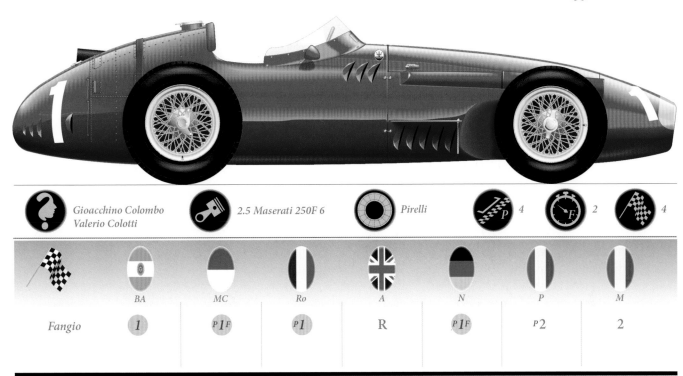

	Gioacchino Colombo Valerio Colotti		2.5 Maserati 250F 6		Pirelli		P 4		F 2		4

	BA	MC	Ro	A	N	P	M
Fangio	1	P 1 F	P 1	R	P 1 F	P 2	2

1957 Vanwall

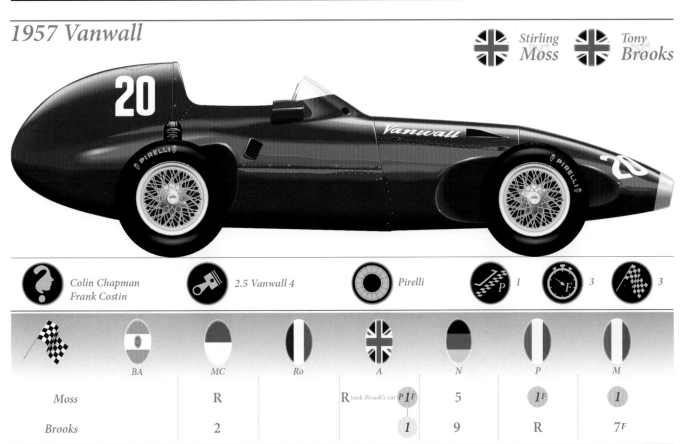

	Colin Chapman Frank Costin		2.5 Vanwall 4		Pirelli		P 1		F 3		3

	BA	MC	Ro	A	N	P	M
Moss		R		R *took Brook's car* P 1 F	5	1 F	1
Brooks		2		1	9	R	7 F

1958 Cooper T43

 Owen Maddock   1.9 Climax 4   Continental   P 0   F 0   1

	BA	MC	Z	S	Re	S	N	O	M	A
Moss	1									

1958 Cooper T45

 Maurice *Trintignant*

 Owen Maddock   2.0 Climax 4
2.2 Climax 4*   Dunlop   P 0   F 0   1

	BA	MC	Z	S	Re	S	N	O	M	A
Trintignant		1	9				3*		R*	R*

1958 Vanwall

Stirling **Moss** Tony **Brooks**

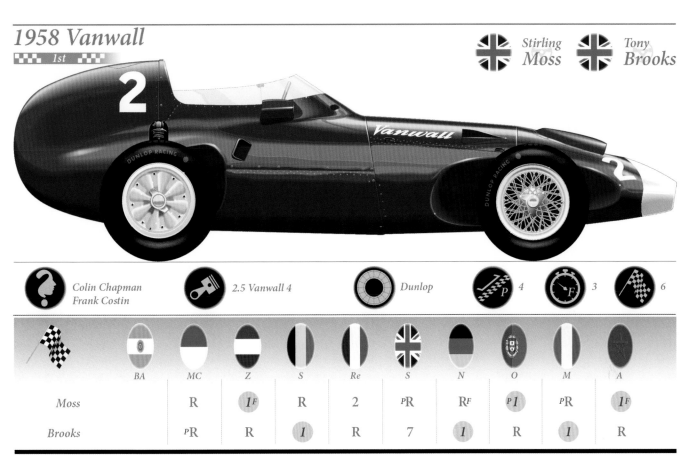

Colin Chapman
Frank Costin | 2.5 Vanwall 4 | Dunlop | P 4 | F 3 | 6

	BA	MC	Z	S	Re	S	N	O	M	A
Moss	R	1F	R	2	PR	RF	P1	PR	1F
Brooks	PR	R	1	R	7	1	R	1	R

1958 Ferrari 246

Mike **Hawthorn** Peter **Collins**

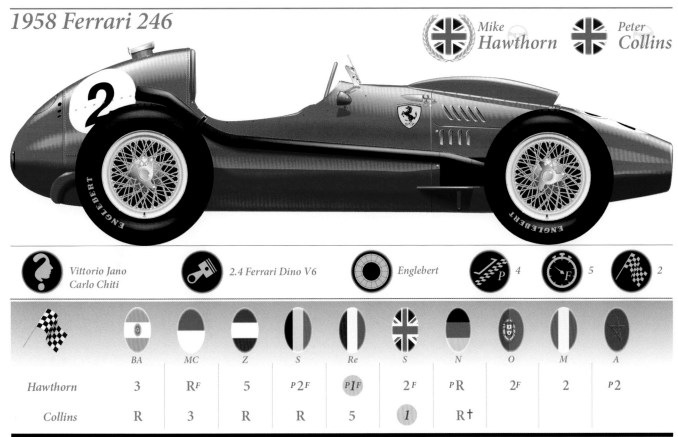

Vittorio Jano
Carlo Chiti | 2.4 Ferrari Dino V6 | Englebert | P 4 | F 5 | 2

	BA	MC	Z	S	Re	S	N	O	M	A
Hawthorn	3	RF	5	P2F	P1F	2F	PR	2F	2	P2
Collins	R	3	R	R	5	1	R†

1959 Cooper T51

 **1st**

 Jack **Brabham**  Stirling **Moss**  Bruce **McLaren**

 Owen Maddock   2.5 Climax 4 / 2.2 Climax 4*   Dunlop   P 5   F 4   5

	MC	Z	Re	A	A	M	M	S
Brabham	1 F	2	3	P 1	R	R	3	4
Moss	P R	R F			R	P 1 F	P 1	P R
McLaren			5 *	3 F	R	R	R	1

1959 BRM P25

 Jo **Bonnier**

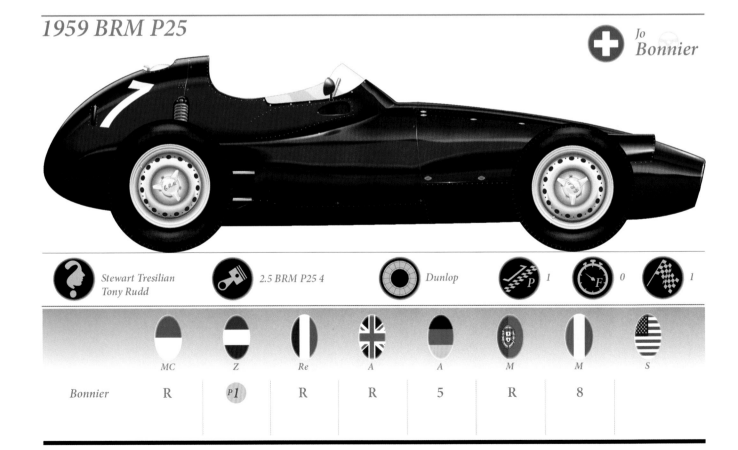

Stewart Tresilian / Tony Rudd 2.5 BRM P25 4 Dunlop P 1 F 0 1

	MC	Z	Re	A	A	M	M	S
Bonnier	R	P 1	R	R	5	R	8	

1959 Ferrari 256

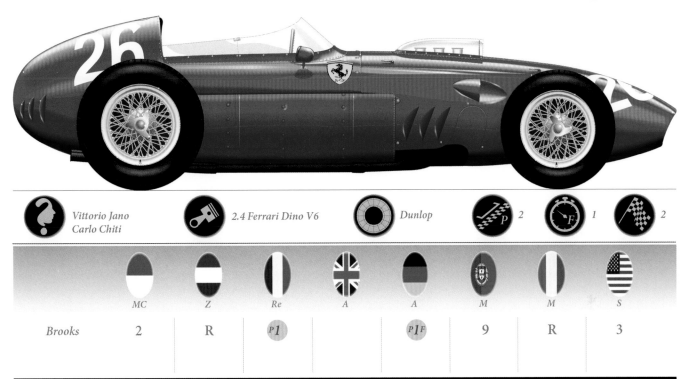

	Vittorio Jano Carlo Chiti		2.4 Ferrari Dino V6		Dunlop		P 2		F 1		2

		MC	Z	Re	A	A	M	M	S
Brooks		2	R	P1		P1F	9	R	3

1960-69

With F1's inherent dangers, drivers of the '60s were still losing their lives. Wolfgang von Trips died when his Ferrari crashed into the Monza fencing, also killing fifteen spectators. Lotus boss Colin Chapman brought us the monocoque chassis, more rigid and lighter than the conventional tubular space-frame chassis, aerodynamic wings and commercial sponsorship with his Lotuses being renamed Gold Leaf Team Lotus after Gold Leaf Cigarettes. He would also be responsible for even more F1 innovations over the years.

New teams started to appear including Matra, McLaren and Brabham, with Jack Brabham becoming the first man to win the World Championship in a car bearing his own name. The Cosworth DFV V8 made its debut in 1967, winning first time out in the hands of Jim Clark and his Lotus 49. The decade saw Clark's rise to fame and then his tragic death while taking part in an F2 race at Hockenheim. Other drivers such as Graham Hill, Jackie Stewart and John Surtees were becoming the British sporting heroes of the era.

1960-1969 Seasons race by race.

	Argentina	Italy	Mexico	Belgium	Monaco	Britain	Portugal	Canada	South Africa	Dutch	Spain	France	Germany	USA
1960	BA	M		S	MC	S	O			Z		Re	R	
1961		M		S	MC	A				Z		Re	WG	N
1962		M		S	MC	A		EL		Z		Ro	WG	N
1963		M	MC	S	MC	S		EL		Z		Re	WG	N
1964		M	Z	MC	S	MC	BH				Z		Ro	WG	N
1965		M		MC	S	MC	S		EL		Z		CF	WG	N
1966		M		MC	S	MC	BH				Z		Re	WG	N
1967		M		MC	S	MC	S		MP	K	Z		LM	WG	N
1968		M		MC	S	MC	BH		SJ	K	Z	Ja	Ro	WG	N
1969		M		MC		MC	S		MP	K	Z	MP	CF	WG	N

for track abbreviations refer to map on pages 6/7

1960 Cooper T51

 Bruce **McLaren**

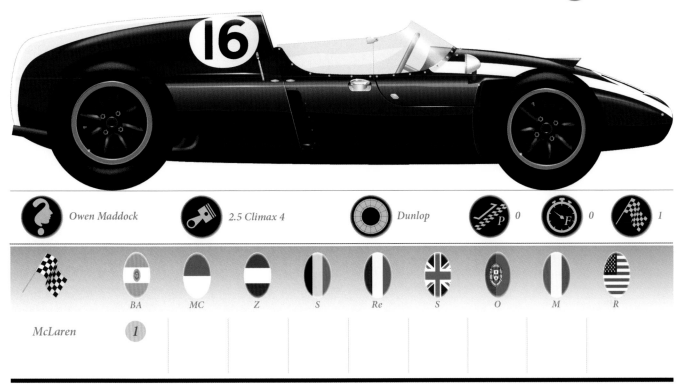

				P	0	F	0		1
Owen Maddock	2.5 Climax 4	Dunlop							

	BA	MC	Z	S	Re	S	O	M	R
McLaren	1								

1960 Lotus 18

 Stirling **Moss**

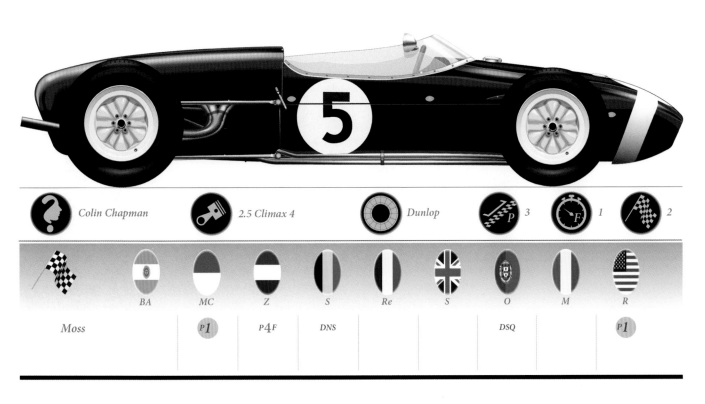

				P	3	F	1		2
Colin Chapman	2.5 Climax 4	Dunlop							

	BA	MC	Z	S	Re	S	O	M	R
Moss	P1	P4F	DNS				DSQ		P1

1960 Cooper T53

Jack
Brabham

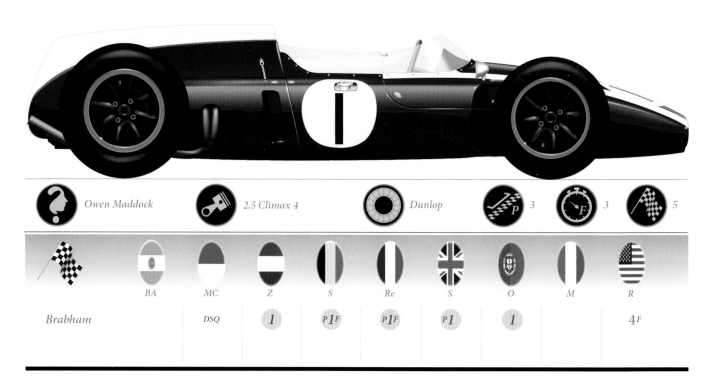

| ❓ Owen Maddock | ⚙️ 2.5 Climax 4 | ⊙ Dunlop | 🏁 P 3 | ⏱ F 3 | 🏁 5 |

🏁	BA	MC	Z	S	Re	S	O	M	R
Brabham		DSQ	*1*	P*1*F	P*1*F	P*1*	*1*		4F

1960 Ferrari 246

Phil
Hill

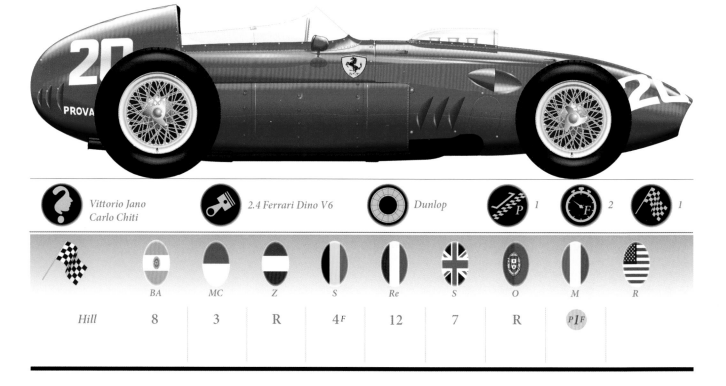

| ❓ Vittorio Jano Carlo Chiti | ⚙️ 2.4 Ferrari Dino V6 | ⊙ Dunlop | 🏁 P 1 | ⏱ F 2 | 🏁 1 |

🏁	BA	MC	Z	S	Re	S	O	M	R
Hill	8	3	R	4F	12	7	R	P*1*F	

1961 Lotus 18

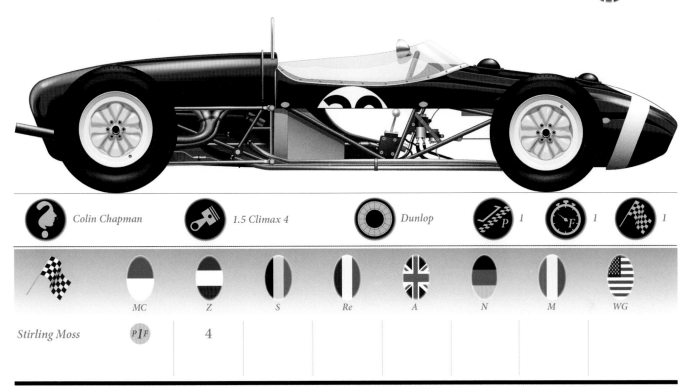

 Colin Chapman	1.5 Climax 4	Dunlop	P 1	F 1	1

	MC	Z	S	Re	A	N	M	WG
Stirling Moss	P*1*F	4						

1961 Ferrari 156

1st

Phil **Hill** — Wolfgang von **Trips** — Giancarlo **Baghetti**

Carlo Chiti	1.5 Ferrari Dino V6	Dunlop	P 6	F 3	5

	MC	Z	S	Re	A	N	M	WG
Hill	3	P2	P1	P9F	P2	P3F	1	
von Trips	R	1	2	R	1	2	PR†	
Baghetti			1	R			RF	

1961 Lotus 18/21

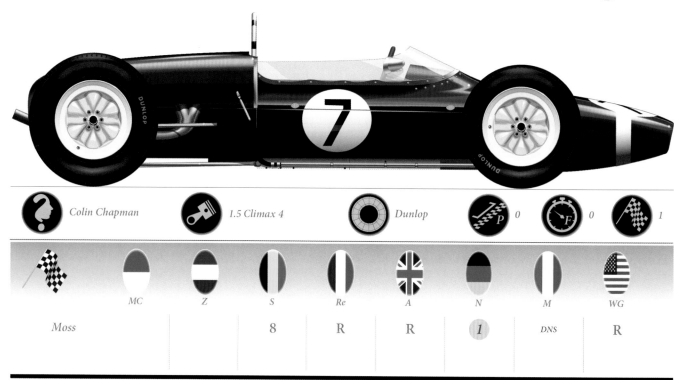

	Colin Chapman		1.5 Climax 4		Dunlop		P	0		F	0			1

	MC	Z	S	Re	A	N	M	WG
Moss			8	R	R	1	DNS	R

1961 Lotus 21

	Colin Chapman		1.5 Climax 4		Dunlop		P	0		F	0			1

	MC	Z	S	Re	A	N	M	WG
Ireland	DNS		R	4	10	R	DNS	1

1962 BRM P57

Graham
Hill

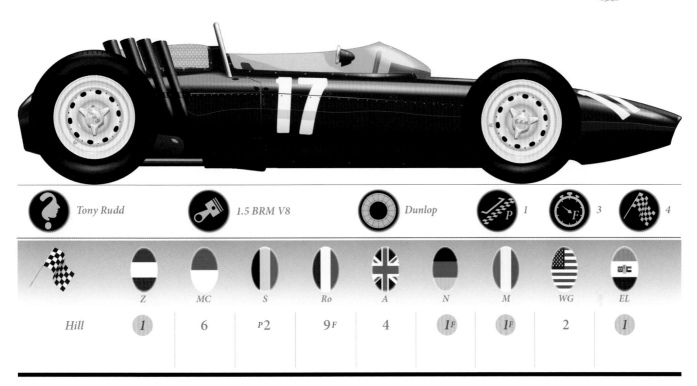

	Tony Rudd		1.5 BRM V8		Dunlop		P	1		F	3			4

		Z	MC	S	Ro	A	N	M	WG	EL
Hill		1	6	P2	9F	4	1F	1F	2	1

1962 Cooper T60

Bruce
McLaren

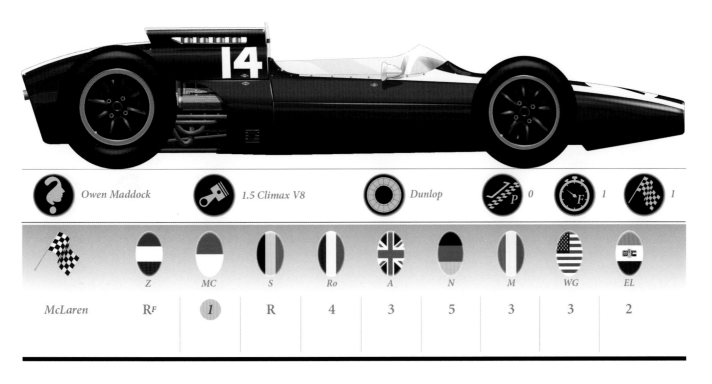

	Owen Maddock		1.5 Climax V8		Dunlop		P	0		F	1			1

		Z	MC	S	Ro	A	N	M	WG	EL
McLaren		RF	1	R	4	3	5	3	3	2

1962 Lotus 25

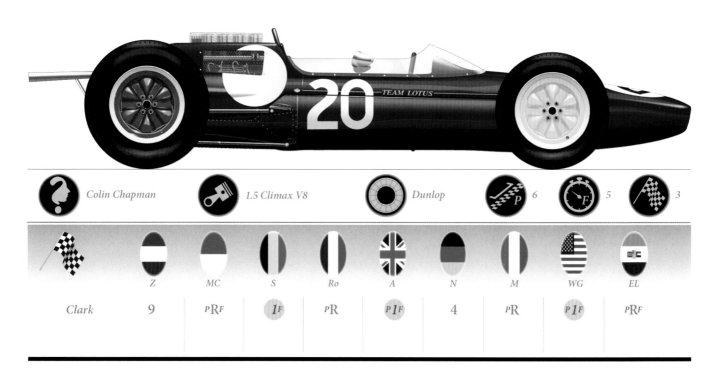

	Colin Chapman		1.5 Climax V8		Dunlop		P 6		F 5		3

	Z	MC	S	Ro	A	N	M	WG	EL
Clark	9	P R F	1 F	P R	P 1 F	4	P R	P 1 F	P R F

1962 Porsche 804

Dan
Gurney

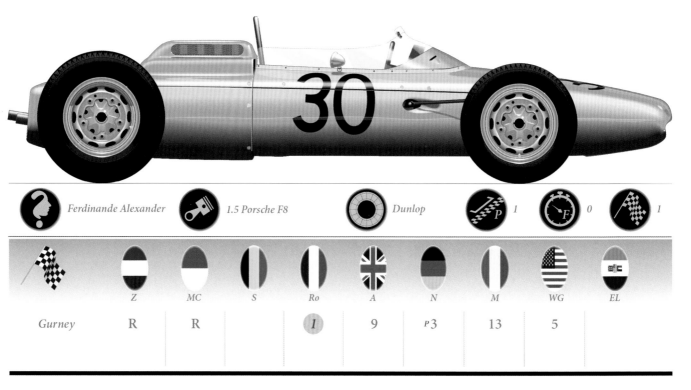

	Ferdinande Alexander		1.5 Porsche F8		Dunlop		P 1		F 0		1

	Z	MC	S	Ro	A	N	M	WG	EL
Gurney	R	R		1	9	P 3	13	5	

1963 BRM P57

Graham *Hill*

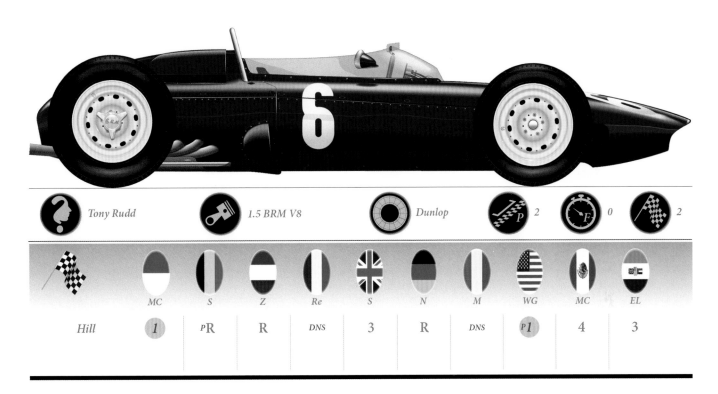

Tony Rudd	1.5 BRM V8	Dunlop	P 2	F 0	2

	MC	S	Z	Re	S	N	M	WG	MC	EL
Hill	1	PR	R	DNS	3	R	DNS	P1	4	3

1963 Lotus 25

 1st

Jim *Clark*

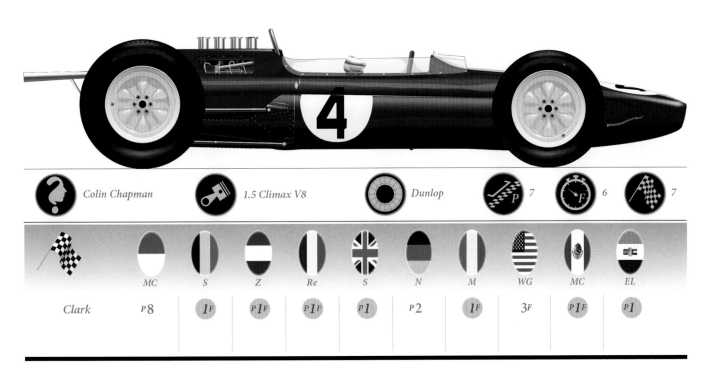

Colin Chapman	1.5 Climax V8	Dunlop	P 7	F 6	7

	MC	S	Z	Re	S	N	M	WG	MC	EL
Clark	P8	1F	P1F	P1F	P1	P2	1F	3F	P1F	P1

1963 Ferrari 156 Aero

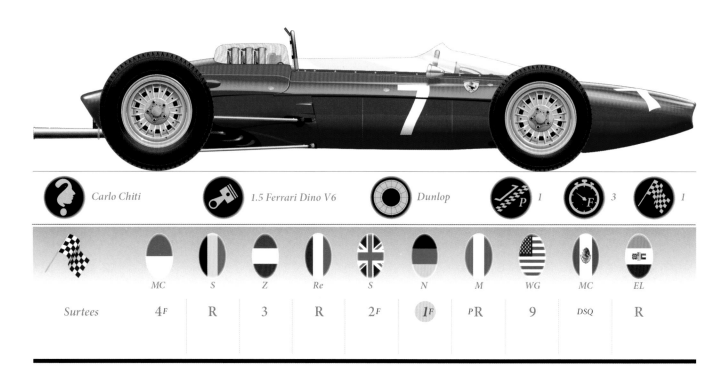

	Carlo Chiti		1.5 Ferrari Dino V6		Dunlop		P 1		F 3		1

	MC	S	Z	Re	S	N	M	WG	MC	EL
Surtees	4 F	R	3	R	2 F	1 F	P R	9	DSQ	R

1964 BRM P261

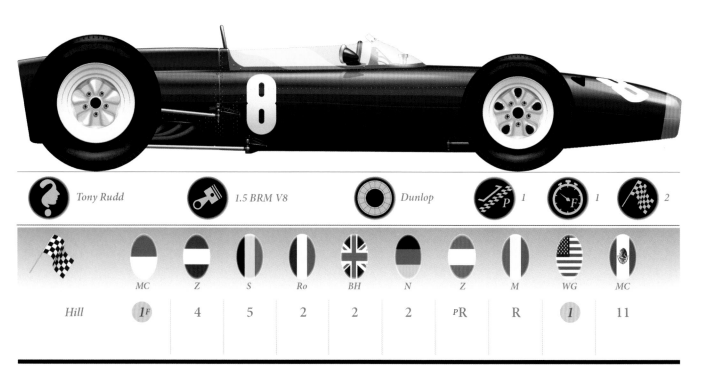

	Tony Rudd		1.5 BRM V8		Dunlop		P 1		F 1		2

	MC	Z	S	Ro	BH	N	Z	M	WG	MC
Hill	1 F	4	5	2	2	2	P R	R	1	11

1964 Lotus 25

Jim
Clark

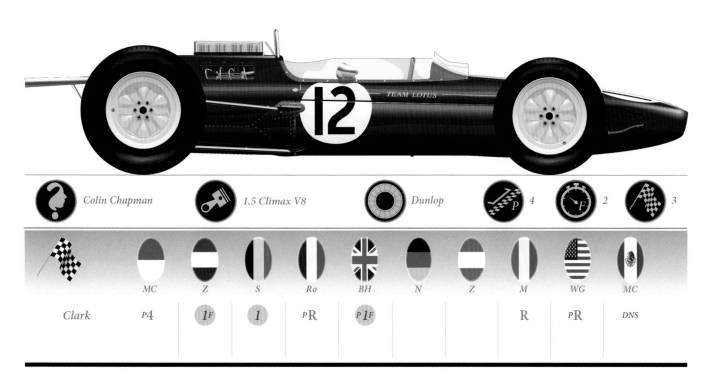

	Colin Chapman		1.5 Climax V8		Dunlop		P 4		F 2		3

	MC	Z	S	Ro	BH	N	Z	M	WG	MC
Clark	P4	1F	1	PR	P1F				R	PR	DNS

1964 Brabham BT7

Dan
Gurney

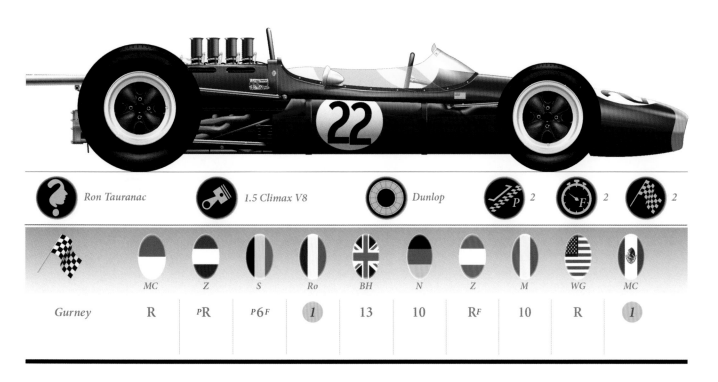

	Ron Tauranac		1.5 Climax V8		Dunlop		P 2		F 2		2

	MC	Z	S	Ro	BH	N	Z	M	WG	MC
Gurney	R	PR	P6F	1	13	10	RF	10	R	1

1964 Ferrari 158 Aero

1st

John
Surtees

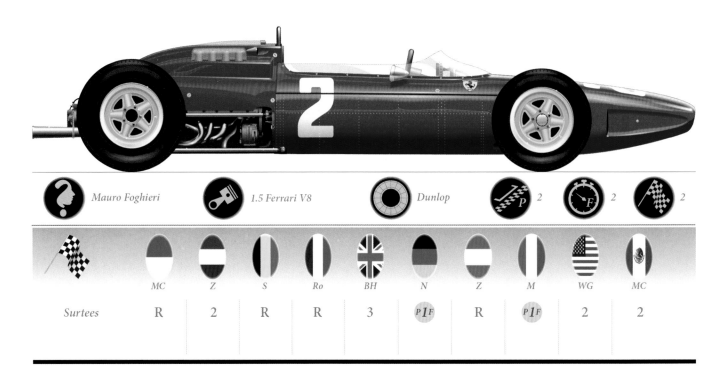

	Mauro Foghieri		1.5 Ferrari V8		Dunlop		P 2		F 2		2

	MC	Z	S	Ro	BH	N	Z	M	WG	MC
Surtees	R	2	R	R	3	P1F	R	P1F	2	2

1964 Ferrari 156 Aero

Lorenzo
Bandini

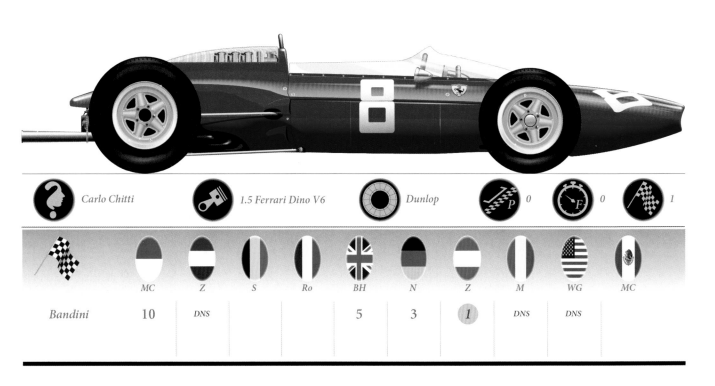

	Carlo Chitti		1.5 Ferrari Dino V6		Dunlop		P 0		F 0		1

	MC	Z	S	Ro	BH	N	Z	M	WG	MC
Bandini	10	DNS			5	3	1	DNS	DNS	

1965 Lotus 33

Jim
Clark

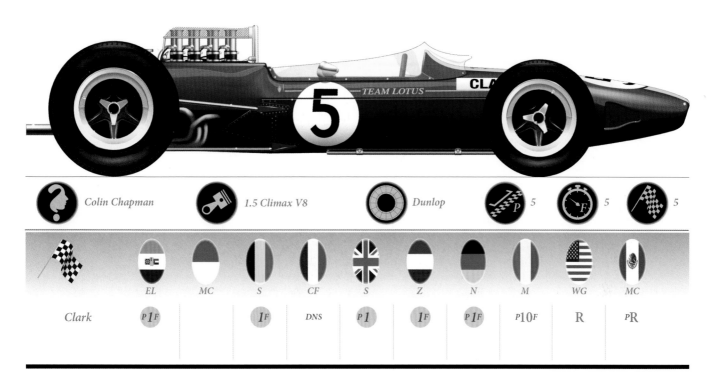

Colin Chapman	1.5 Climax V8	Dunlop	*P* 5	*F* 5	5

	EL	MC	S	CF	S	Z	N	M	WG	MC
Clark	*P* 1*F*		1*F*	DNS	*P* 1	1*F*	*P* 1*F*	*P* 10*F*	R	*P* R

1965 Lotus 25

Jim
Clark

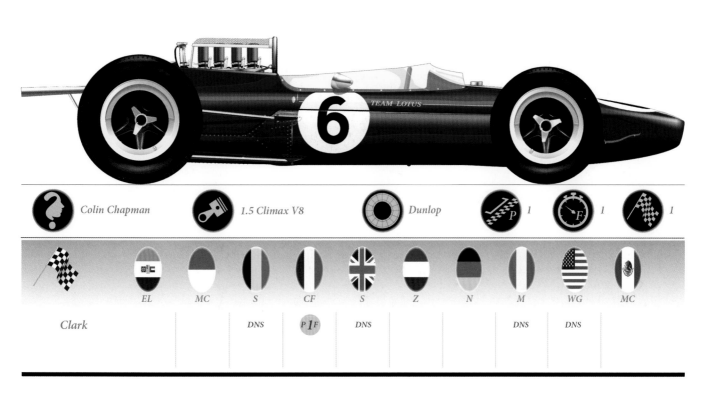

Colin Chapman	1.5 Climax V8	Dunlop	*P* 1	*F* 1	1

	EL	MC	S	CF	S	Z	N	M	WG	MC
Clark			DNS	*P* 1*F*	DNS			DNS	DNS	

1965 BRM P261

 Graham **Hill**  Jackie **Stewart**

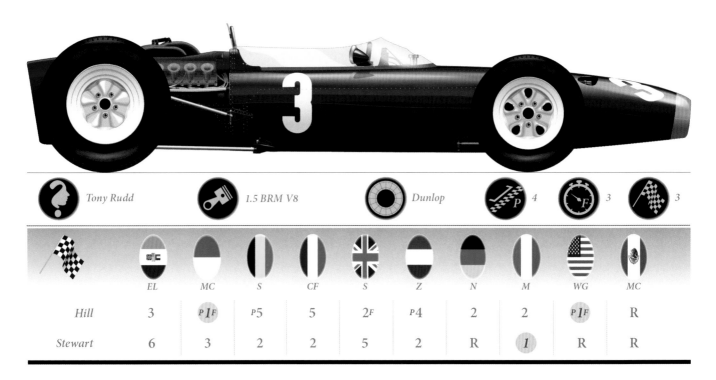

	Tony Rudd		1.5 BRM V8		Dunlop	P	4	F	3	🏁	3

🏁	EL	MC	S	CF	S	Z	N	M	WG	MC
Hill	3	P1F	P5	5	2F	P4	2	2	P1F	R
Stewart	6	3	2	2	5	2	R	1	R	R

1965 Honda RA272

 Richie **Ginther**

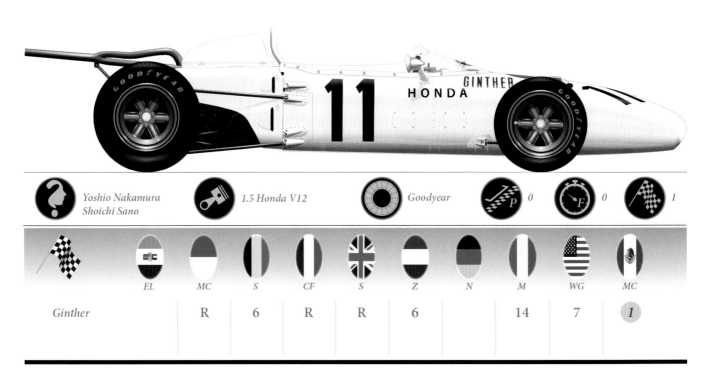

	Yoshio Nakamura Shoichi Sano		1.5 Honda V12		Goodyear	P	0	F	0	🏁	1

🏁	EL	MC	S	CF	S	Z	N	M	WG	MC
Ginther		R	6	R	R	6		14	7	1

1966 BRM P261

Jackie
Stewart

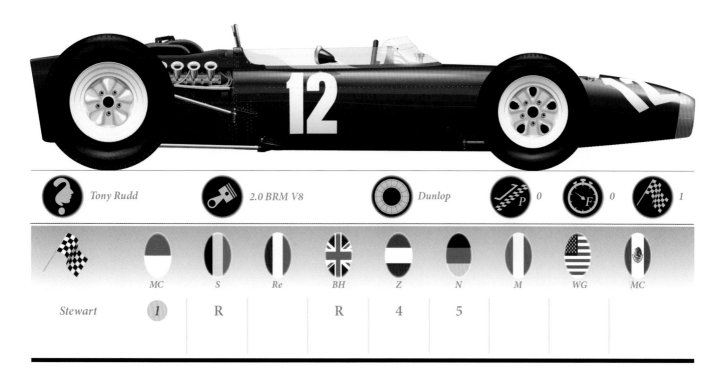

? Tony Rudd	2.0 BRM V8	Dunlop	P 0	F 0	🏁 1

	MC	S	Re	BH	Z	N	M	WG	MC
Stewart	*1*	R		R	4	5			

1966 Ferrari 312/66

John **Surtees**   *Ludovici* **Scarfiotti**

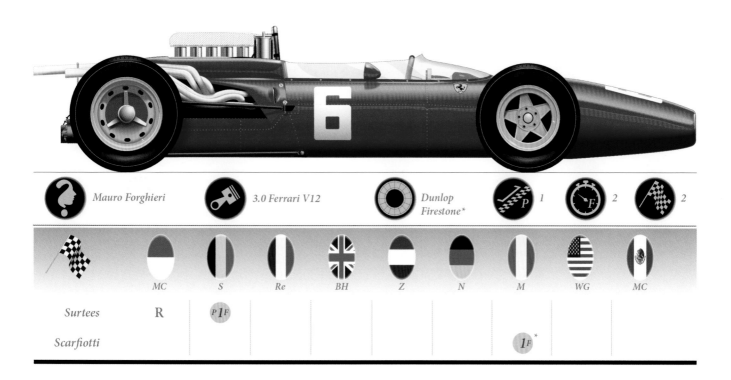

? Mauro Forghieri	3.0 Ferrari V12	Dunlop Firestone*	P 1	F 2	🏁 2

	MC	S	Re	BH	Z	N	M	WG	MC
Surtees	R	P *1* F							
Scarfiotti							*1* F *		

1966 Brabham BT19

Jack **Brabham**

1st

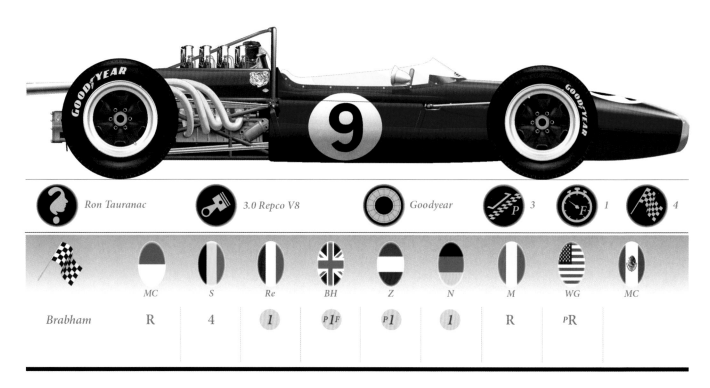

| | Ron Tauranac | | 3.0 Repco V8 | | Goodyear | P | 3 | F | 1 | | 4 |

Brabham	MC	S	Re	BH	Z	N	M	WG	MC
	R	4	*1*	P*1*F	P*1*	*1*	R	PR	

1966 Lotus 43 BRM

Jim **Clark**

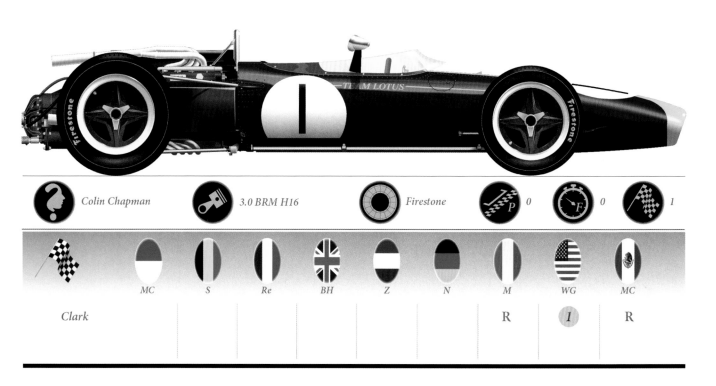

| | Colin Chapman | | 3.0 BRM H16 | | Firestone | P | 0 | F | 0 | | 1 |

Clark	MC	S	Re	BH	Z	N	M	WG	MC
							R	*1*	R

1966 Cooper T81

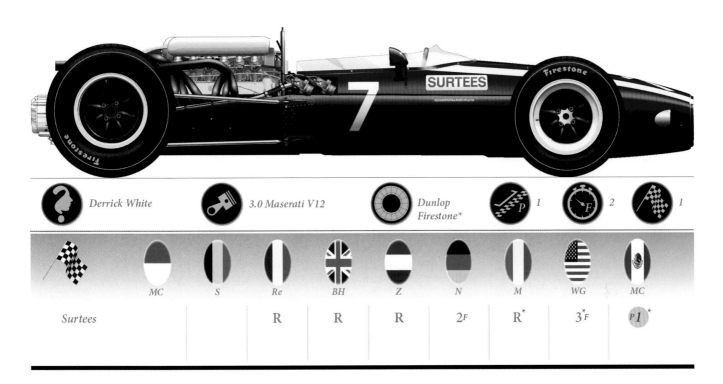

John *Surtees*

	Derrick White		3.0 Maserati V12		Dunlop Firestone*		P 1		F 2		1

		MC	S	Re	BH	Z	N	M	WG	MC
Surtees			R	R	R	2_F	R^*	3^*_F	$P1^*$

1967 Cooper T81

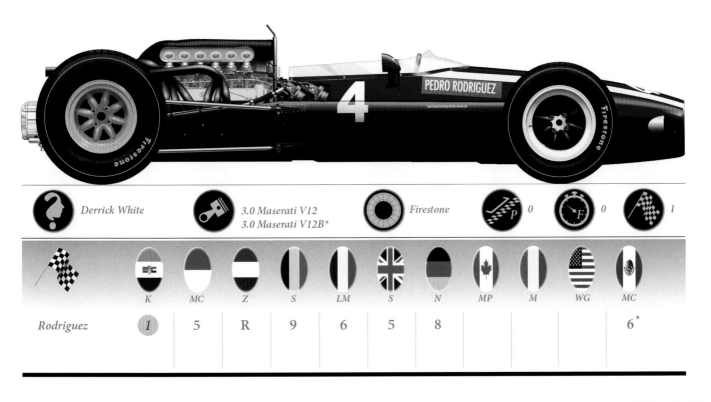

Pedro *Rodriguez*

	Derrick White		3.0 Maserati V12 3.0 Maserati V12B*		Firestone		P 0		F 0		1

		K	MC	Z	S	LM	S	N	MP	M	WG	MC
Rodriguez		*1*	5	R	9	6	5	8				6^*

1967 Brabham BT20

 Denny *Hulme*  Jack *Brabham*

	Ron Tauranac		3.0 Repco V8		Goodyear		P 1		F 1		1

	K	MC	Z	S	LM	S	N	MP	M	WG	MC
Hulme	4 F	1	3								
Brabham	P 6										

1967 Lotus 49

 Jim *Clark*

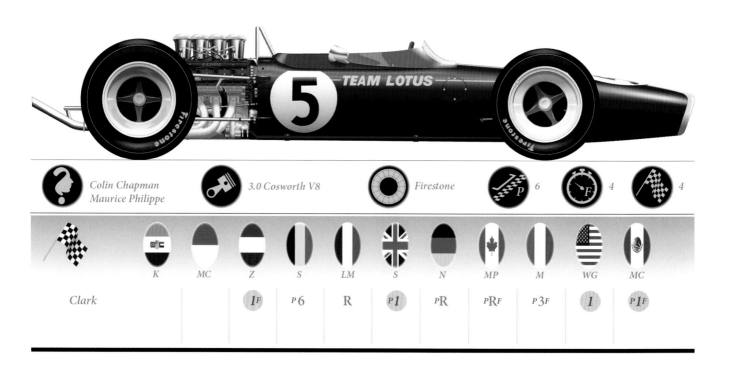

	Colin Chapman Maurice Philippe		3.0 Cosworth V8		Firestone		P 6		F 4		4

	K	MC	Z	S	LM	S	N	MP	M	WG	MC
Clark		1 F	P 6	R	P 1	P R	P R F	P 3 F	1	P 1 F	

1967 Eagle T1G

 Dan **Gurney**

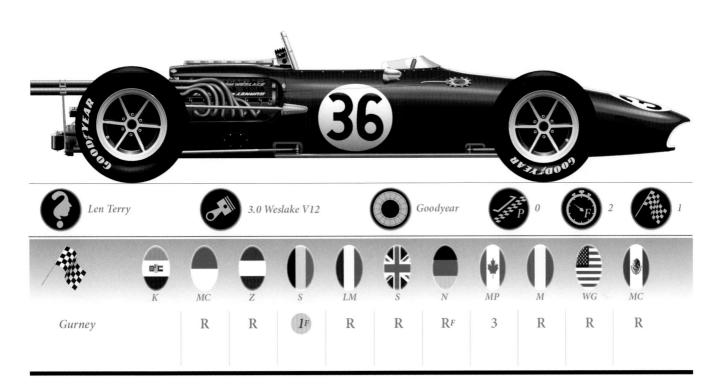

	Len Terry		3.0 Weslake V12		Goodyear	P	0	F	2		1

		K	MC	Z	S	LM	S	N	MP	M	WG	MC
Gurney			R	R	1F	R	R	RF	3	R	R	R

1967 Brabham BT24

 1st

Denny **Hulme**   Jack **Brabham**

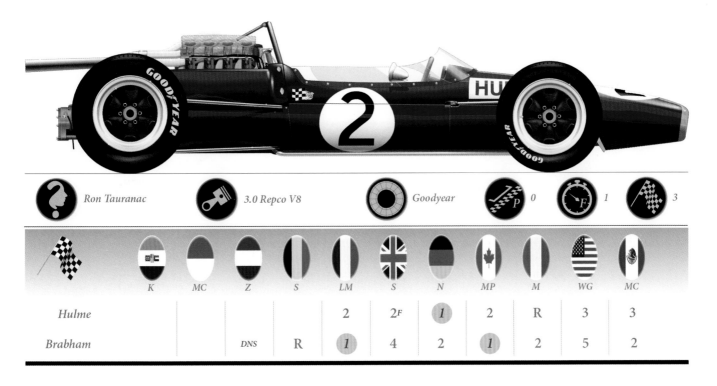

	Ron Tauranac		3.0 Repco V8		Goodyear	P	0	F	1		3

		K	MC	Z	S	LM	S	N	MP	M	WG	MC
Hulme						2	2F	1	2	R	3	3
Brabham			DNS	R	1	4	2	1	2	5	2

1967 Honda RA300

John *Surtees*

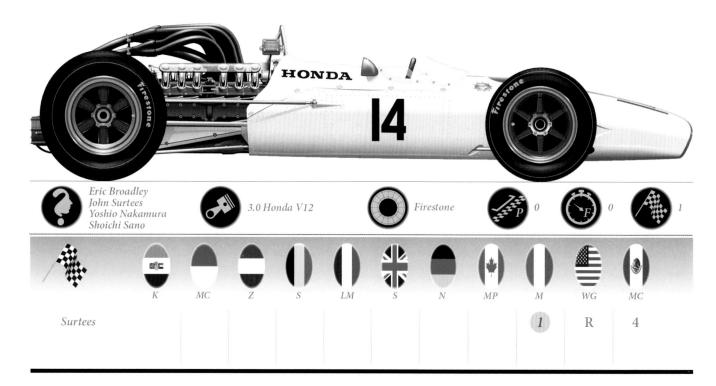

?	Eric Broadley John Surtees Yoshio Nakamura Shoichi Sano		3.0 Honda V12		Firestone		P 0		F 0		1

	K	MC	Z	S	LM	S	N	MP	M	WG	MC
Surtees								1		R	4

1968 Lotus 49

Jim *Clark*

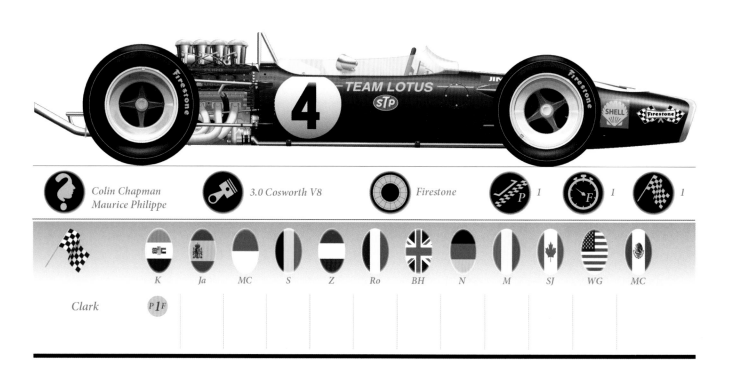

?	Colin Chapman Maurice Philippe		3.0 Cosworth V8		Firestone		P 1		F 1		1

	K	Ja	MC	S	Z	Ro	BH	N	M	SJ	WG	MC
Clark	P 1 F											

1968 Lotus 49 *Gold Leaf*

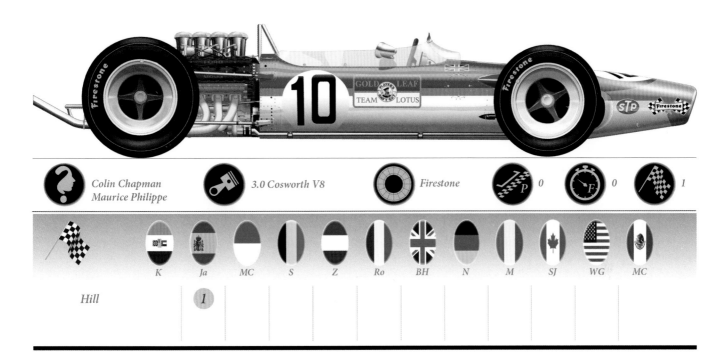

| | Colin Chapman Maurice Philippe | | 3.0 Cosworth V8 | | Firestone | | P 0 | | F 0 | | 1 |

		K	Ja	MC	S	Z	Ro	BH	N	M	SJ	WG	MC
Hill			1										

1968 Lotus 49B *Gold Leaf*

 1st

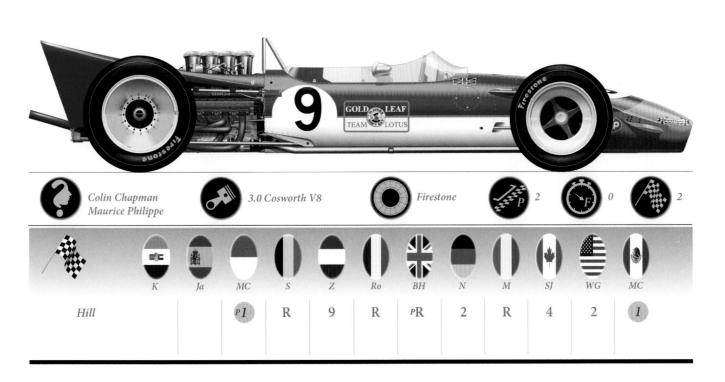

| | Colin Chapman Maurice Philippe | | 3.0 Cosworth V8 | | Firestone | | P 2 | | F 0 | | 2 |

		K	Ja	MC	S	Z	Ro	BH	N	M	SJ	WG	MC
Hill				P1	R	9	R	PR	2	R	4	2	1

1968 McLaren M7A

 Bruce **McLaren**

 Denny **Hulme**

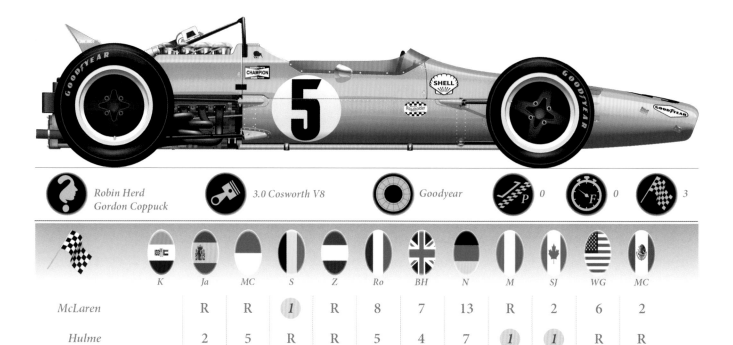

	Robin Herd Gordon Coppuck		3.0 Cosworth V8		Goodyear		P 0		F 0		3

	K	Ja	MC	S	Z	Ro	BH	N	M	SJ	WG	MC
McLaren	R	R	*1*	R	8	7	13	R	2	6	2
Hulme	2	5	R	R	5	4	7	*1*	*1*	R	R

1968 Matra MS10

 Jackie **Stewart**

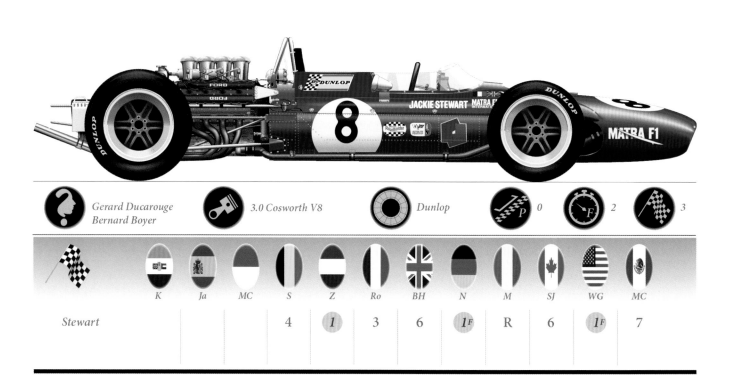

	Gerard Ducarouge Bernard Boyer		3.0 Cosworth V8		Dunlop		P 0		F 2		3

	K	Ja	MC	S	Z	Ro	BH	N	M	SJ	WG	MC
Stewart				4	*1*	3	6	*1*F	R	6	*1*F	7

1968 Ferrari 312 68

Jacky
Ickx

	Mauro Forghieri		3.0 Ferrari V12		Firestone		P 1		F 0		1

	K	Ja	MC	S	Z	Ro	BH	N	M	SJ	WG	MC
Ickx					4	1	3	P4	3	DNS		R

1968 Lotus 49B *Rob Walker/Jack Durlacher Racing*

Jo
Siffert

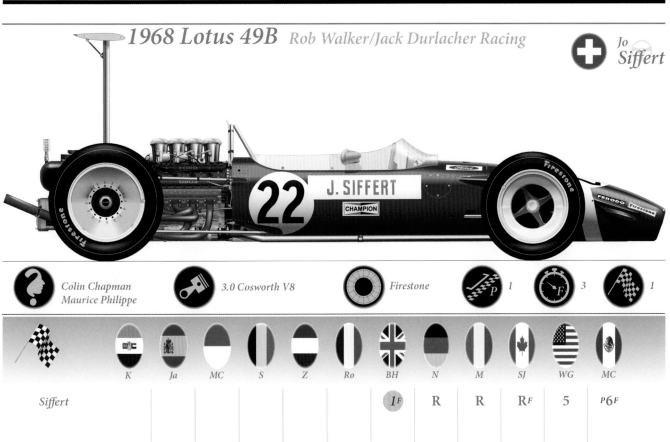

	Colin Chapman Maurice Philippe		3.0 Cosworth V8		Firestone		P 1		F 3		1

	K	Ja	MC	S	Z	Ro	BH	N	M	SJ	WG	MC
Siffert							1F	R	R	RF	5	P6F

1969 Matra MS10

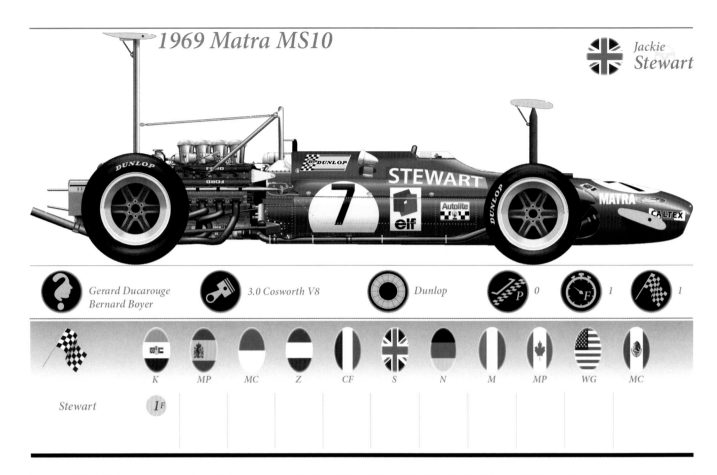

	Gerard Ducarouge Bernard Boyer	3.0 Cosworth V8	Dunlop	P 0	F 1	1

	K	MP	MC	Z	CF	S	N	M	MP	WG	MC
Stewart	1F										

1969 Matra MS80

 *1st*

Jackie *Stewart*

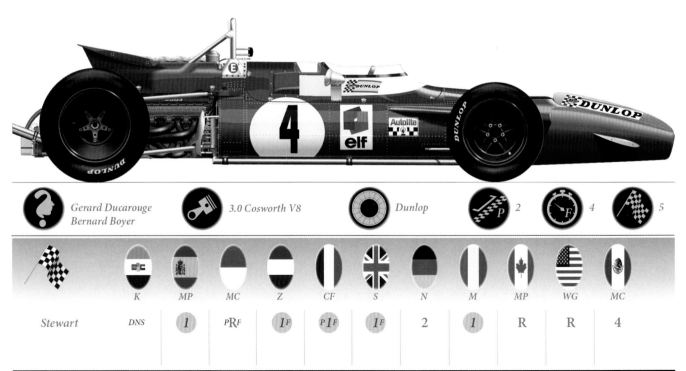

	Gerard Ducarouge Bernard Boyer	3.0 Cosworth V8	Dunlop	P 2	F 4	5

	K	MP	MC	Z	CF	S	N	M	MP	WG	MC
Stewart	DNS	1	PRF	1F	P1F	1F	2	1	R	R	4

1969 Lotus 49B *Gold Leaf*

 Graham **Hill**  Jochen **Rindt**

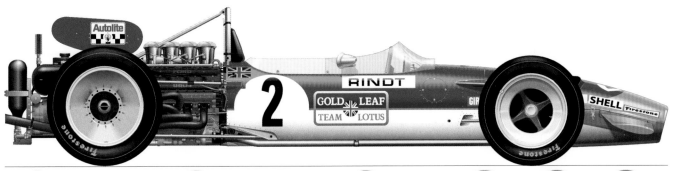

| | Colin Chapman Maurice Philippe | | 3.0 Cosworth V8 | | Firestone | | P 5 | | F 2 | | 2 |

		K	MP	MC	Z	CF	S	N	M	MP	WG	MC
Hill		2	R	*1*	7	6	7	4	9	R	R	
Rindt		R	ᴾR ꜰ		ᴾR	R	ᴾ4	R	ᴾ2	3	ᴾ1ꜰ	R

1969 Brabham BT26A

 Jacky **Ickx**

| | Ron Tauranac | | 3.0 Cosworth V8 | | Goodyear | | P 2 | | F 3 | | 2 |

		K	MP	MC	Z	CF	S	N	M	MP	WG	MC
Ickx		R	6	R	5	3	2	ᴾ1ꜰ	10	ᴾ1ꜰ	R	2ꜰ

1969 McLaren M7A

Denny
Hulme

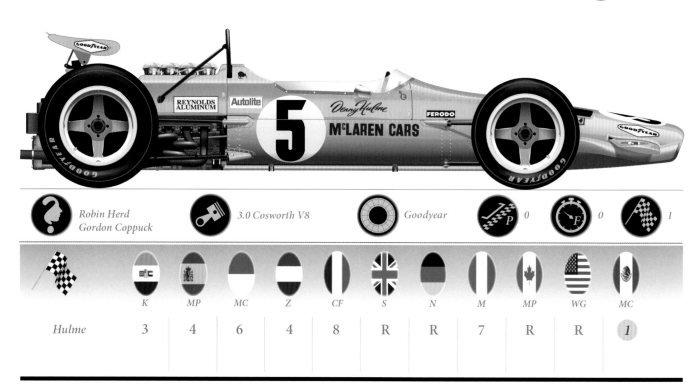

	Robin Herd Gordon Coppuck		3.0 Cosworth V8		Goodyear		P	0		F	0		1

		K	MP	MC	Z	CF	S	N	M	MP	WG	MC
Hulme		3	4	6	4	8	R	R	7	R	R	*1*

1970-79

The new Lotus 72 debuted at the 1970 Spanish GP, and once perfected, Jochen Rindt scored four successive victories, only to die after crashing his Lotus at Monza during practice. Having amassed enough points, Formula 1 had its first and only posthumous World Champion. In 1973, David Purley tried in vain to save Roger Williamson from his overturned burning car at Zandvoort, and we also lost François Cevert who died in practice at Watkins Glen. In November 1975, returning from testing at Paul Ricard, Graham Hill and five members of his Embassy team were killed, including driver Tony Brise, when the light plane flown by Hill crashed in fog near Elstree airfield. 1976 saw Tyrrell introduce their six-wheeler, the P34, Jody Scheckter managing to bring it home in first place in the Swedish GP. In the same year, Niki Lauda crashed heavily in the German GP at the Nürburgring, after which his car burst into flames. Against the odds he was racing again five weeks later, taking 4th place at Monza, still badly burned around his head. 1977 saw Lotus debut the Lotus 78 'wing car', and in the South African GP, Tom Pryce lost his life when he struck and killed a marshal who was crossing the track. 1978 saw Niki Lauda move to Brabham-Alfa Romeo, winning in Sweden, driving the infamous 'fan-car' which used a huge fan to generate downforce. Lotus also debuted the Lotus 79, which won Mario Andretti the 1978 driver's crown. Clay Regazzoni brought Williams his first taste of many victories at the 1979 British GP, and Ferrari's Jody Scheckter saw the decade out by clinching the World Championship crown.

1970-1979 Seasons race by race.

Year	Argentina	Italy	Austria	Japan	Brazil	Mexico	Belgium	Monaco	Britain	South Africa	Canada	Spain	Dutch	Sweden	France	USA West	Germany	USA
1970		M	Ö			MC	S	MC	BH	K	SJ	Ja	Z		CF		H	WG
1971		M	Ö					MC	S	K	MP	MP	Z		PR		N	WG
1972	BA	M	Ö				N	MC	BH	K	MP	Ja			CF		N	WG
1973	BA	M	Ö		I		Z	MC	S	K	MP	MP	Z	A	PR		N	WG
1974	BA	M	Ö		I		N	MC	BH	K	MP	Ja	Z	A	D		N	WG
1975	BA	M	Ö		I		Z	MC	S	K		MP	Z	A	PR		N	WG
1976		M	Ö	F	I		Z	MC	BH	K	MP	Ja	Z	A	PR	LB	N	WG
1977	BA	M	Ö	F	I		Z	MC	S	K	MP	Ja	Z	A	D	LB	H	WG
1978	BA	M	Ö		J		Z	MC	BH	K	M	Ja	Z	A	PR	LB	H	WG
1979	BA	M	Ö		I		Z	MC	S	K	M	Ja	Z		D	LB	H	WG

for track abbreviations refer to map on pages 6/7

1970 Brabham BT33

Jack
Brabham

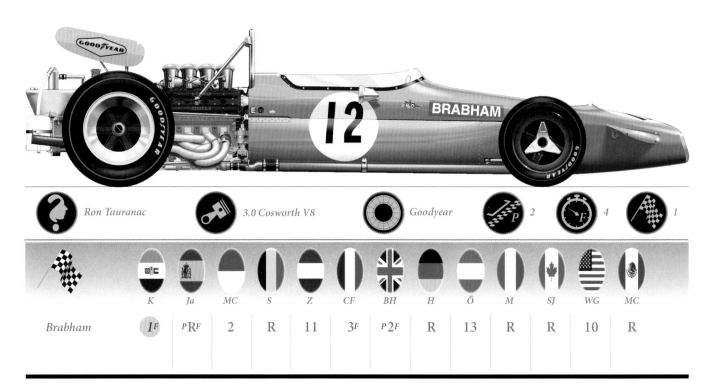

Ron Tauranac	3.0 Cosworth V8	Goodyear	P 2	F 4	1

	K	Ja	MC	S	Z	CF	BH	H	Ö	M	SJ	WG	MC
Brabham	1F	P RF	2	R	11	3F	P 2F	R	13	R	R	10	R

1970 March 701

Jackie
Stewart

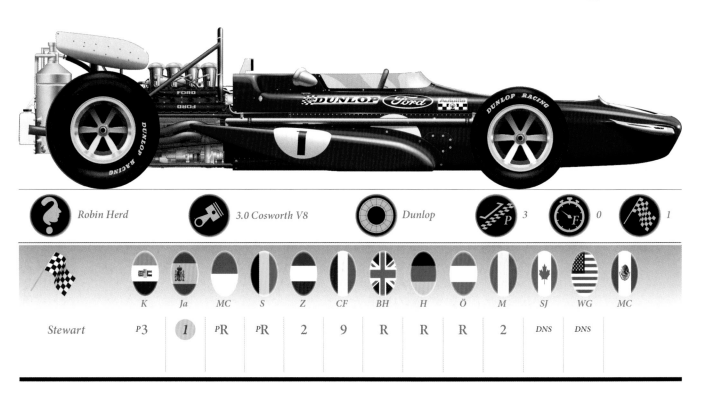

Robin Herd	3.0 Cosworth V8	Dunlop	P 3	F 0	1

	K	Ja	MC	S	Z	CF	BH	H	Ö	M	SJ	WG	MC
Stewart	P 3	1	P R	P R	2	9	R	R	R	2	DNS	DNS	

1970 Lotus 49C

Jochen
Rindt

Colin Chapman	3.0 Cosworth V8	Firestone	P 0	F 1	1

	K	Ja	MC	S	Z	CF	BH	H	Ö	M	SJ	WG	MC
Rindt	13		1ᶠ	R									

1970 BRM P153

Pedro
Rodriguez

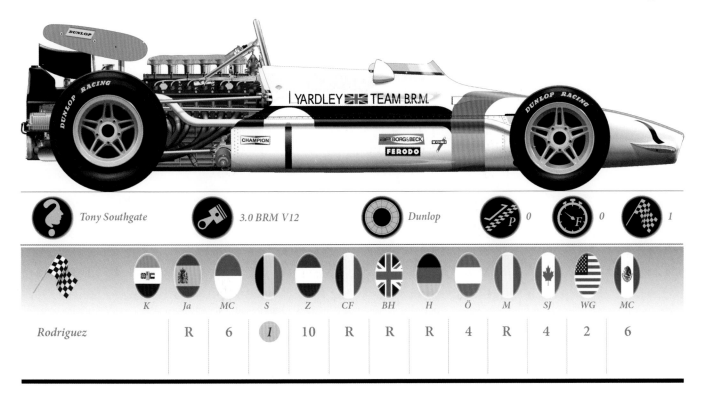

Tony Southgate	3.0 BRM V12	Dunlop	P 0	F 0	1

	K	Ja	MC	S	Z	CF	BH	H	Ö	M	SJ	WG	MC
Rodriguez	R	6	1	10	R	R	R	4	R	4	2	6	

1970 Lotus 72C

1st

 Jochen **Rindt**    Emerson **Fittipaldi**

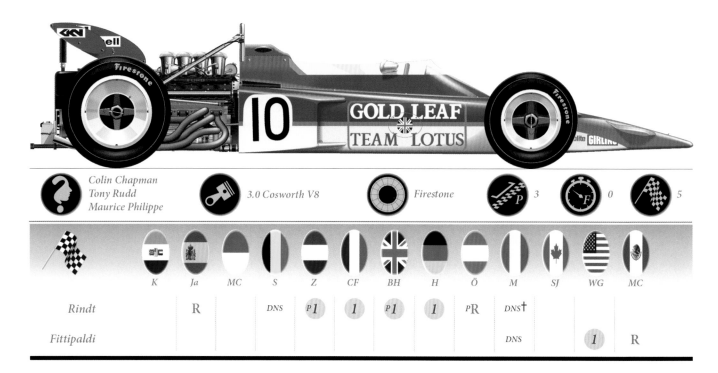

Colin Chapman
Tony Rudd
Maurice Philippe | 3.0 Cosworth V8 | Firestone | P 3 | F 0 | 5

	K	Ja	MC	S	Z	CF	BH	H	Ö	M	SJ	WG	MC
Rindt		R		DNS	P1	1	P1	1	PR	DNS†			
Fittipaldi										DNS		1	R

1970 Ferrari 312B

Jacky **Ickx**   Clay **Regazzoni**

Mauro Forghieri | 3.0 Ferrari Flat 12 | Firestone | P 5 | F 6 | 4

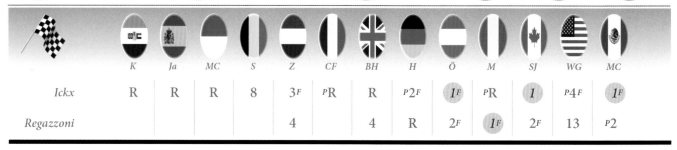

	K	Ja	MC	S	Z	CF	BH	H	Ö	M	SJ	WG	MC
Ickx	R	R	R	8	3F	PR	R	P2F	1F	PR	1	P4F	1F
Regazzoni					4		4	R	2F	1F	2F	13	P2

1971 Ferrari 312B

Mario
Andretti

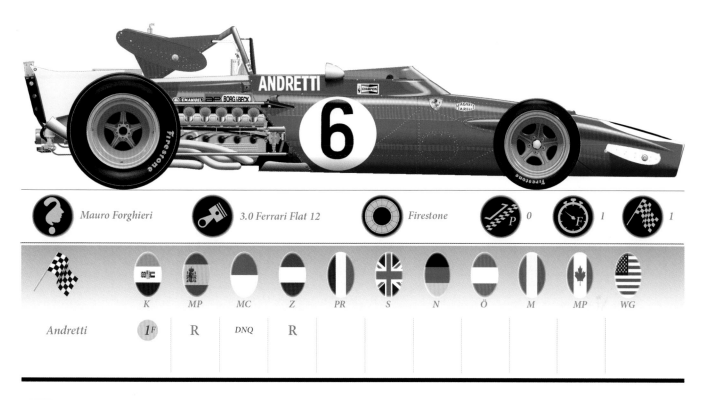

Mauro Forghieri	3.0 Ferrari Flat 12	Firestone	P 0	F 1	1

		K	MP	MC	Z	PR	S	N	Ö	M	MP	WG
Andretti		1ᶠ	R	DNQ	R							

1971 Tyrrell 003

Jackie
Stewart

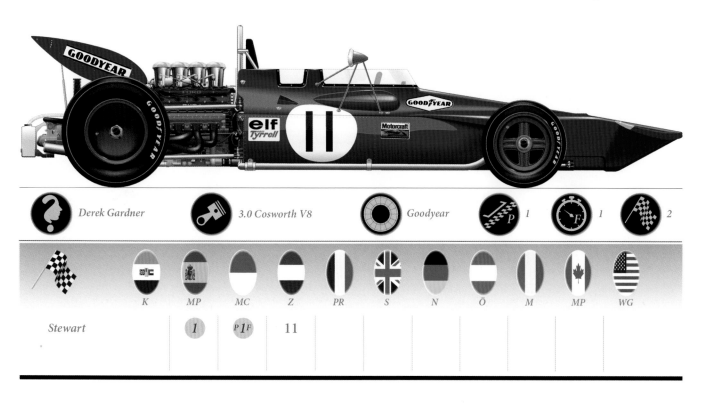

Derek Gardner	3.0 Cosworth V8	Goodyear	P 1	F 1	2

		K	MP	MC	Z	PR	S	N	Ö	M	MP	WG
Stewart		1	P 1ᶠ	11								

1971 Ferrari 312B2

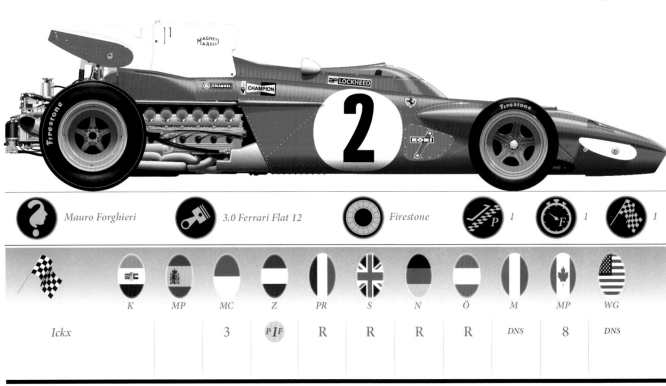

	Mauro Forghieri		3.0 Ferrari Flat 12		Firestone		P 1		F 1		1

		K	MP	MC	Z	PR	S	N	Ö	M	MP	WG
Ickx				3	P1F	R	R	R	R	DNS	8	DNS

1971 Tyrrell 003

1st

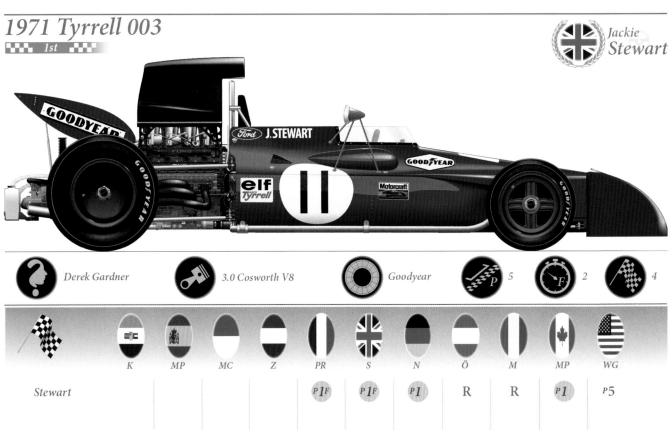

	Derek Gardner		3.0 Cosworth V8		Goodyear		P 5		F 2		4

		K	MP	MC	Z	PR	S	N	Ö	M	MP	WG
Stewart						P1F	P1F	P1	R	R	P1	P5

1971 BRM P160

Jo **Siffert**

Peter **Gethin**

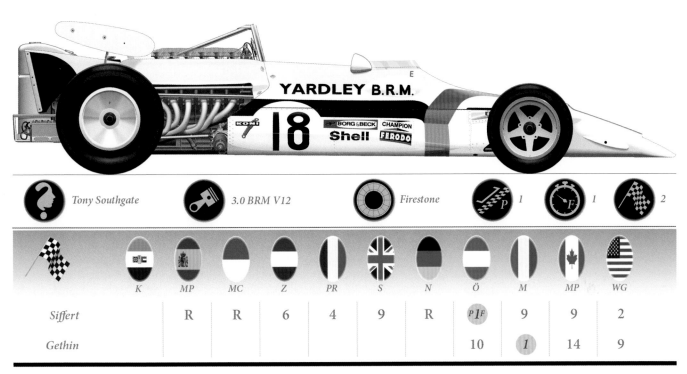

	Tony Southgate		3.0 BRM V12		Firestone		P 1		F 1		2

		K	MP	MC	Z	PR	S	N	Ö	M	MP	WG
Siffert		R	R	6	4	9	R	P1F	9	9	2
Gethin									10	1	14	9

1971 Tyrrell 002

François **Cevert**

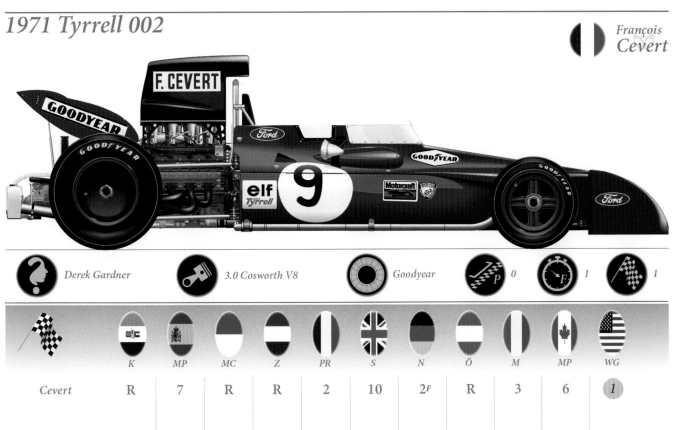

	Derek Gardner		3.0 Cosworth V8		Goodyear		P 0		F 1		1

		K	MP	MC	Z	PR	S	N	Ö	M	MP	WG
Cevert		R	7	R	R	2	10	2F	R	3	6	1

1972 Tyrrell 003

Jackie
Stewart

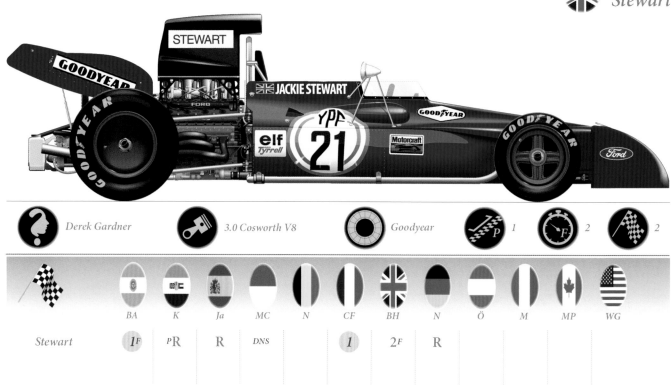

? Derek Gardner		🔧 3.0 Cosworth V8		⊙ Goodyear		🏁 P 1		⏱ F 2		🏁 2		

		BA	K	Ja	MC	N	CF	BH	N	Ö	M	MP	WG
Stewart		1F	PR	R	DNS		1	2F	R				

1972 McLaren M19A

Denny
Hulme

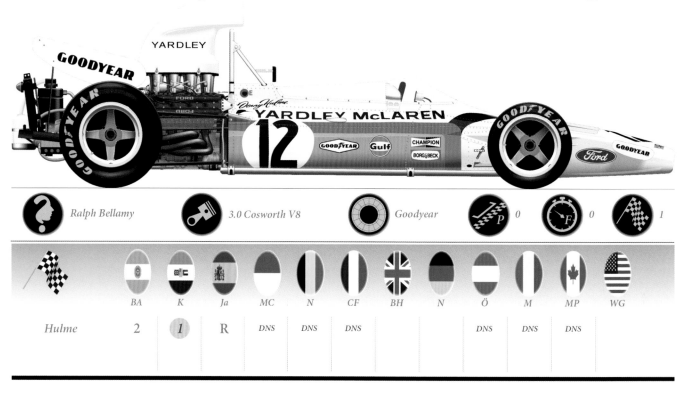

? Ralph Bellamy		🔧 3.0 Cosworth V8		⊙ Goodyear		🏁 P 0		⏱ F 0		🏁 1		

	BA	K	Ja	MC	N	CF	BH	N	Ö	M	MP	WG
Hulme	2	1	R	DNS	DNS	DNS			DNS	DNS	DNS	

1972 Lotus 72D

Emerson
Fittipaldi

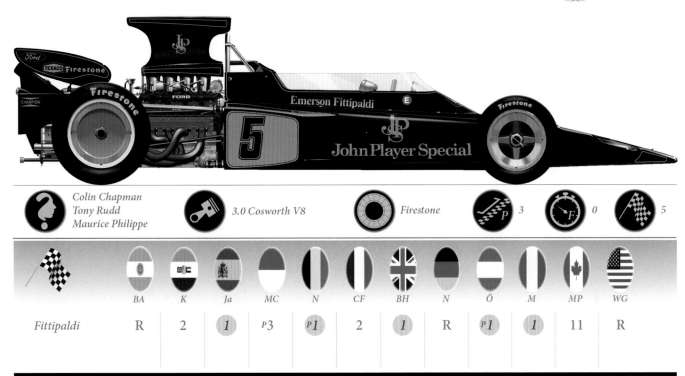

Colin Chapman
Tony Rudd
Maurice Philippe

3.0 Cosworth V8

Firestone

P 3   F 0   5

	BA	K	Ja	MC	N	CF	BH	N	Ö	M	MP	WG
Fittipaldi	R	2	*1*	P3	P1	2	*1*	R	P1	*1*	11	R

1972 BRM P160B

Jean-Pierre
Beltoise

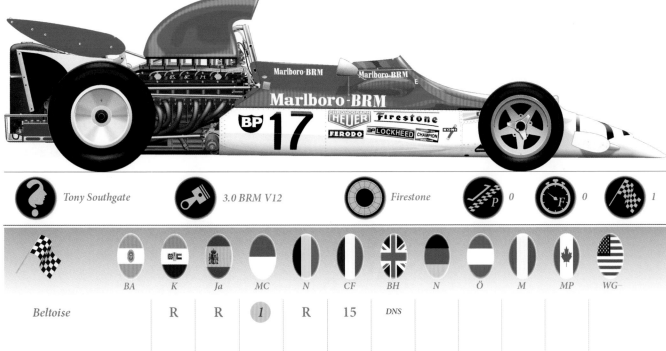

Tony Southgate

3.0 BRM V12

Firestone

P 0   F 0   1

	BA	K	Ja	MC	N	CF	BH	N	Ö	M	MP	WG
Beltoise	R	R	*1*	R	15	DNS						

1972 Ferrari 312B2

Jacky
Ickx

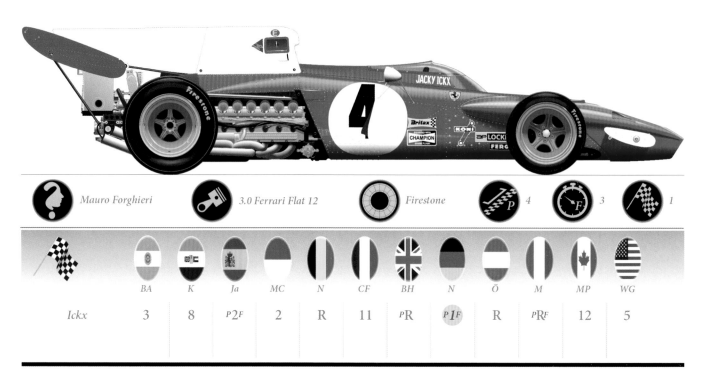

	Mauro Forghieri		3.0 Ferrari Flat 12		Firestone		P 4		F 3		1

	BA	K	Ja	MC	N	CF	BH	N	Ö	M	MP	WG
Ickx	3	8	P2F	2	R	11	PR	P1F	R	PRF	12	5

1972 Tyrrell 005

Jackie
Stewart

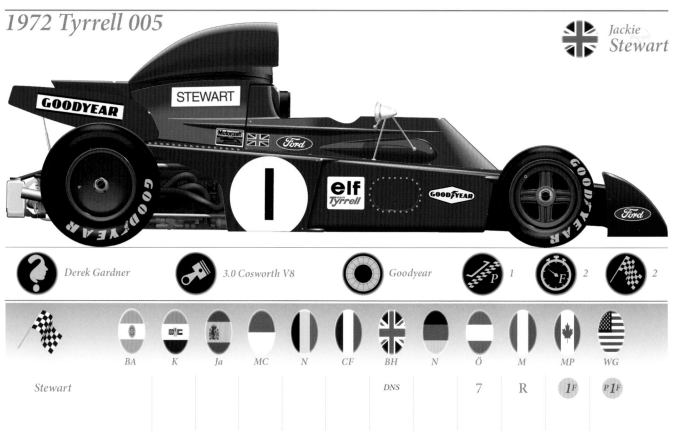

	Derek Gardner		3.0 Cosworth V8		Goodyear		P 1		F 2		2

	BA	K	Ja	MC	N	CF	BH	N	Ö	M	MP	WG
Stewart							DNS		7	R	1F	P1F

1973 Lotus 72D

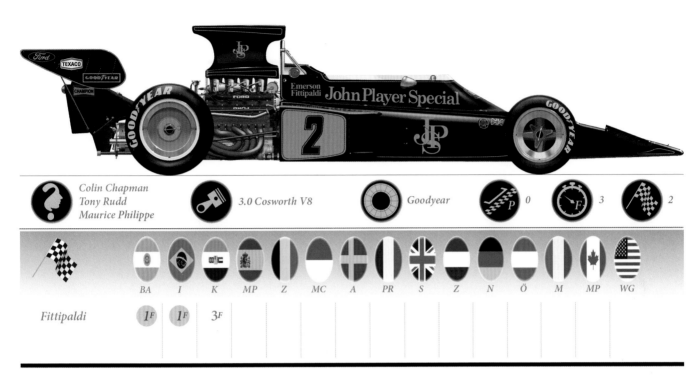

Emerson *Fittipaldi*

| ? | Colin Chapman
Tony Rudd
Maurice Philippe | ⚙ | 3.0 Cosworth V8 | ◎ | Goodyear | 🏁P | 0 | ⏱F | 3 | 🏁 | 2 |

🏁		BA	I	K	MP	Z	MC	A	PR	S	Z	N	Ö	M	MP	WG
Fittipaldi		1F	1F	3F												

1973 Tyrrell 006

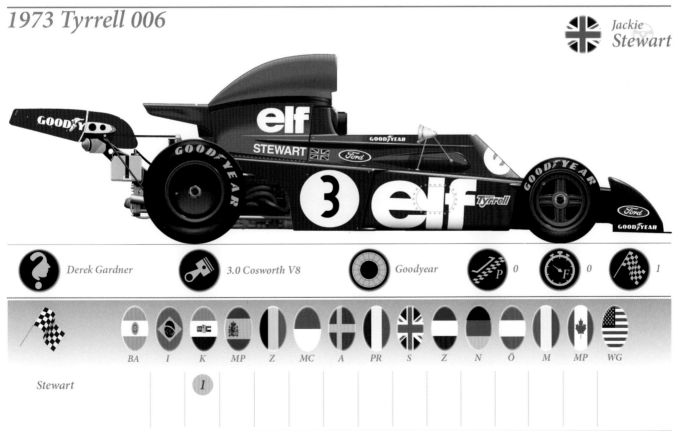

Jackie *Stewart*

| ? | Derek Gardner | ⚙ | 3.0 Cosworth V8 | ◎ | Goodyear | 🏁P | 0 | ⏱F | 0 | 🏁 | 1 |

🏁		BA	I	K	MP	Z	MC	A	PR	S	Z	N	Ö	M	MP	WG
Stewart			1													

1973 Lotus 72E
1st

Emerson **Fittipaldi**
Ronnie **Peterson**

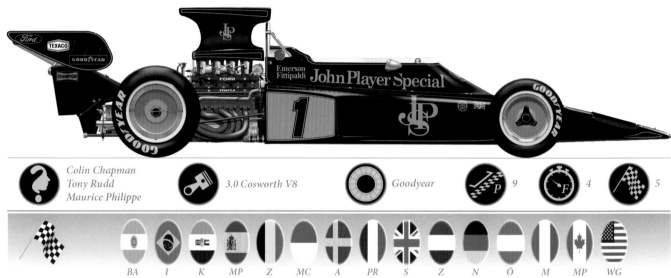

Colin Chapman / Tony Rudd / Maurice Philippe	3.0 Cosworth V8	Goodyear	P 9	F 4	5

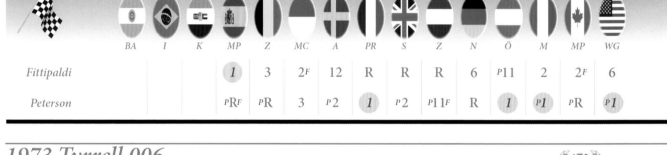

	BA	I	K	MP	Z	MC	A	PR	S	Z	N	Ö	M	MP	WG
Fittipaldi				1	3	2F	12	R	R	R	6	P11	2	2F	6
Peterson				PRF	PR	3	P2	1	P2	P11F	R	1	P1	PR	P1

1973 Tyrrell 006

Jackie **Stewart**

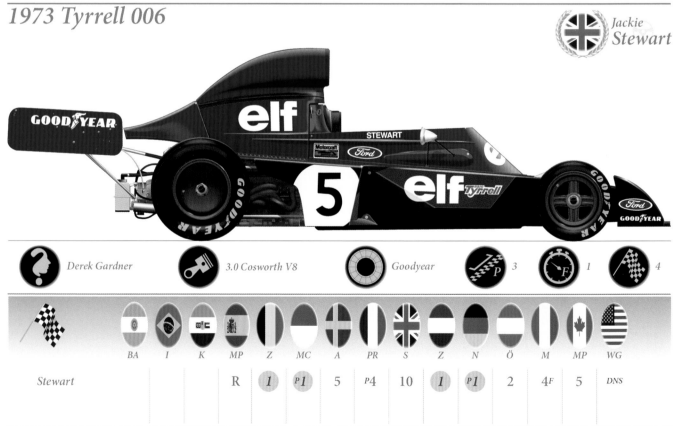

Derek Gardner	3.0 Cosworth V8	Goodyear	P 3	F 1	4

	BA	I	K	MP	Z	MC	A	PR	S	Z	N	Ö	M	MP	WG
Stewart				R	1	P1	5	P4	10	1	P1	2	4F	5	DNS

1973 McLaren M23

 Denny *Hulme*    Peter *Revson*

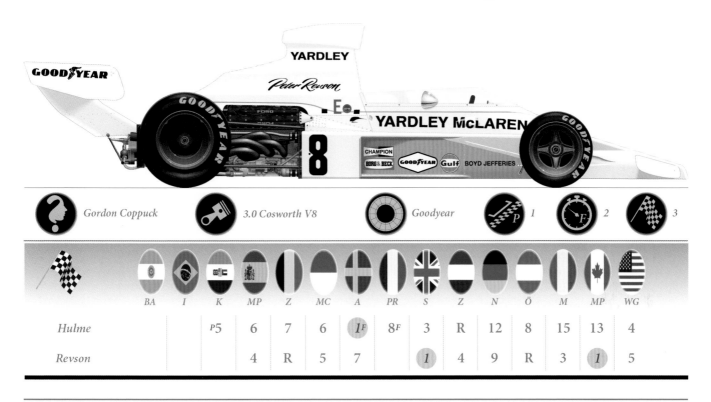

Gordon Coppuck	3.0 Cosworth V8	Goodyear	P 1	F 2	3

	BA	I	K	MP	Z	MC	A	PR	S	Z	N	Ö	M	MP	WG
Hulme		P5	6	7	6	1F	8F	3	R	12	8	15	13	4
Revson			4	R	5	7		1	4	9	R	3	1	5

1974 McLaren M23

 Emerson *Fittipaldi*    Denny *Hulme*

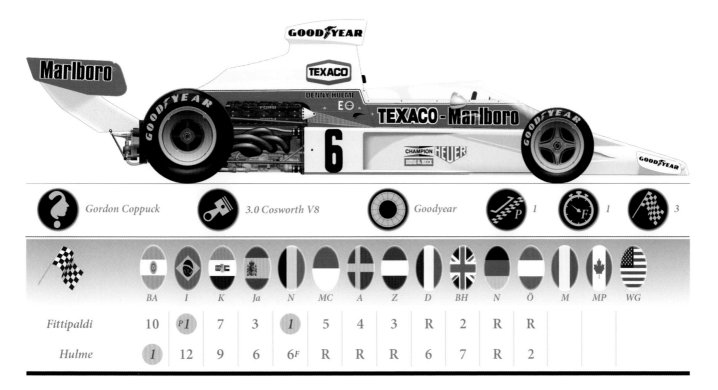

Gordon Coppuck	3.0 Cosworth V8	Goodyear	P 1	F 1	3

	BA	I	K	Ja	N	MC	A	Z	D	BH	N	Ö	M	MP	WG
Fittipaldi	10	P1	7	3	1	5	4	3	R	2	R	R			
Hulme	1	12	9	6	6F	R	R	R	6	7	R	2			

1974 Lotus 72E

Ronnie *Peterson*

| | Colin Chapman Tony Rudd Maurice Philippe | | 3.0 Cosworth V8 | | Goodyear | | P 2 | | F 2 | | 3 |

		BA	I	K	Ja	N	MC	A	Z	D	BH	N	Ö	M	MP	WG
Peterson		P13	6	DNS		DNS	1F	R	8F	1	P10	DNS	R	1	3	R

1974 Brabham BT44

Carlos *Reutemann*

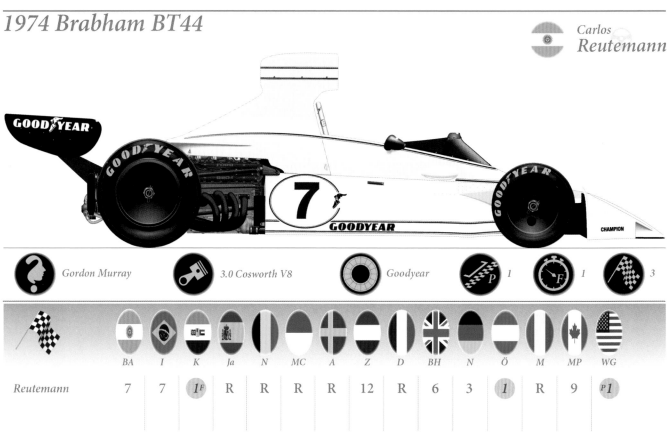

| | Gordon Murray | | 3.0 Cosworth V8 | | Goodyear | | P 1 | | F 1 | | 3 |

		BA	I	K	Ja	N	MC	A	Z	D	BH	N	Ö	M	MP	WG
Reutemann		7	7	1F	R	R	R	R	12	R	6	3	1	R	9	P1

1974 Ferrari 312B3

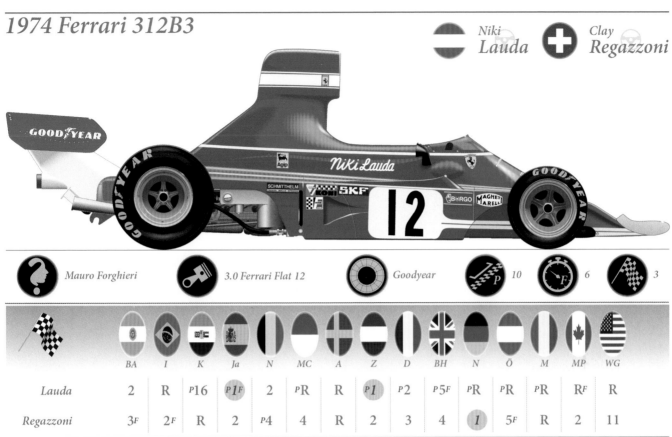

Niki **Lauda**   Clay **Regazzoni**

Mauro Forghieri   3.0 Ferrari Flat 12   Goodyear   P 10   F 6   3

	BA	I	K	Ja	N	MC	A	Z	D	BH	N	Ö	M	MP	WG
Lauda	2	R	P16	P1F	2	PR	R	P1	P2	P5F	PR	PR	PR	RF	R
Regazzoni	3F	2F	R	2	P4	4	R	2	3	4	1	5F	R	2	11

1974 Tyrrell 007

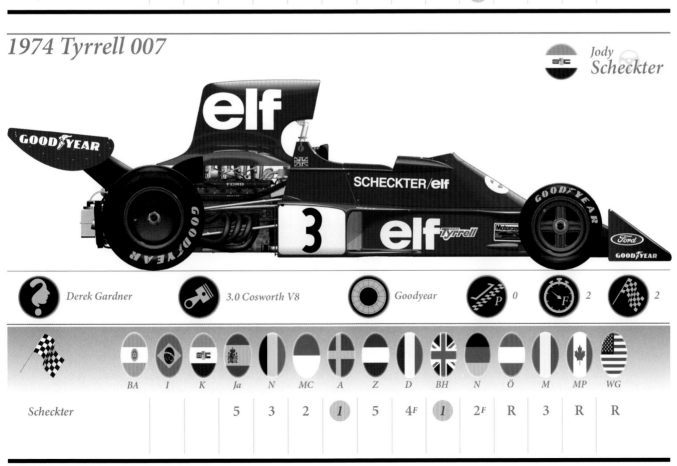

Jody **Scheckter**

Derek Gardner   3.0 Cosworth V8   Goodyear   P 0   F 2   2

	BA	I	K	Ja	N	MC	A	Z	D	BH	N	Ö	M	MP	WG
Scheckter					5	3	2	1	5	4F	1	2F	R	3	R	R

1974 McLaren M23B
1st

 Emerson *Fittipaldi*  Denny *Hulme*

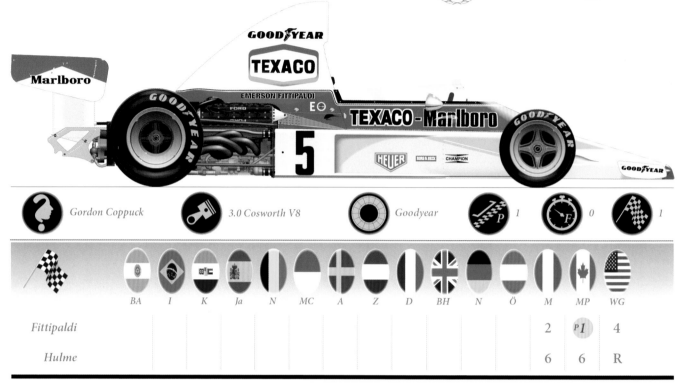

| | Gordon Coppuck | | 3.0 Cosworth V8 | | Goodyear | P 1 | F 0 | 1 |

		BA	I	K	Ja	N	MC	A	Z	D	BH	N	Ö	M	MP	WG
Fittipaldi															2	P1	4
Hulme															6	6	R

1975 McLaren M23C

 Emerson *Fittipaldi*   Jochen *Mass*

| | Gordon Coppuck | | 3.0 Cosworth V8 | | Goodyear | P 0 | F 2 | 3 |

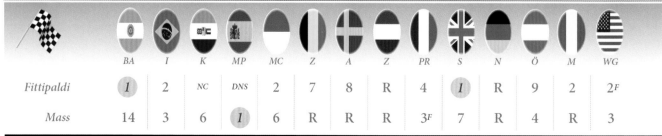

	BA	I	K	MP	MC	Z	A	Z	PR	S	N	Ö	M	WG
Fittipaldi	1	2	NC	DNS	2	7	8	R	4	1	R	9	2	2F
Mass	14	3	6	1	6	R	R	R	3F	7	R	4	R	3

1975 Tyrrell 007

Jody **Scheckter**

Derek Gardner	3.0 Cosworth V8	Goodyear	P 0	F 0	1

	BA	I	K	MP	MC	Z	A	Z	PR	S	N	Ö	M	WG
Scheckter	11	R	*1*	R	7	2	7	16	9	3	R	8	8	6

1975 Brabham BT44B

Carlos **Pace**   *Carlos* **Reutemann**

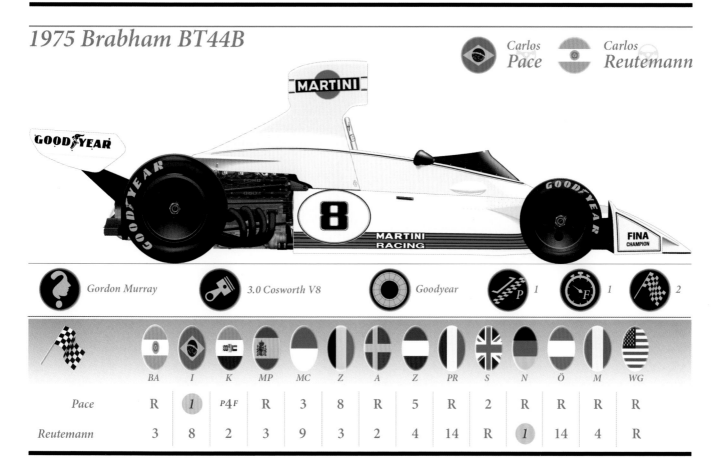

Gordon Murray	3.0 Cosworth V8	Goodyear	P 1	F 1	2

	BA	I	K	MP	MC	Z	A	Z	PR	S	N	Ö	M	WG
Pace	R	*1*	P4F	R	3	8	R	5	R	2	R	R	R	R
Reutemann	3	8	2	3	9	3	2	4	14	R	*1*	14	4	R

1975 Ferrari 312T

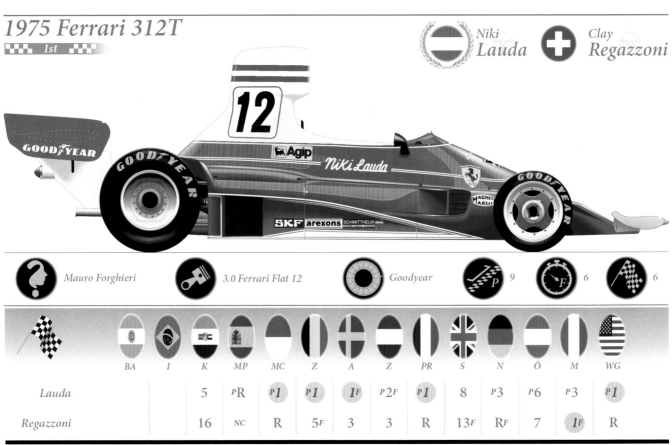

1st

Niki **Lauda**   Clay **Regazzoni**

| | Mauro Forghieri | | 3.0 Ferrari Flat 12 | | Goodyear | | P 9 | | F 6 | | 6 |

	BA	I	K	MP	MC	Z	A	Z	PR	S	N	Ö	M	WG
Lauda	5	PR	P1	P1	1F	P2F	P1	8	P3	P6	P3	P1		
Regazzoni	16	NC	R	5F	3	3	R	13F	RF	7	1F	R		

1975 Hesketh 308B

James **Hunt**

| | Harvey Postlethwaite | | 3.0 Cosworth V8 | | Goodyear | | P 0 | | F 1 | | 1 |

	BA	I	K	MP	MC	Z	A	Z	PR	S	N	Ö	M	WG
Hunt	2F	6	R	R	R	R	R	1	2	4	R	2	DNS	

1975 March 751

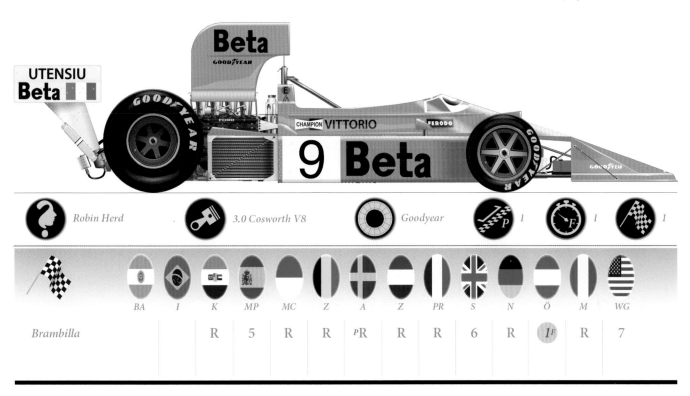

	Robin Herd		3.0 Cosworth V8		Goodyear		P 1		F 1		1

		BA	I	K	MP	MC	Z	A	Z	PR	S	N	Ö	M	WG
Brambilla			R	5	R	R	PR	R	R	6	R	1F	R	7

1976 Ferrari 312T

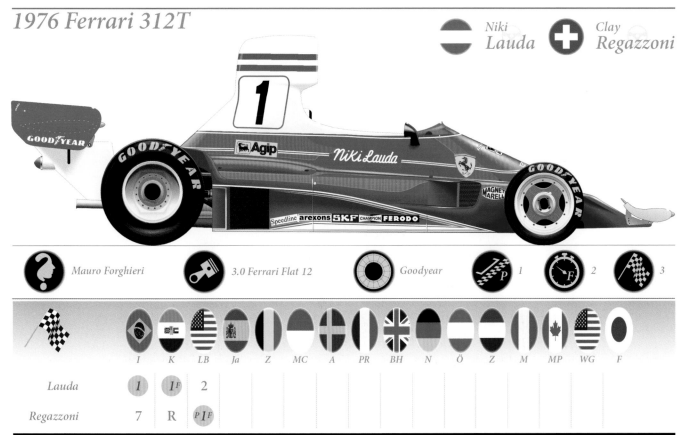

	Mauro Forghieri		3.0 Ferrari Flat 12		Goodyear		P 1		F 2		3

	I	K	LB	Ja	Z	MC	A	PR	BH	N	Ö	Z	M	MP	WG	F
Lauda	1	1F	2													
Regazzoni	7	R	P1F													

1976 Ferrari 312T2

Niki
Lauda

▰▰ **1st** ▰▰

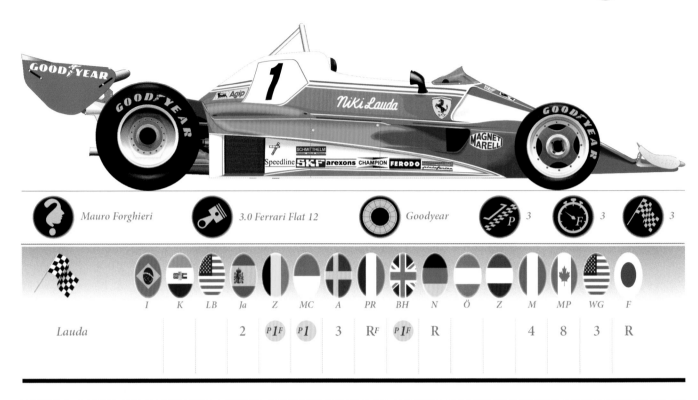

	Mauro Forghieri		3.0 Ferrari Flat 12		Goodyear		P 3		F 3		3

		I	K	LB	Ja	Z	MC	A	PR	BH	N	Ö	Z	M	MP	WG	F
Lauda						2	P1F	P1	3	RF	P1F	R		4	8	3	R

1976 Tyrrell P34

Jody
Scheckter

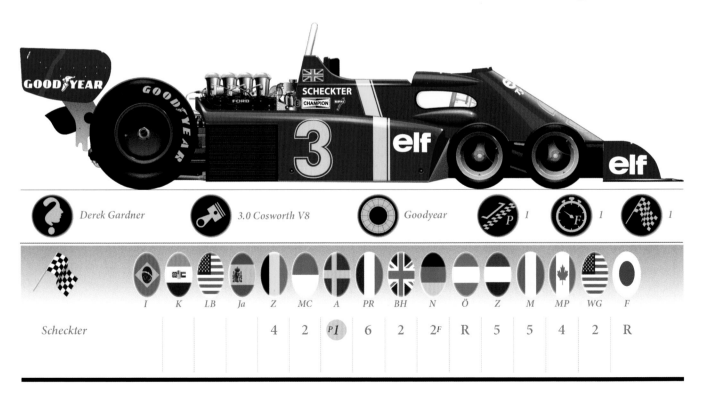

	Derek Gardner		3.0 Cosworth V8		Goodyear		P 1		F 1		1

		I	K	LB	Ja	Z	MC	A	PR	BH	N	Ö	Z	M	MP	WG	F
Scheckter						4	2	P1	6	2	2F	R	5	5	4	2	R

1976 McLaren M23D

James **Hunt**

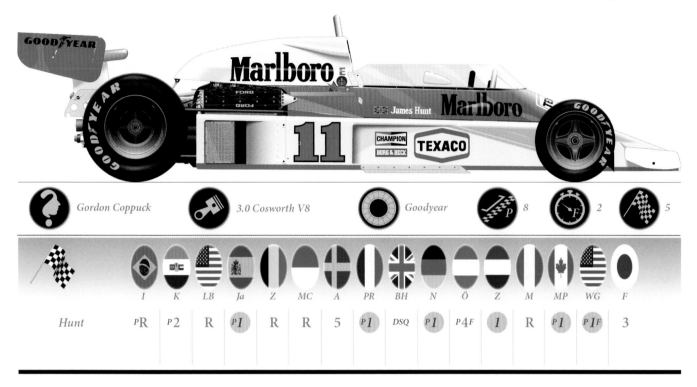

	Gordon Coppuck		3.0 Cosworth V8		Goodyear		P 8		F 2		5

	I	K	LB	Ja	Z	MC	A	PR	BH	N	Ö	Z	M	MP	WG	F
Hunt	PR	P2	R	P1	R	R	5	P1	DSQ	P1	P4F	1	R	P1	P1F	3

1976 Penske PC4

John **Watson**

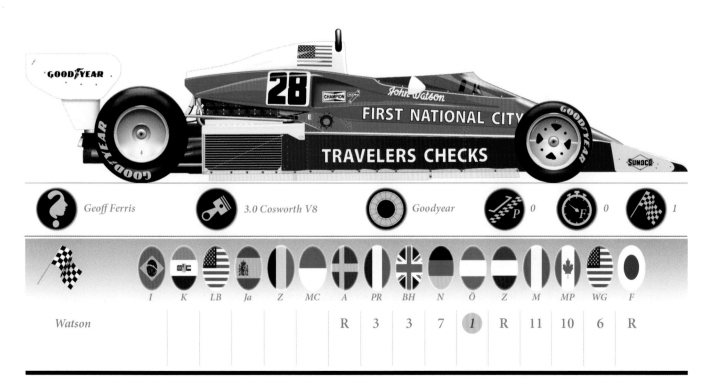

	Geoff Ferris		3.0 Cosworth V8		Goodyear		P 0		F 0		1

	I	K	LB	Ja	Z	MC	A	PR	BH	N	Ö	Z	M	MP	WG	F
Watson							R	3	3	7	1	R	11	10	6	R

1976 March 761

Ronnie
Peterson

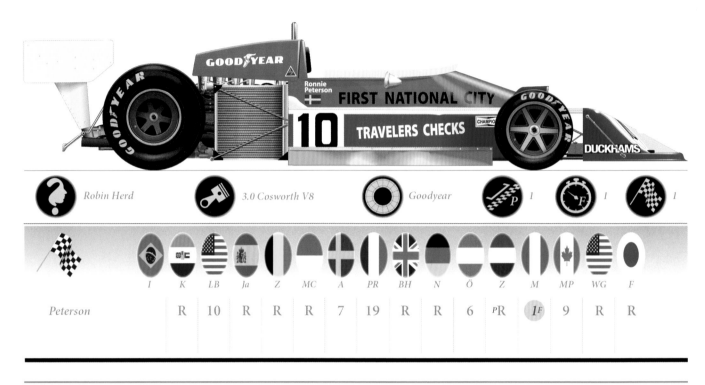

| | Robin Herd | | 3.0 Cosworth V8 | | Goodyear | | P 1 | | F 1 | | 1 |

		I	K	LB	Ja	Z	MC	A	PR	BH	N	Ö	Z	M	MP	WG	F
Peterson		R	10	R	R	R	7	19	R	R	6	PR	1F	9	R	R

1976 Lotus 77

Mario
Andretti

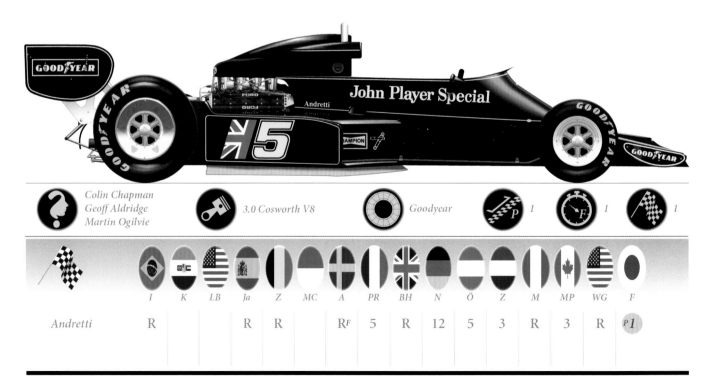

| | Colin Chapman Geoff Aldridge Martin Ogilvie | | 3.0 Cosworth V8 | | Goodyear | | P 1 | | F 1 | | 1 |

		I	K	LB	Ja	Z	MC	A	PR	BH	N	Ö	Z	M	MP	WG	F
Andretti		R		R	R		RF	5	R	12	5	3	R	3	R	P 1

1977 Wolf WR 1, 2, 3
* ** ***

Jody **Scheckter**

? Harvey Postlethwaite	🔧 3.0 Cosworth V8	⭕ Goodyear	🏁P 1	⏱F 2	🏁 3

🏁	BA	I	K	LB	Ja	MC	Z	A	D	S	H	Ö	Z	M	WG	MP	F
Scheckter	1 *	R *	2 *	3 *	3 **	1F *	R ***	R *	R ***	R *	P2 **	R ***	3 **	R *	3 **	1 *	10F ***

1977 Ferrari 312T2

1st

Niki **Lauda**   Carlos **Reutemann**

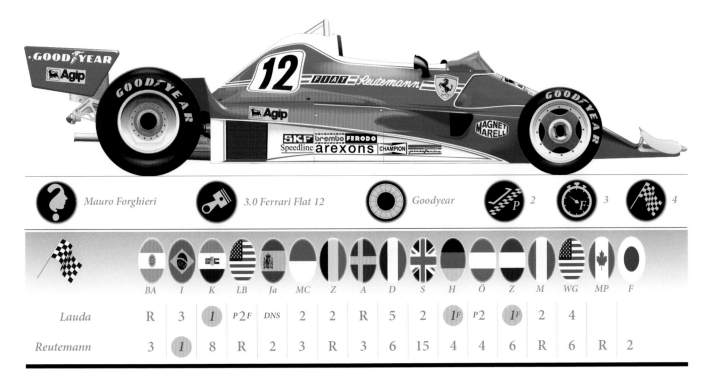

? Mauro Forghieri	🔧 3.0 Ferrari Flat 12	⭕ Goodyear	🏁P 2	⏱F 3	🏁 4

🏁	BA	I	K	LB	Ja	MC	Z	A	D	S	H	Ö	Z	M	WG	MP	F
Lauda	R	3	1	P2F	DNS	2	2	R	5	2	1F	P2	1F	2	4		
Reutemann	3	1	8	R	2	3	R	3	6	15	4	4	6	R	6	R	2

1977 Lotus 78

 Mario *Andretti*  Gunnar *Nilsson*

	Colin Chapman Peter Wright Martin Ogilvie		3.0 Cosworth V8		Goodyear		P 7		F 5		5

	BA	I	K	LB	Ja	MC	Z	A	D	S	H	Ö	Z	M	WG	MP	F
Andretti	5	R	R	*1*	P*1*	5	PR	P6F	P*1F*	14	R	R	PR	*1F*	2	P9F	PR
Nilsson	DNS	5	12	8	5	R	*1F*	19	4	3	R	R	R	R	R	R	R

1977 Ligier JS7

 Jacques *Laffite*

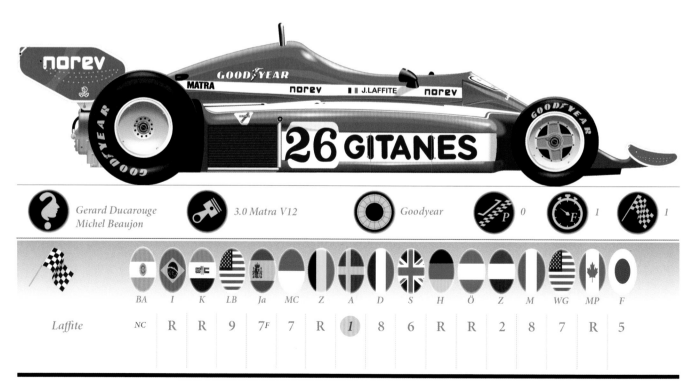

	Gerard Ducarouge Michel Beaujon		3.0 Matra V12		Goodyear		P 0		F 1		1

	BA	I	K	LB	Ja	MC	Z	A	D	S	H	Ö	Z	M	WG	MP	F
Laffite	NC	R	R	9	7F	7	R	*1*	8	6	R	R	2	8	7	R	5

1977 McLaren M26

James *Hunt*

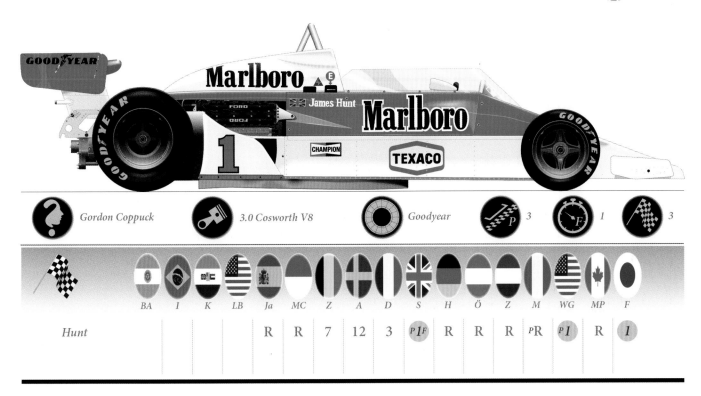

Gordon Coppuck | 3.0 Cosworth V8 | Goodyear | P 3 | F 1 | 🏁 3

	BA	I	K	LB	Ja	MC	Z	A	D	S	H	Ö	Z	M	WG	MP	F
Hunt					R	R	7	12	3	P1F	R	R	R	PR	P1	R	1

1977 Shadow DN8

Alan *Jones*

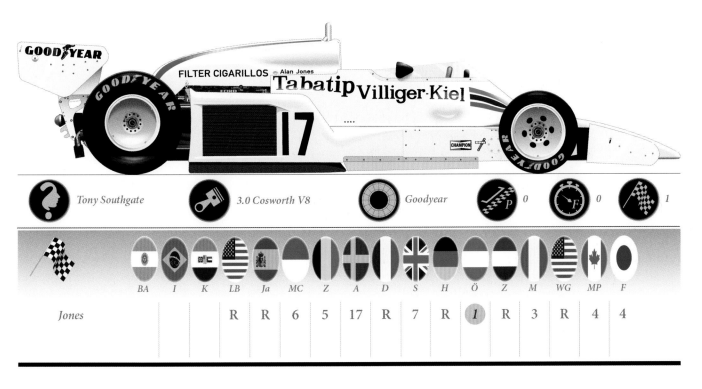

Tony Southgate | 3.0 Cosworth V8 | Goodyear | P 0 | F 0 | 🏁 1

	BA	I	K	LB	Ja	MC	Z	A	D	S	H	Ö	Z	M	WG	MP	F
Jones				R	R	6	5	17	R	7	R	1	R	3	R	4	4

1978 Lotus 78

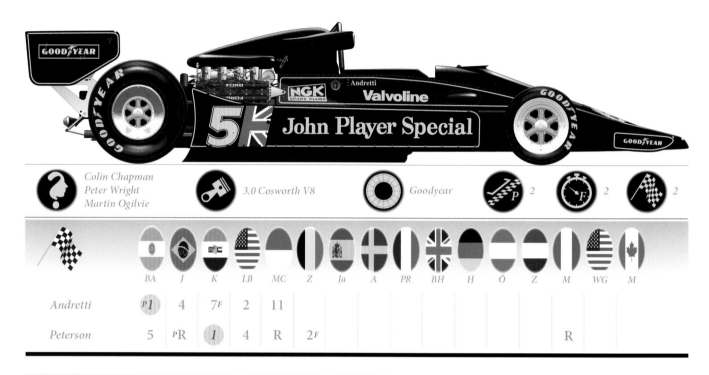

	Colin Chapman Peter Wright Martin Ogilvie		3.0 Cosworth V8		Goodyear		P 2		F 2		2

		BA	J	K	LB	MC	Z	Ja	A	PR	BH	H	Ö	Z	M	WG	M
Andretti		P1	4	7F	2	11											
Peterson		5	PR	1	4	R	2F								R		

1978 Ferrari 312T2

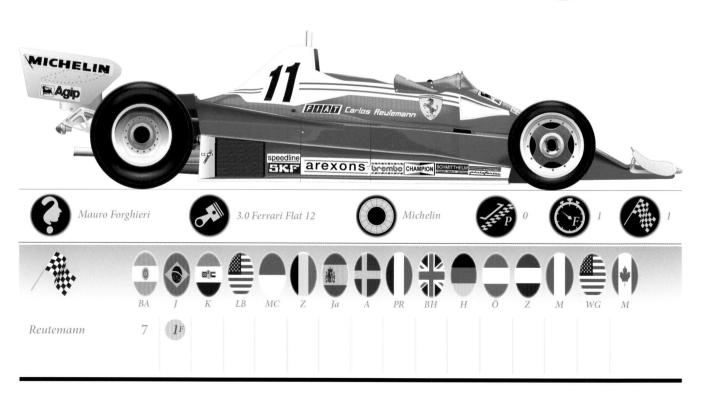

	Mauro Forghieri		3.0 Ferrari Flat 12		Michelin		P 0		F 1		1

		BA	J	K	LB	MC	Z	Ja	A	PR	BH	H	Ö	Z	M	WG	M
Reutemann		7	1F														

1978 Ferrari 312T3

 Carlos **Reutemann**  Gilles **Villeneuve**

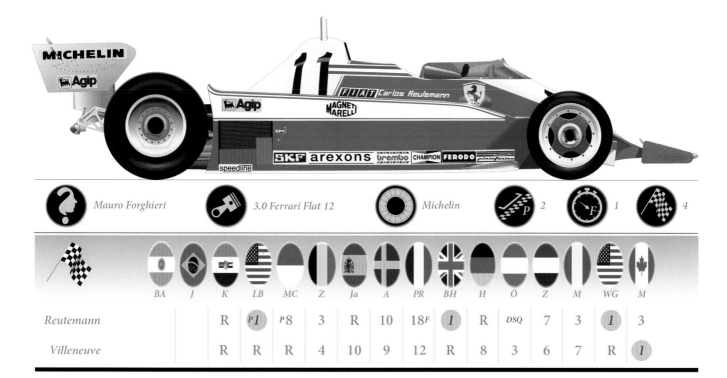

	Mauro Forghieri		3.0 Ferrari Flat 12		Michelin		P 2		F 1		4

	BA	J	K	LB	MC	Z	Ja	A	PR	BH	H	Ö	Z	M	WG	M
Reutemann			R	P1	P8	3	R	10	18F	1	R	DSQ	7	3	1	3
Villeneuve			R	R	R	4	10	9	12	R	8	3	6	7	R	1

1978 Tyrrell 008

 Patrick **Depailler**

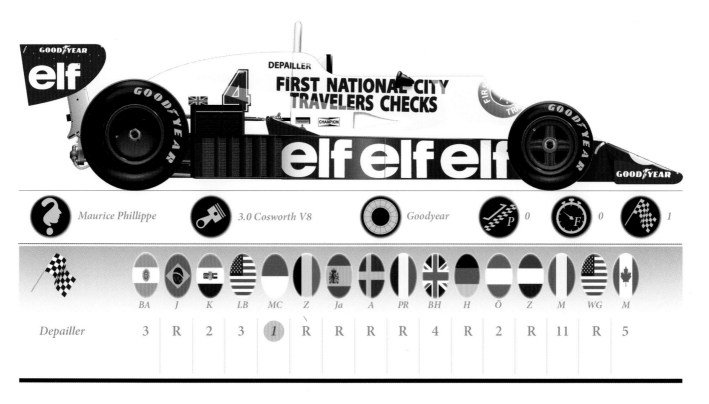

	Maurice Phillippe		3.0 Cosworth V8		Goodyear		P 0		F 0		1

	BA	J	K	LB	MC	Z	Ja	A	PR	BH	H	Ö	Z	M	WG	M
Depailler	3	R	2	3	1	R	R	R	R	4	R	2	R	11	R	5

MICK HILL ©

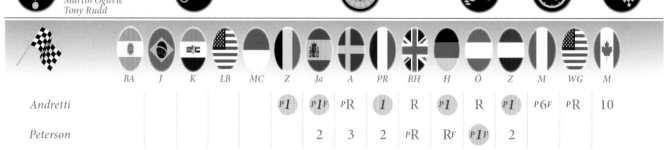

Colin Chapman
Peter Wright
Geoff Aldridge
Martin Ogilvie
Tony Rudd

3.0 Cosworth V8

Goodyear

P 9

F 4

6

	BA	J	K	LB	MC	Z	Ja	A	PR	BH	H	Ö	Z	M	WG	M
Andretti						P1	P1F	PR	1	R	P1	R	P1	P6F	PR	10
Peterson							2	3	2	PR	RF	P1F	2			

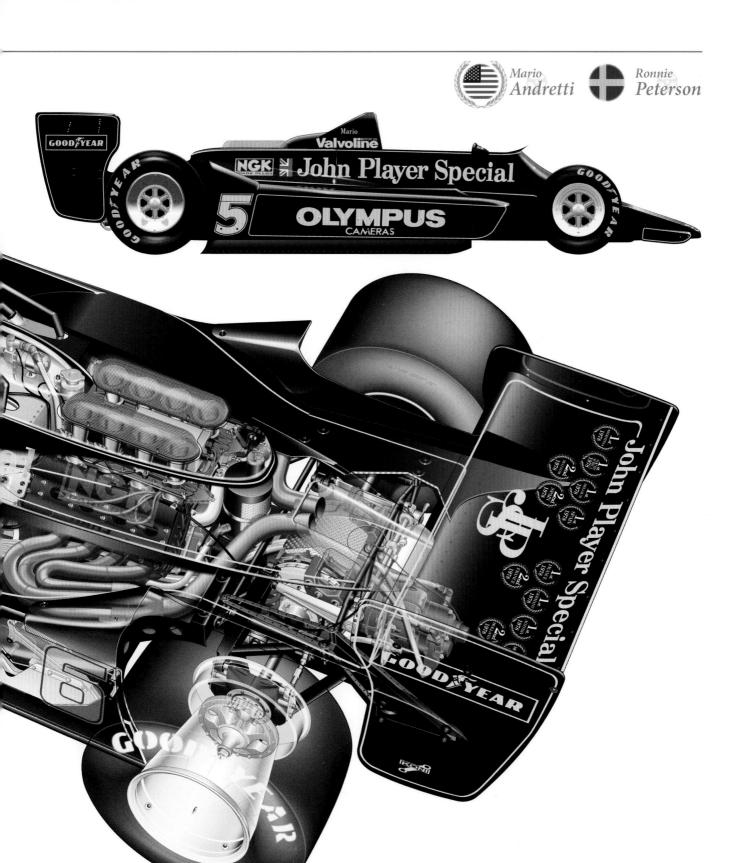

1978 Brabham BT46B *(fan car)*

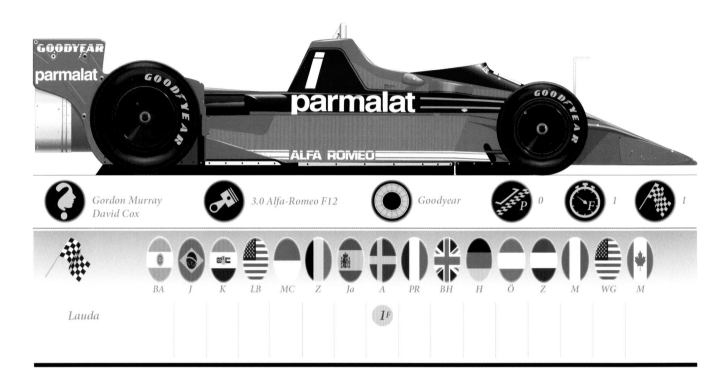

	Gordon Murray David Cox		3.0 Alfa-Romeo F12		Goodyear		P 0		F 1		1

	BA	J	K	LB	MC	Z	Ja	A	PR	BH	H	Ö	Z	M	WG	M
Lauda							1^F									

1978 Brabham BT46

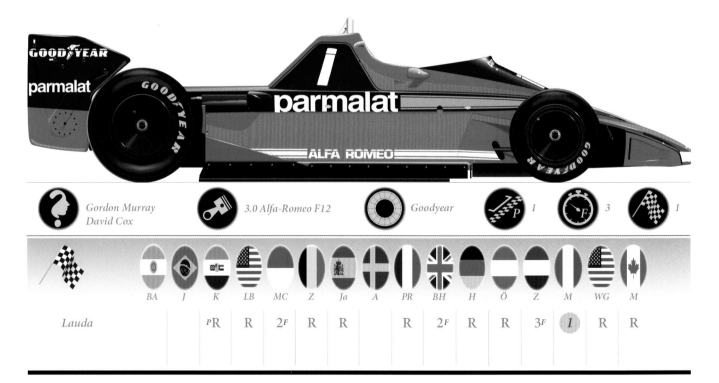

	Gordon Murray David Cox		3.0 Alfa-Romeo F12		Goodyear		P 1		F 3		1

	BA	J	K	LB	MC	Z	Ja	A	PR	BH	H	Ö	Z	M	WG	M
Lauda		^PR	R	2^F	R	R		R	2^F	R	R	3^F	*1*	R	R	

1979 Ligier JS11

Jacques **Laffite** Patrick **Depailler**

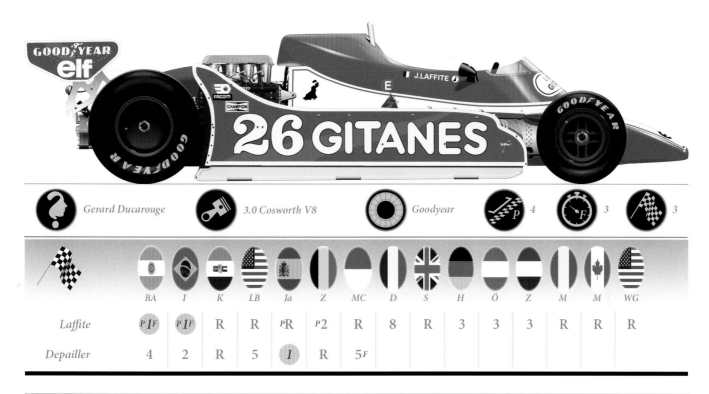

Gerard Ducarouge	3.0 Cosworth V8	Goodyear	P 4	F 3	🏁 3

🏁	BA	I	K	LB	Ja	Z	MC	D	S	H	Ö	Z	M	M	WG
Laffite	P1F	P1F	R	R	PR	P2	R	8	R	3	3	3	R	R	R
Depailler	4	2	R	5	1	R	5F								

1979 Ferrari 312T4

1st

Jody **Scheckter** Gilles **Villeneuve**

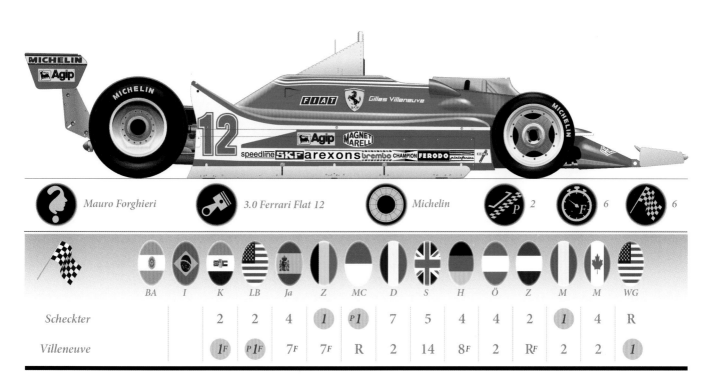

Mauro Forghieri	3.0 Ferrari Flat 12	Michelin	P 2	F 6	🏁 6

🏁	BA	I	K	LB	Ja	Z	MC	D	S	H	Ö	Z	M	M	WG
Scheckter			2	2	4	1	P1	7	5	4	4	2	1	4	R
Villeneuve			1F	P1F	7F	7F	R	2	14	8F	2	RF	2	2	1

1979 Renault RS10

Jean-Pierre *Jabouille*

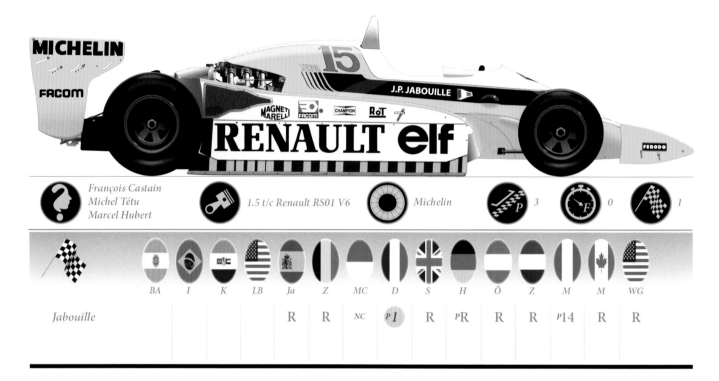

François Castain Michel Tétu Marcel Hubert	1.5 t/c Renault RS01 V6	Michelin	P 3 F 0 1

	BA	I	K	LB	Ja	Z	MC	D	S	H	Ö	Z	M	M	WG
Jabouille					R	R	NC	P1	R	PR	R	R	P14	R	R

1979 Williams FW07

Clay *Regazzoni*   Alan *Jones*

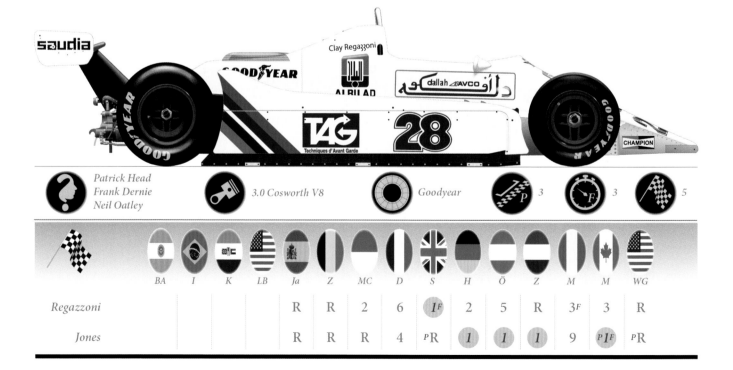

Patrick Head Frank Dernie Neil Oatley	3.0 Cosworth V8	Goodyear	P 3 F 3 5

	BA	I	K	LB	Ja	Z	MC	D	S	H	Ö	Z	M	M	WG
Regazzoni					R	R	2	6	1F	2	5	R	3F	3	R
Jones					R	R	R	4	PR	1	1	1	9	P1F	PR

1980-89

The 1980s was to be a tumultuous era with the governing body FISA and the Bernie Ecclestone-led constructors' body, FOCA, at loggerheads for most of the season.

In 1980 Alan Jones won in Spain only for the race not to count in the championship, with the same happening in the 1981 South African GP, again won by Jones. The San Marino GP in '82 saw the mainly British-based FOCA teams boycott the race, leaving Ferrari's Didier Pironi to take the honours.

With the dangers of motor racing still apparent, Ferrari driver Gilles Villeneuve was killed in practice at Zolder, and Pironi suffered career-ending injuries in practice for the German GP a few months later.

Niki Lauda came out of retirement in 1982 and went on to win the 1984 Drivers' title by just half a point from Alain Prost – the closest World Championship-winning margin of all time.

The first carbon-fibre monocoque chassis appeared in the form of a McLaren MP4/1, and in 1988 the McLaren MP4/4 became the most successful F1 car of all time, winning fifteen of the sixteen GPs that season. The biggest duel of the decade was between McLaren teammates Ayrton Senna and Alain Prost, which continued long after Prost moved to Ferrari.

1980-1989 Seasons race by race.

Year	Argentina	Japan	Australia	Mexico	Austria	Monaco	Brazil	Portugal	Belgium	San Marino	Britian	Spain	Canada	South Africa	Dutch	Swiss	European	Caesars Palace	French	Dallas	German	Detroit	Hungary	USA West	Italy	USA
1980	BA				Ö	MC	I		Z		BH		M	K	Z				PR		H			LB	I	WG
1981	BA				Ö	MC	J		Z	I	S	Ja	M		Z			LV	D		H			LB	M	
1982					Ö	MC	J		Z	I	BH		M	K	Z	D		LV	PR		H	De		LB	M	
1983					Ö	MC	J		S	I	S		M	K	Z		BH		PR		H	De		LB	M	
1984					Ö	MC	J	E	Z	I	BH		M	K	Z		N		D	Da	H	De			M	
1985			A		Ö	MC	J	E	S	I	S		M	K	Z		BH		PR		N	De			M	
1986			A	MC	Ö	MC	J	E	S	I	BH	Je	M						PR		H	De	H		M	
1987		S	A	MC	Ö	MC	J	E	S	I	S	Je							PR		H	De	H		M	
1988		S	A	MC		MC	J	E	S	I	S	Je	M						PR		H	De	H		M	
1989		S	A	MC		MC	J	E	S	I	S	Je	M						PR		H		H		M	P

for track abbreviations refer to map on pages 6/7

1980 Williams FW07

Alan
Jones

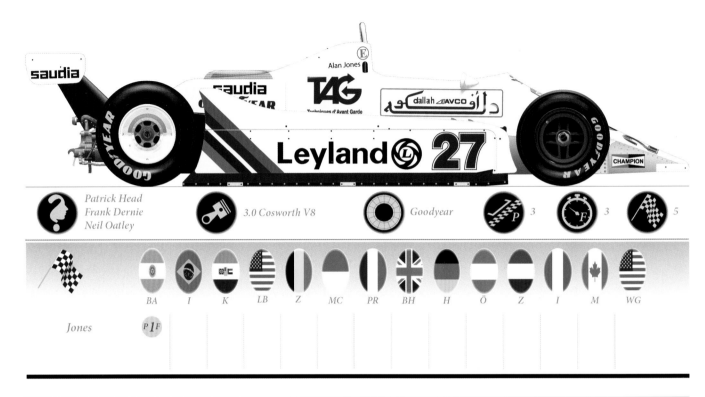

Patrick Head Frank Dernie Neil Oatley	3.0 Cosworth V8	Goodyear

P 3   F 3   5

	BA	I	K	LB	Z	MC	PR	BH	H	Ö	Z	I	M	WG
Jones	P**1**F													

1980 Renault RE20

René
Arnoux

Jean-Pierre
Jabouille

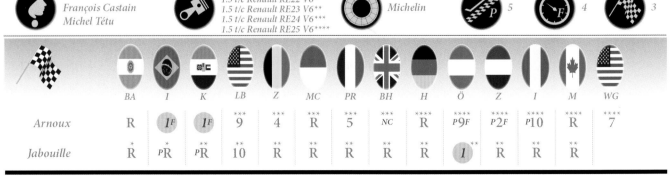

François Castain Michel Tétu	1.5 t/c Renault RE21 V6 1.5 t/c Renault RE22 V6* 1.5 t/c Renault RE23 V6** 1.5 t/c Renault RE24 V6*** 1.5 t/c Renault RE25 V6****	Michelin

P 5   F 4   3

	BA	I	K	LB	Z	MC	PR	BH	H	Ö	Z	I	M	WG
Arnoux	R	**1**F	**1**F	9***	4***	R***	5***	NC***	R****	P**9**F****	P**2**F****	P**10******	R****	7****
Jabouille	R*	P R*	P R**	10	R**	R	R**	R	R**	**1****	R**	R**	R**	

1980 Brabham BT49

Nelson *Piquet*

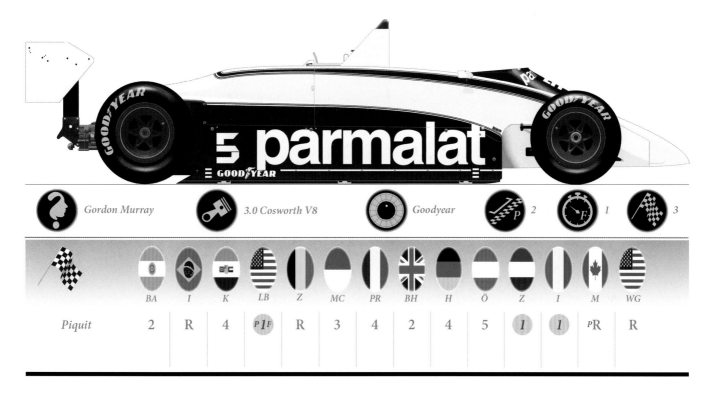

? Gordon Murray	🔧 3.0 Cosworth V8	⊙ Goodyear	🏁 P 2	⏱ F 1	🏁 3

🏁		BA	I	K	LB	Z	MC	PR	BH	H	Ö	Z	I	M	WG
Piquit		2	R	4	P1F	R	3	4	2	4	5	1	1	PR	R

1980 Ligier JS11/15

Didier *Pironi*   Jacques *Laffite*

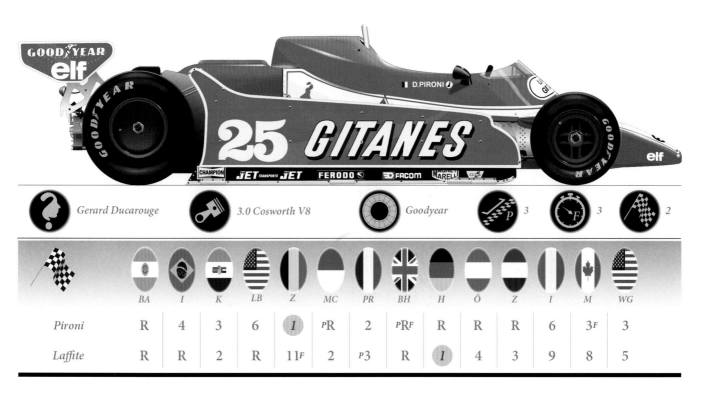

? Gerard Ducarouge	🔧 3.0 Cosworth V8	⊙ Goodyear	🏁 P 3	⏱ F 3	🏁 2

🏁		BA	I	K	LB	Z	MC	PR	BH	H	Ö	Z	I	M	WG
Pironi		R	4	3	6	1	PR	2	PRF	R	R	R	6	3F	3
Laffite		R	R	2	R	11F	2	P3	R	1	4	3	9	8	5

1980 Williams FW07B

Alan **Jones**

Carlos **Reutemann**

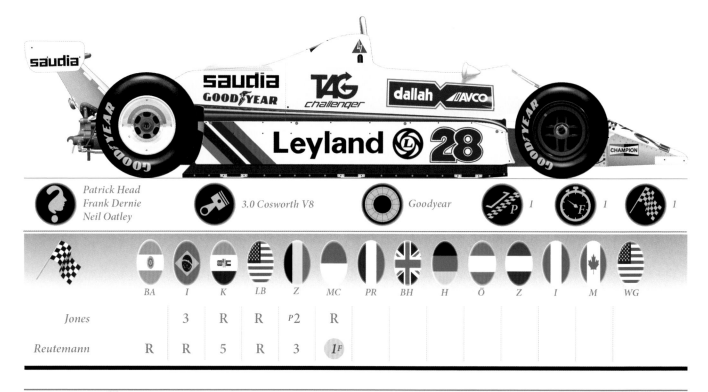

	Patrick Head / Frank Dernie / Neil Oatley	3.0 Cosworth V8	Goodyear	P 1	F 1	1

	BA	I	K	LB	Z	MC	PR	BH	H	Ö	Z	I	M	WG
Jones		3	R	R	P2	R								
Reutemann	R	R	5	R	3	1F								

1980 Williams FW07B

1st

Alan **Jones**

Carlos **Reutemann**

	Patrick Head / Frank Dernie / Neil Oatley	3.0 Cosworth V8	Goodyear	P 1	F 4	5

	BA	I	K	LB	Z	MC	PR	BH	H	Ö	Z	I	M	WG
Jones							1F	1	P3F	2	11	2F	1	1F
Reutemann							6	3	2	3	4	3	2	2

1981 Williams FW07C

1st

Alan **Jones** Carlos **Reutemann**

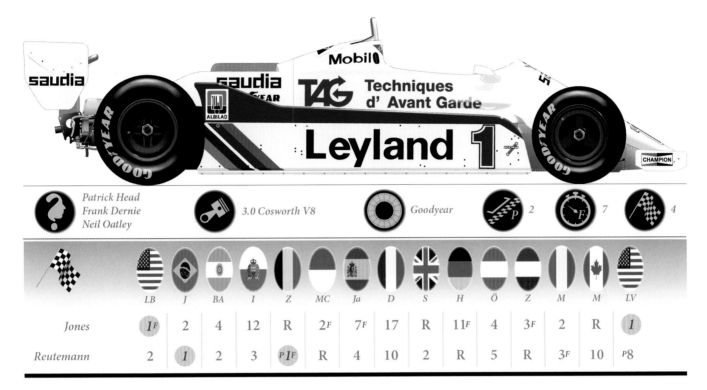

Patrick Head Frank Dernie Neil Oatley	3.0 Cosworth V8	Goodyear	P 2 F 7 4

	LB	J	BA	I	Z	MC	Ja	D	S	H	Ö	Z	M	M	LV
Jones	1F	2	4	12	R	2F	7F	17	R	11F	4	3F	2	R	1
Reutemann	2	1	2	3	P1F	R	4	10	2	R	5	R	3F	10	P8

1981 Brabham BT49C

Nelson **Piquet**

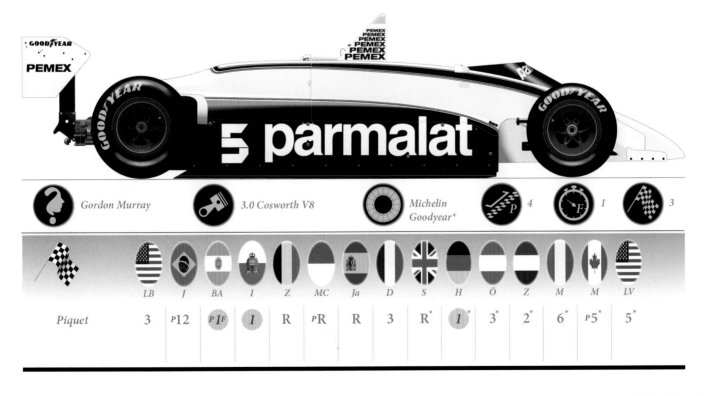

Gordon Murray	3.0 Cosworth V8	Michelin Goodyear*	P 4 F 1 3

	LB	J	BA	I	Z	MC	Ja	D	S	H	Ö	Z	M	M	LV
Piquet	3	P12	P1F	1	R	PR	R	3	R*	1*	3*	2*	6*	P5*	5*

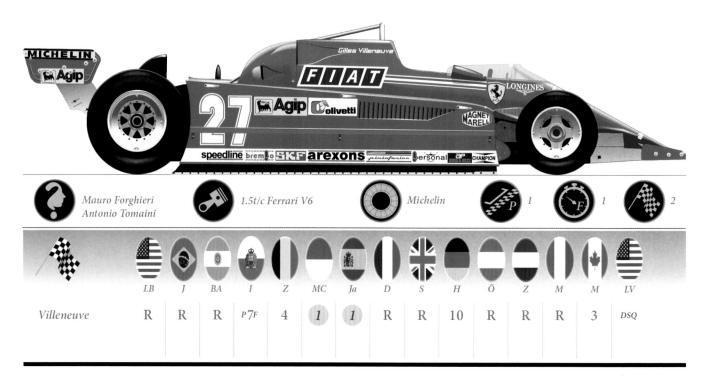

Mauro Forghieri Antonio Tomaini	1.5t/c Ferrari V6	Michelin	P 1 F 1 2

	LB	J	BA	I	Z	MC	Ja	D	S	H	Ö	Z	M	M	LV
Villeneuve	R	R	R	P7F	4	1	1	R	R	10	R	R	R	3	DSQ

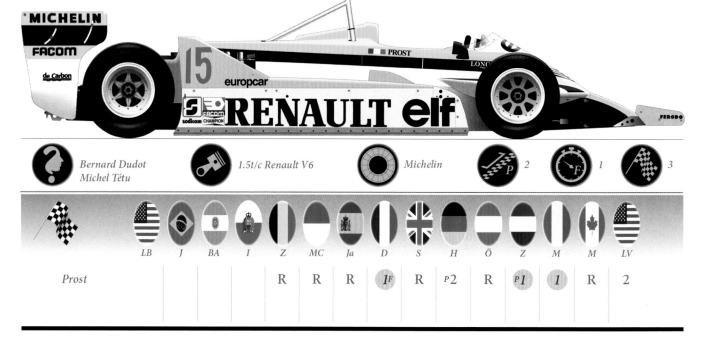

Bernard Dudot Michel Tétu	1.5t/c Renault V6	Michelin	P 2 F 1 3

	LB	J	BA	I	Z	MC	Ja	D	S	H	Ö	Z	M	M	LV
Prost			R	R	R	1F	R	P2	R	P1	1	R	2		

1981 McLaren MP4

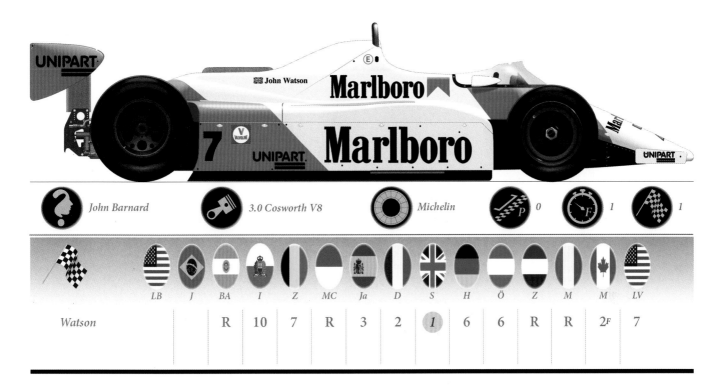

	John Barnard		3.0 Cosworth V8		Michelin	P	0	F	1		1

		LB	J	BA	I	Z	MC	Ja	D	S	H	Ö	Z	M	M	LV
Watson		R	10	7	R	3	2		1	6	6	R	R	2F	7

1981 Ligier JS17

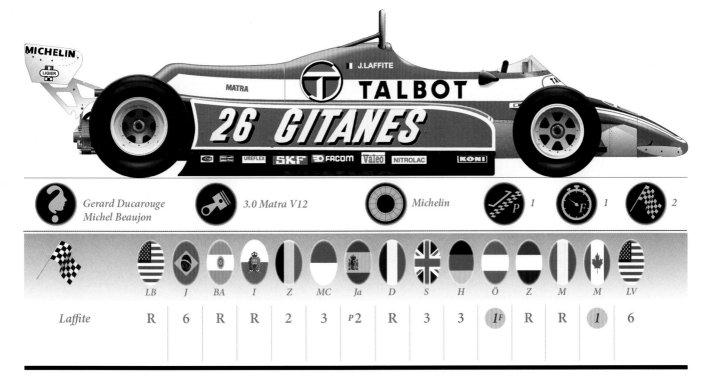

	Gerard Ducarouge Michel Beaujon		3.0 Matra V12		Michelin	P	1	F	1		2

		LB	J	BA	I	Z	MC	Ja	D	S	H	Ö	Z	M	M	LV
Laffite		R	6	R	R	2	3	P2	R	3	3	1F	R	R	1	6

1982 Renault RE30B

Alain **Prost** René **Arnoux**

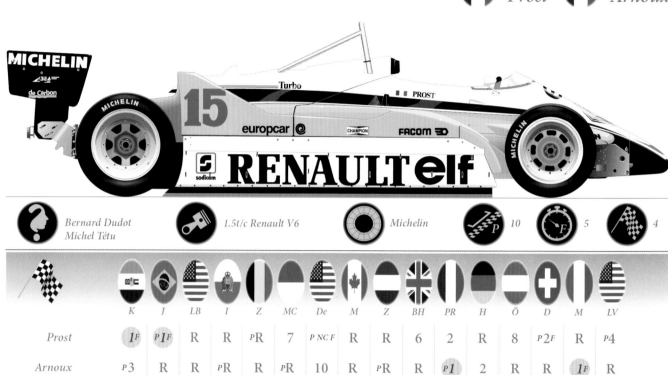

| Bernard Dudot Michel Tétu | 1.5t/c Renault V6 | Michelin | P 10 | F 5 | 4 |

	K	J	LB	I	Z	MC	De	M	Z	BH	PR	H	Ö	D	M	LV
Prost	1F	P1F	R	R	PR	7	P NC F	R	R	6	2	R	8	P2F	R	P4
Arnoux	P3	R	R	PR	R	PR	10	R	PR	R	P1	2	R	R	1F	R

1982 McLaren MP4B

Niki **Lauda** John **Watson**

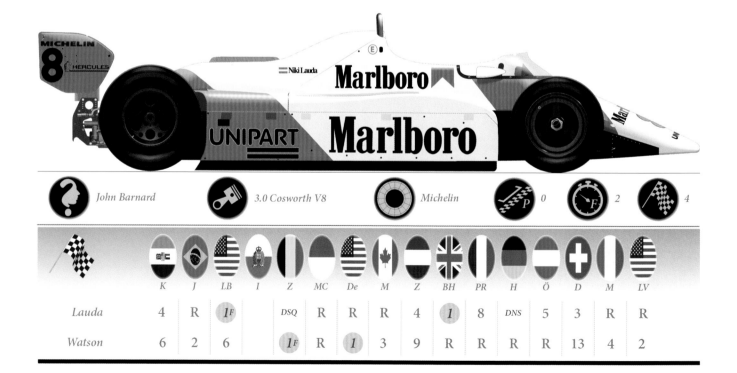

| John Barnard | 3.0 Cosworth V8 | Michelin | P 0 | F 2 | 4 |

	K	J	LB	I	Z	MC	De	M	Z	BH	PR	H	Ö	D	M	LV
Lauda	4	R	1F		DSQ	R	R	R	4	1	8	DNS	5	3	R	R
Watson	6	2	6		1F	R	1	3	9	R	R	R	13	4		2

1982 Ferrari 126C2
🏁 **1st** 🏁

 Didier **Pironi**  Patrick **Tambay**

 Mauro Forghirei / Harvey Postlethwaite   1.5t/c Ferrari V6   Goodyear   P 1   F 2   3

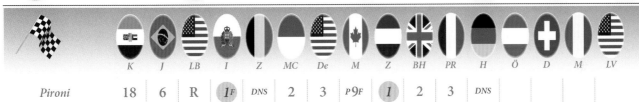

	K	J	LB	I	Z	MC	De	M	Z	BH	PR	H	Ö	D	M	LV
Pironi	18	6	R	1F	DNS	2	3	P9F	1	2	3	DNS				
Tambay									8	3	4	1	4	DNS	2	DNS

1982 Brabham BT49D

 Riccardo **Patrese**

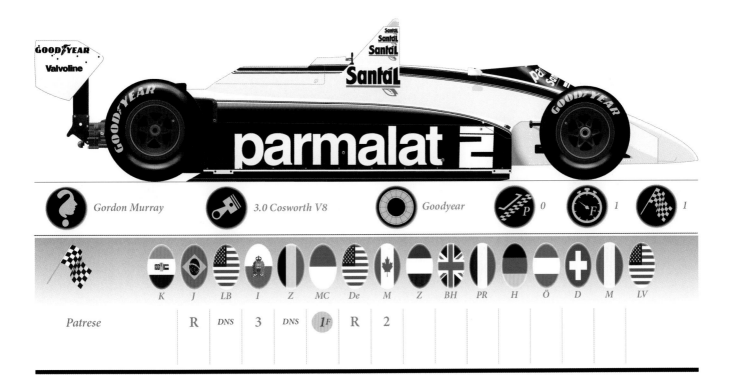

 Gordon Murray 1 3.0 Cosworth V8 1 Goodyear P 0 F 1 1

	K	J	LB	I	Z	MC	De	M	Z	BH	PR	H	Ö	D	M	LV
Patrese			R	DNS	3	DNS	1F	R	2							

1982 Brabham BT50

Nelson
Piquet

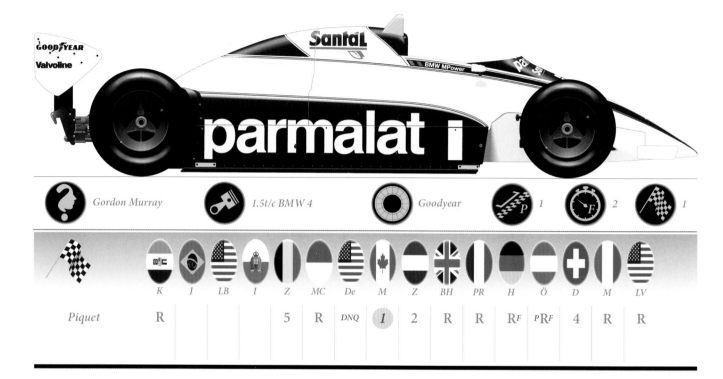

? Gordon Murray	1.5t/c BMW 4	Goodyear	P 1	F 2	1

	K	J	LB	I	Z	MC	De	M	Z	BH	PR	H	Ö	D	M	LV
Piquet	R				5	R	DNQ	*1*	2	R	R	RF	PRF	4	R	R

1982 Lotus 91

Elio de
Angelis

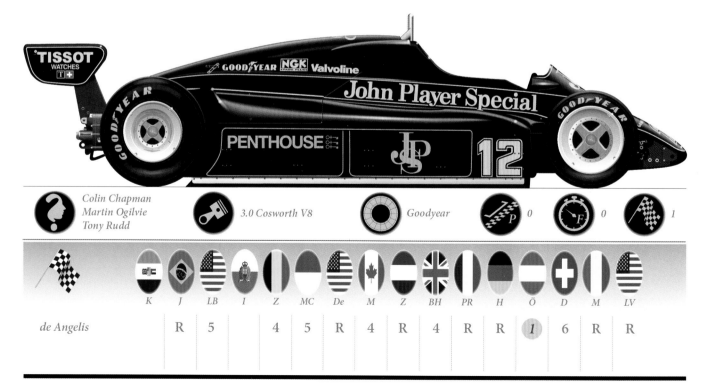

? Colin Chapman Martin Ogilvie Tony Rudd	3.0 Cosworth V8	Goodyear	P 0	F 0	1

	K	J	LB	I	Z	MC	De	M	Z	BH	PR	H	Ö	D	M	LV
de Angelis		R	5		4	5	R	4	R	4	R	R	*1*	6	R	R

1982 Williams FW08

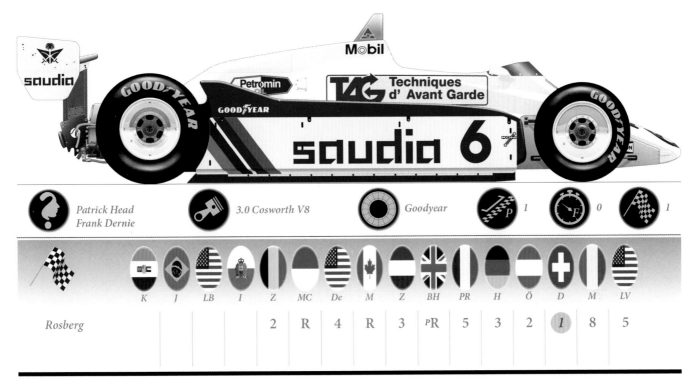

	Patrick Head Frank Dernie		3.0 Cosworth V8		Goodyear		P 1		F 0		1

		K	J	LB	I	Z	MC	De	M	Z	BH	PR	H	Ö	D	M	LV
Rosberg						2	R	4	R	3	PR	5	3	2	1	8	5

1982 Tyrrell 011

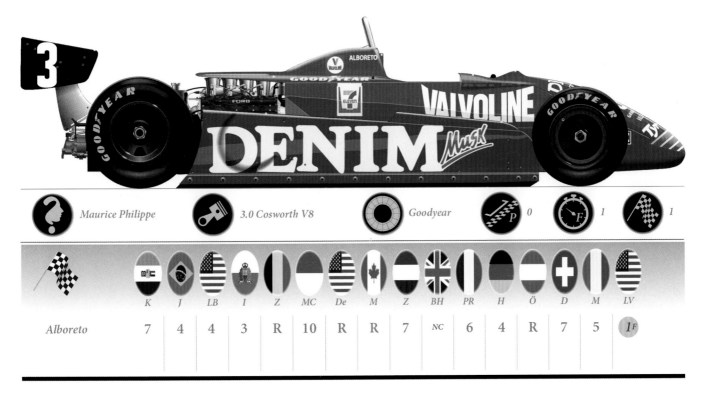

	Maurice Philippe		3.0 Cosworth V8		Goodyear		P 0		F 1		1

		K	J	LB	I	Z	MC	De	M	Z	BH	PR	H	Ö	D	M	LV
Alboreto		7	4	4	3	R	10	R	R	7	NC	6	4	R	7	5	1F

1983 Brabham BT52

Nelson
Piquet

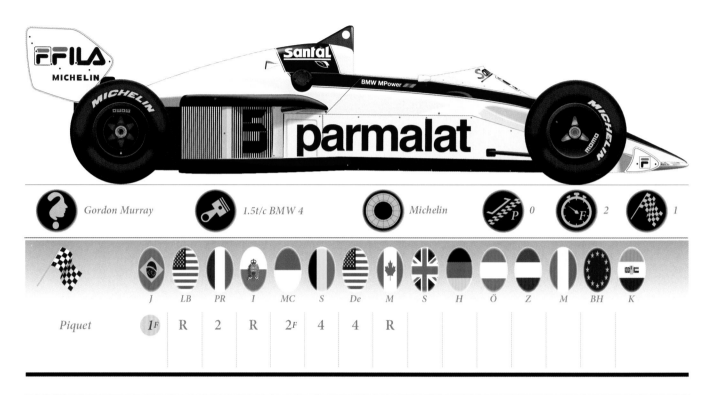

	Gordon Murray		1.5t/c BMW 4		Michelin		0		2		1

		J	LB	PR	I	MC	S	De	M	S	H	Ö	Z	M	BH	K
Piquet		1F	R	2	R	2F	4	4	R							

1983 McLaren MP4/1C

John
Watson

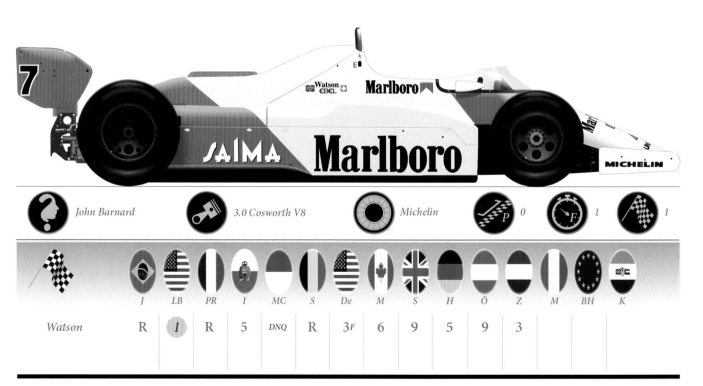

	John Barnard		3.0 Cosworth V8		Michelin		0		1		1

		J	LB	PR	I	MC	S	De	M	S	H	Ö	Z	M	BH	K
Watson		R	1	R	5	DNQ	R	3F	6	9	5	9	3			

1983 Renault RE40

Alain
Prost

	Bernard Dudot Michel Tétu Jean-Claude Migeot		1.5t/c Renault V6		Michelin		P 3		F 3		4

		J	LB	PR	I	MC	S	De	M	S	H	Ö	Z	M	BH	K
Prost		11	P1F	2	P3	P1	8	5	1F	4	1F	R	R	2	R

1983 Ferrari 126C2B

Patrick
Tambay

René
Arnoux

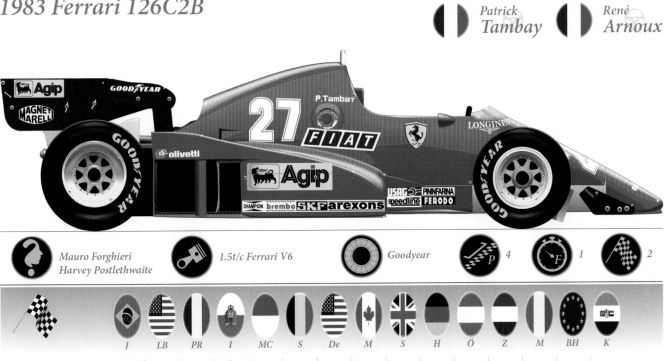

	Mauro Forghieri Harvey Postlethwaite		1.5t/c Ferrari V6		Goodyear		P 4		F 1		2

		J	LB	PR	I	MC	S	De	M	S	H	Ö	Z	M	BH	K
Tambay		5	PR	4	1	4	2	R	3F						
Arnoux		10	3	7	P3	R	R	PR	P1						

1983 Williams FW08C

Keke
Rosberg

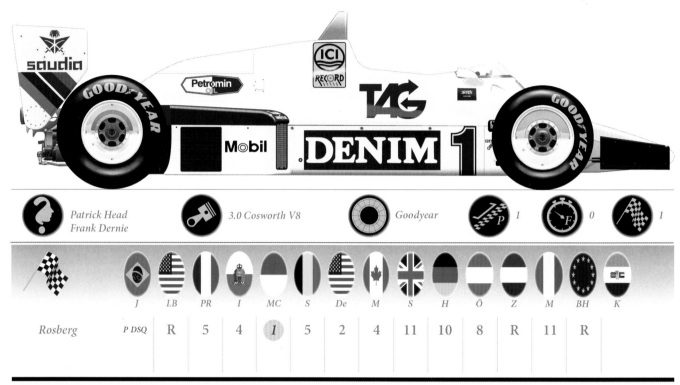

	Patrick Head Frank Dernie		3.0 Cosworth V8		Goodyear		P 1		F 0		1

		J	LB	PR	I	MC	S	De	M	S	H	Ö	Z	M	BH	K
Rosberg	P DSQ	R	5	4	*1*	5	2	4	11	10	8	R	11	R		

1983 Tyrrell 011

Michele
Alboreto

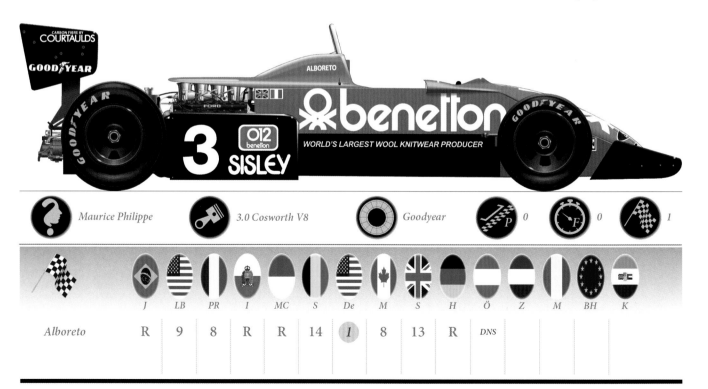

	Maurice Philippe		3.0 Cosworth V8		Goodyear		P 0		F 0		1

	J	LB	PR	I	MC	S	De	M	S	H	Ö	Z	M	BH	K
Alboreto	R	9	8	R	R	14	*1*	8	13	R	*DNS*				

1983 Ferrari 126C3

1st

René *Arnoux*

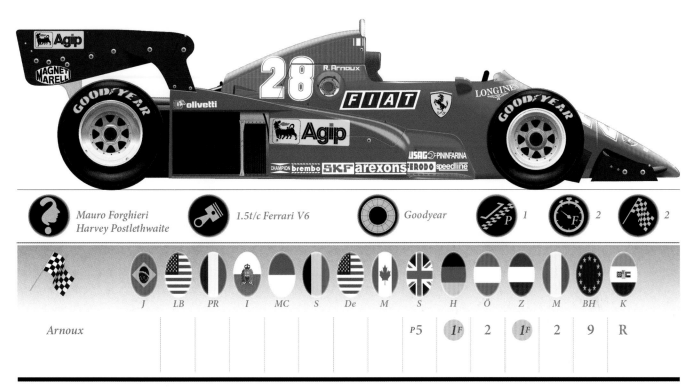

| | Mauro Forghieri Harvey Postlethwaite | | 1.5t/c Ferrari V6 | | Goodyear | | P 1 | | F 2 | | 2 |

	J	LB	PR	I	MC	S	De	M	S	H	Ö	Z	M	BH	K
Arnoux									P5	1F	2	1F	2	9	R

1983 Brabham BT52B

Nelson *Piquet*   Riccardo *Patrese*

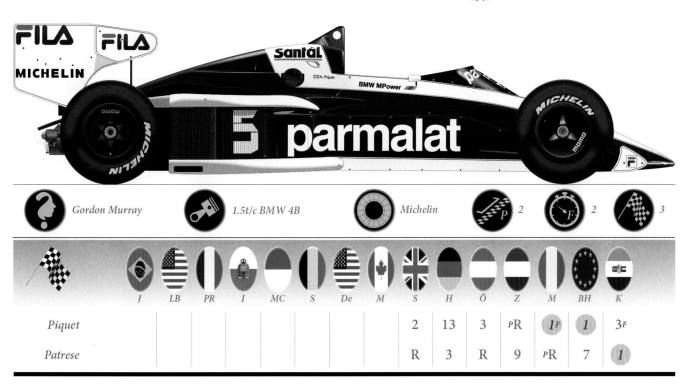

| | Gordon Murray | | 1.5t/c BMW 4B | | Michelin | | P 2 | | F 2 | | 3 |

	J	LB	PR	I	MC	S	De	M	S	H	Ö	Z	M	BH	K
Piquet									2	13	3	PR	1F	1	3F
Patrese									R	3	R	9	PR	7	1

1984 McLaren MP4/2

Niki **Lauda** *Alain* **Prost**

1st

 John Barnard   1.5t/c TAG Porsche V6   Michelin   P 3   F 8   12

	J	K	Z	I	D	MC	M	De	Da	BH	H	Ö	Z	M	N	E
Lauda	R	1	R	R	1	R	2	R	9F	1F	2	1F	2	1F	4	2F
Prost	1F	2	R	1	7F	P1	3	4	R	R	P1F	R	P1	R	1	1

1984 Ferrari 126C4

Michele **Alboreto**

 Mauro Forghieri
Harvey Postlethwaite   1.5t/c Ferrari V6   Goodyear   P 1   F 1   1

	J	K	Z	I	D	MC	M	De	Da	BH	H	Ö	Z	M	N	E
Alboreto	R	11	P1	R	R	6	R	R	R	5	R	3	R	2	2F	4

1984 Brabham BT53

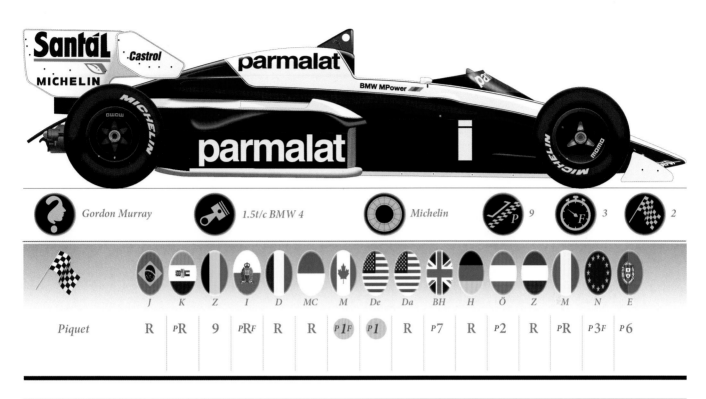

	Gordon Murray		1.5t/c BMW 4		Michelin	P	9	F	3		2

		J	K	Z	I	D	MC	M	De	Da	BH	H	Ö	Z	M	N	E
Piquet		R	ᴾR	9	ᴾRF	R	R	ᴾ1F	ᴾ1	R	ᴾ7	R	ᴾ2	R	ᴾR	ᴾ3F	ᴾ6

1984 Williams FW09

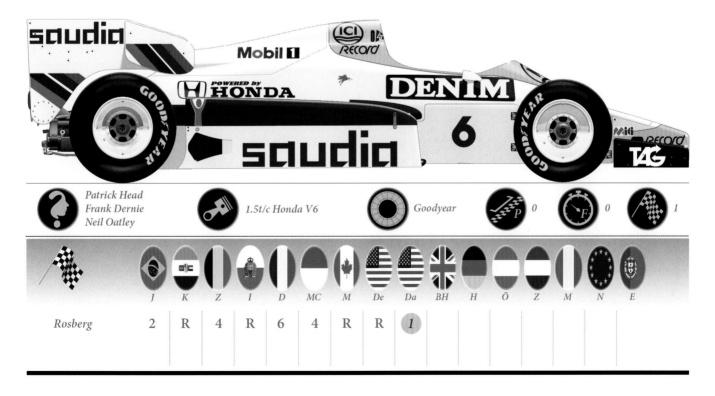

	Patrick Head Frank Dernie Neil Oatley		1.5t/c Honda V6		Goodyear	P	0	F	0		1

		J	K	Z	I	D	MC	M	De	Da	BH	H	Ö	Z	M	N	E
Rosberg		2	R	4	R	6	4	R	R	1							

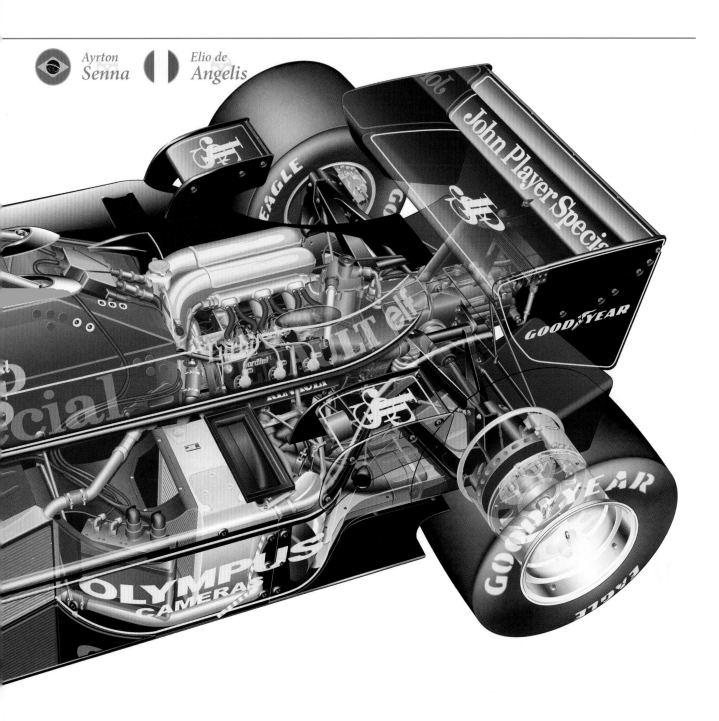

Ayrton **Senna** Elio de **Angelis**

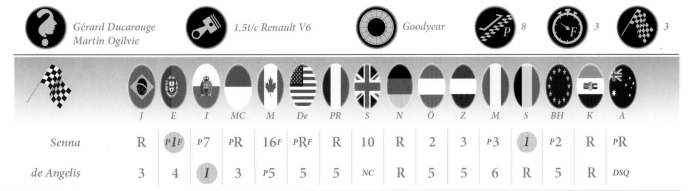

Gérard Ducarouge
Martin Ogilvie

1.5t/c Renault V6

Goodyear

P 8

F 3

3

	J	E	I	MC	M	De	PR	S	N	Ö	Z	M	S	BH	K	A
Senna	R	P1F	P7	PR	16F	PRF	R	10	R	2	3	P3	1	P2	R	PR
de Angelis	3	4	1	3	P5	5	5	NC	R	5	5	6	R	5	R	DSQ

1985 McLaren MP4/2B

1st

 Alain **Prost**  Niki **Lauda**

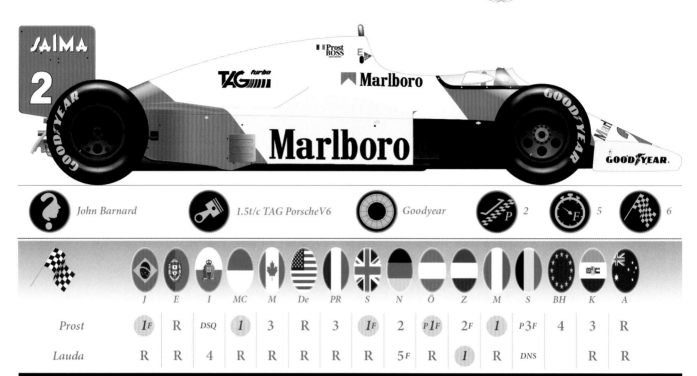

| | John Barnard | | 1.5t/c TAG Porsche V6 | | Goodyear | | P 2 | | F 5 | | 6 |

	J	E	I	MC	M	De	PR	S	N	Ö	Z	M	S	BH	K	A
Prost	1F	R	DSQ	1	3	R	3	1F	2	P1F	2F	1	P3F	4	3	R
Lauda	R	R	4	R	R	R	R	R	5F	R	1	R	DNS		R	R

1985 Ferrari 156/85

 Michele **Alboreto**

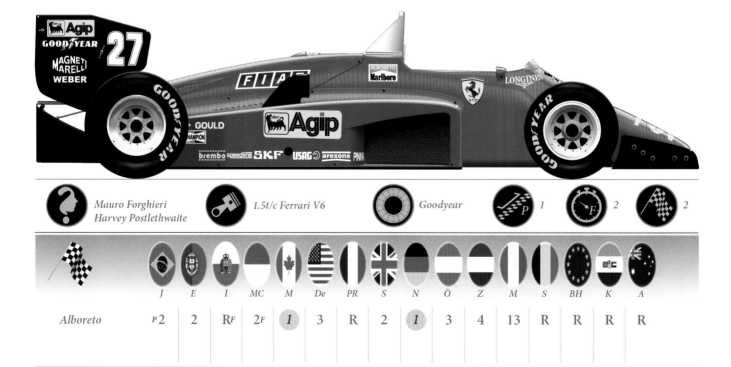

| | Mauro Forghieri Harvey Postlethwaite | | 1.5t/c Ferrari V6 | | Goodyear | | P 1 | | F 2 | | 2 |

	J	E	I	MC	M	De	PR	S	N	Ö	Z	M	S	BH	K	A
Alboreto	P2	2	RF	2F	1	3	R	2	1	3	4	13	R	R	R	R

1985 Williams FW10

 Keke **Rosberg**  Nigel **Mansell**

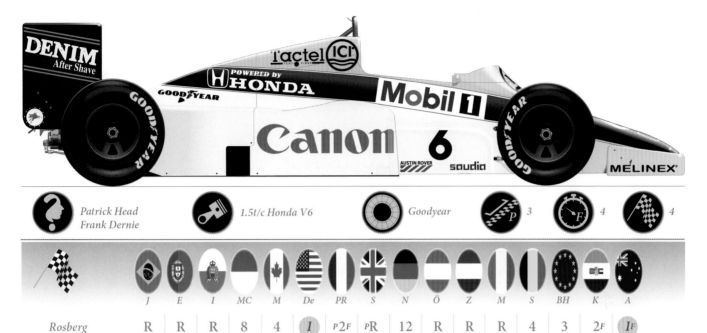

Patrick Head Frank Dernie	1.5t/c Honda V6	Goodyear	P 3	F 4	4

	J	E	I	MC	M	De	PR	S	N	Ö	Z	M	S	BH	K	A
Rosberg	R	R	R	8	4	1	P2F	PR	12	R	R	R	4	3	2F	1F
Mansell	R	5	5	7	6	R	DNS	R	6	R	6	11F	2	1	P1	R

1985 Brabham BT54

 Nelson **Piquet**

Gordon Murray	1.5t/c BMW 4	Pirelli	P 1	F 0	1

	J	E	I	MC	M	De	PR	S	N	Ö	Z	M	S	BH	K	A
Piquet	R	R	8	R	R	6	1	4	R	R	P8	2	5	R	R	R

 Nelson **Piquet**  Nigel **Mansell**

1st

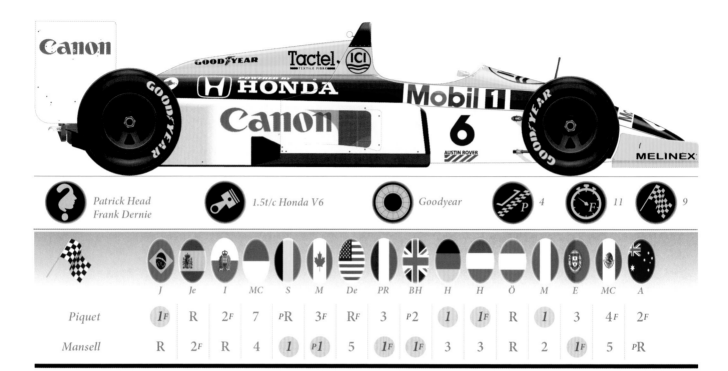

Patrick Head Frank Dernie	1.5t/c Honda V6	Goodyear	P 4	F 11	9

	J	Je	I	MC	S	M	De	PR	BH	H	H	Ö	M	E	MC	A
Piquet	1F	R	2F	7	PR	3F	RF	3	P2	1	1F	R	1	3	4F	2F
Mansell	R	2F	R	4	1	P1	5	1F	1F	3	3	R	2	1F	5	PR

1986 Lotus 98T

 Ayrton **Senna**

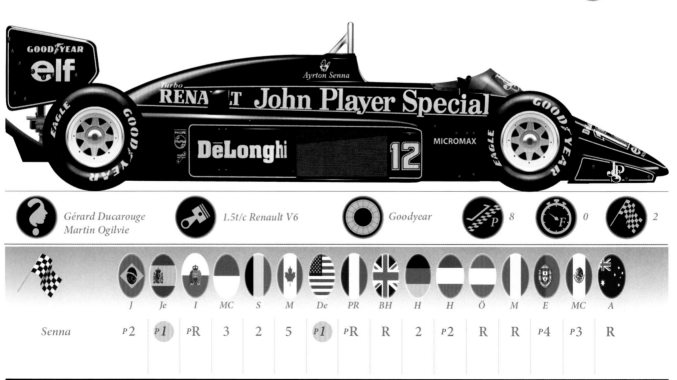

Gérard Ducarouge Martin Ogilvie	1.5t/c Renault V6	Goodyear	P 8	F 0	2

	J	Je	I	MC	S	M	De	PR	BH	H	H	Ö	M	E	MC	A
Senna	P2	P1	PR	3	2	5	P1	PR	R	2	P2	R	R	P4	P3	R

1986 McLaren MP4/2C

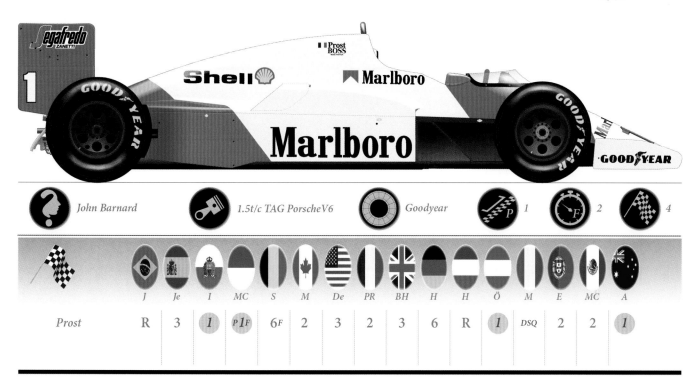

	John Barnard		1.5t/c TAG Porsche V6		Goodyear		P	1		F	2			4

	J	Je	I	MC	S	M	De	PR	BH	H	H	Ö	M	E	MC	A
Prost	R	3	*1*	P *1F*	6F	2	3	2	3	6	R	*1*	DSQ	2	2	*1*

1986 Benetton B186

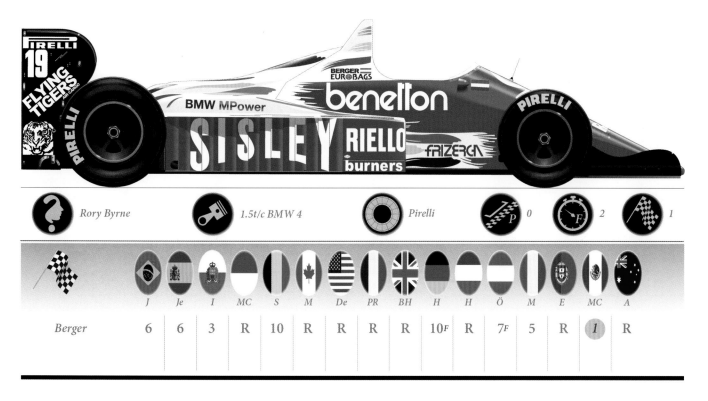

	Rory Byrne		1.5t/c BMW 4		Pirelli		P	0		F	2			1

	J	Je	I	MC	S	M	De	PR	BH	H	H	Ö	M	E	MC	A
Berger	6	6	3	R	10	R	R	R	R	10F	R	7F	5	R	*1*	R

1987 McLaren MP4/3

Alain **Prost**

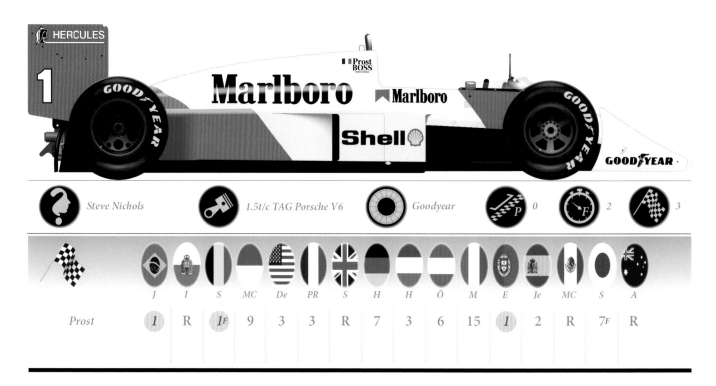

	Steve Nichols		1.5t/c TAG Porsche V6		Goodyear		P 0		F 2		3

	J	I	S	MC	De	PR	S	H	H	Ö	M	E	Je	MC	S	A
Prost	1	R	1F	9	3	3	R	7	3	6	15	1	2	R	7F	R

1987 Williams FW11B

 1st

Nigel **Mansell** Nelson **Piquet**

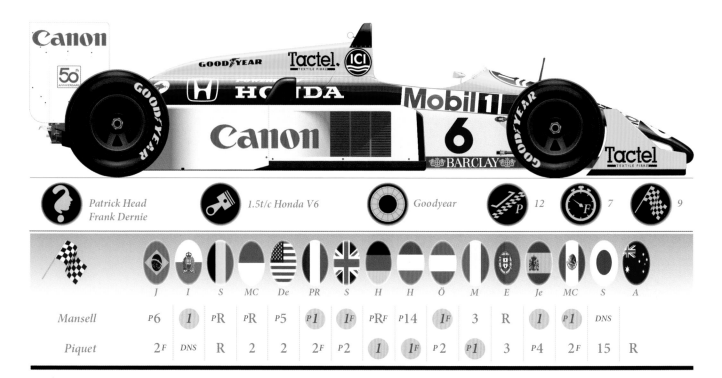

	Patrick Head Frank Dernie		1.5t/c Honda V6		Goodyear		P 12		F 7		9

	J	I	S	MC	De	PR	S	H	H	Ö	M	E	Je	MC	S	A
Mansell	P6	1	PR	PR	P5	P1	1F	PRF	P14	1F	3	R	1	P1	DNS	
Piquet	2F	DNS	R	2	2	2F	P2	1	1F	P2	P1	3	P4	2F	15	R

1987 Lotus 99T

Ayrton *Senna*

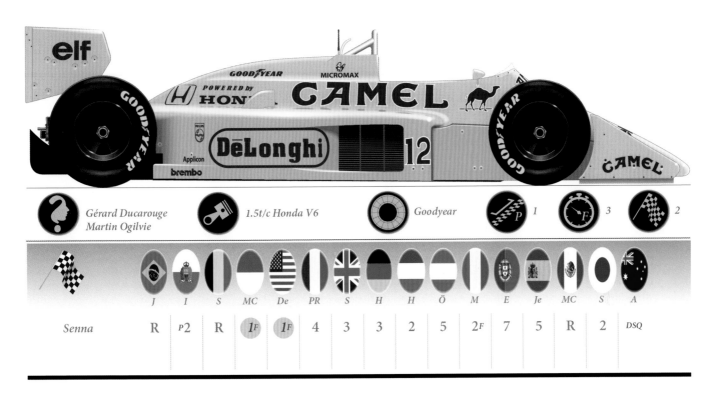

| ? | Gérard Ducarouge Martin Ogilvie | ⚙ | 1.5t/c Honda V6 | ◯ | Goodyear | P | 1 | F | 3 | 🏁 | 2 |

🏁		J	I	S	MC	De	PR	S	H	H	Ö	M	E	Je	MC	S	A
Senna		R	P2	R	1F	1F	4	3	3	2	5	2F	7	5	R	2	DSQ

1987 Ferrari F1/87

Gerhard *Berger*

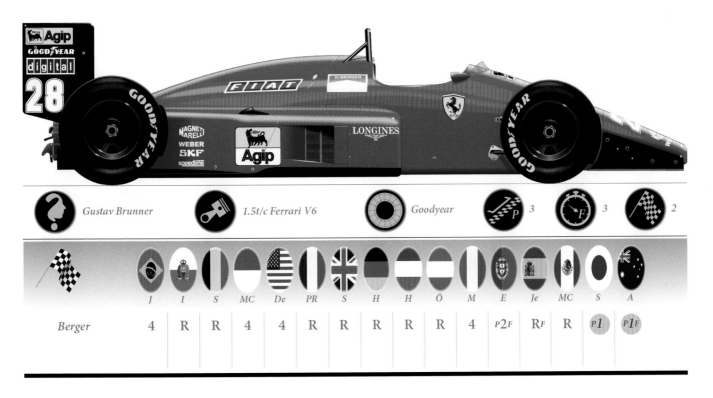

| ? | Gustav Brunner | ⚙ | 1.5t/c Ferrari V6 | ◯ | Goodyear | P | 3 | F | 3 | 🏁 | 2 |

🏁		J	I	S	MC	De	PR	S	H	H	Ö	M	E	Je	MC	S	A
Berger		4	R	R	4	4	R	R	R	R	R	4	P2F	RF	R	P1	P1F

1988 McLaren MP4/4

Alain **Prost** Ayrton **Senna**

1st

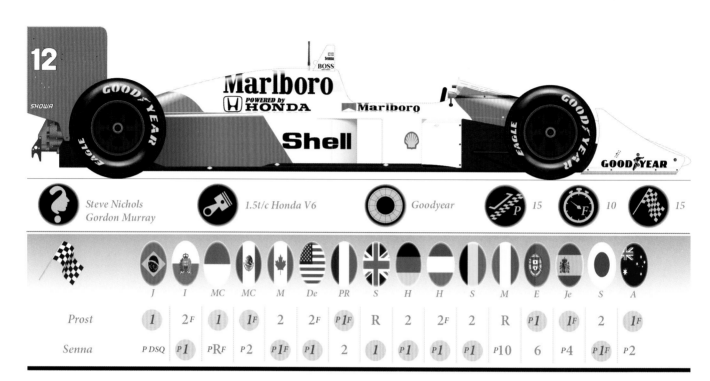

Steve Nichols Gordon Murray	1.5t/c Honda V6	Goodyear	P 15 F 10 15

	J	I	MC	MC	M	De	PR	S	H	H	S	M	E	Je	S	A
Prost	1	2F	1	1F	2	2F	P1F	R	2	2F	2	R	P1	1F	2	1F
Senna	P DSQ	P1	PRF	P2	P1F	P1	2	1	P1	P1	P1	P10	6	P4	P1F	P2

1988 Ferrari F1/87/88C

Gerhard **Berger**

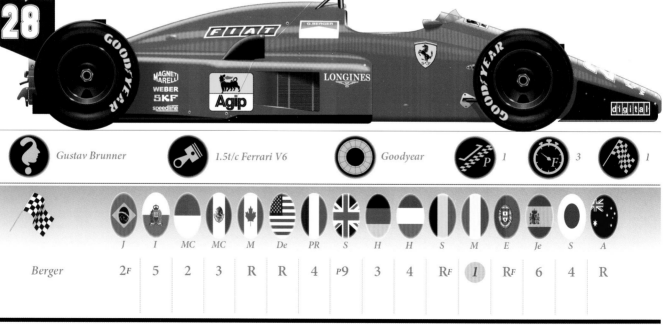

Gustav Brunner	1.5t/c Ferrari V6	Goodyear	P 1 F 3 1

	J	I	MC	MC	M	De	PR	S	H	H	S	M	E	Je	S	A
Berger	2F	5	2	3	R	R	4	P9	3	4	RF	1	RF	6	4	R

1989 Ferrari 640

Nigel **Mansell**

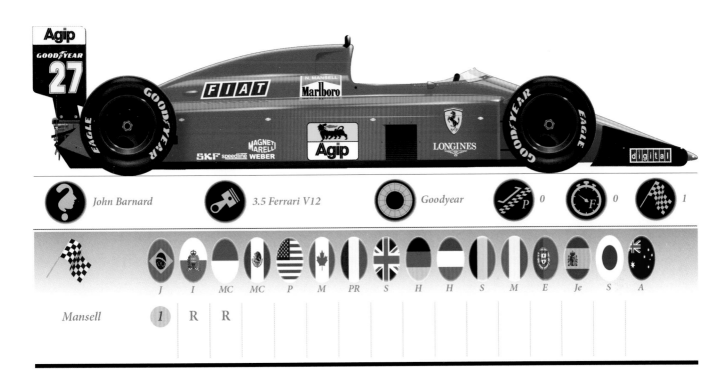

	John Barnard		3.5 Ferrari V12		Goodyear		P 0		F 0		1

	J	I	MC	MC	P	M	PR	S	H	H	S	M	E	Je	S	A
Mansell	1	R	R													

1989 McLaren MP4/5

 1st

Ayrton **Senna**   Alain **Prost**

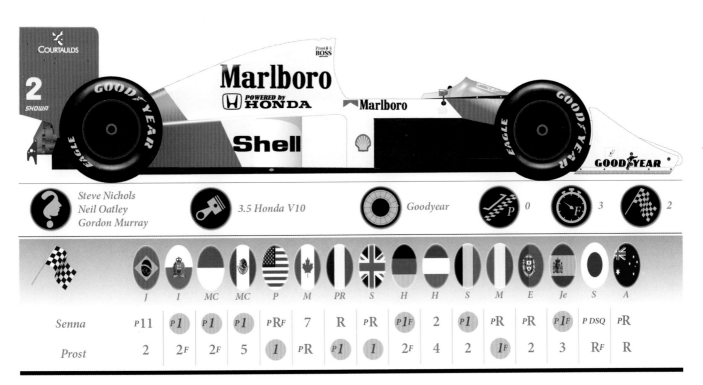

	Steve Nichols Neil Oatley Gordon Murray		3.5 Honda V10		Goodyear		P 0		F 3		2

	J	I	MC	MC	P	M	PR	S	H	H	S	M	E	Je	S	A
Senna	P11	P1	P1	P1	PRF	7	R	PR	P1F	2	P1	PR	PR	P1F	P DSQ	PR
Prost	2	2F	2F	5	1	PR	P1	1	2F	4	2	1F	2	3	RF	R

1989 Williams FW12C

Thierry
Boutsen

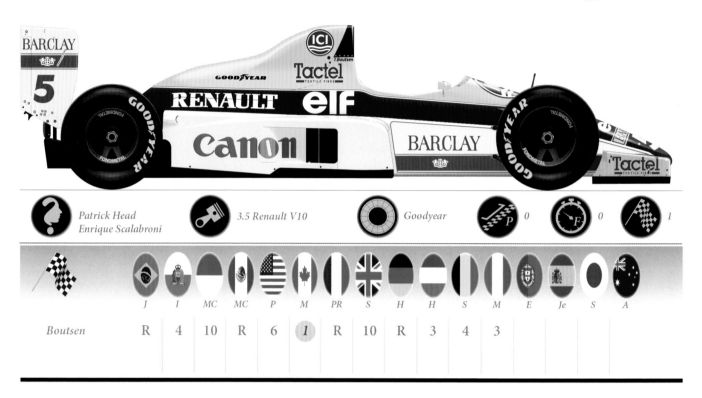

| | Patrick Head Enrique Scalabroni | | 3.5 Renault V10 | | Goodyear | | P 0 | | F 0 | | 1 |

		J	I	MC	MC	P	M	PR	S	H	H	S	M	E	Je	S	A
Boutsen		R	4	10	R	6	1	R	10	R	3	4	3				

1989 Ferrari 640/2

Nigel
Mansell

Gerhard
Berger

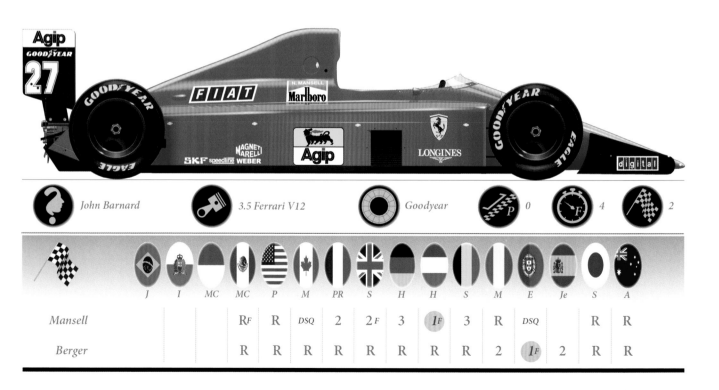

| | John Barnard | | 3.5 Ferrari V12 | | Goodyear | | P 0 | | F 4 | | 2 |

		J	I	MC	MC	P	M	PR	S	H	H	S	M	E	Je	S	A
Mansell				RF	R	DSQ	2	2F	3	1F	3	R	DSQ			R	R
Berger				R	R	R	R	R	R	R	R	2	1F	2		R	R

1989 Benetton B189

Alessandro **Nannini**

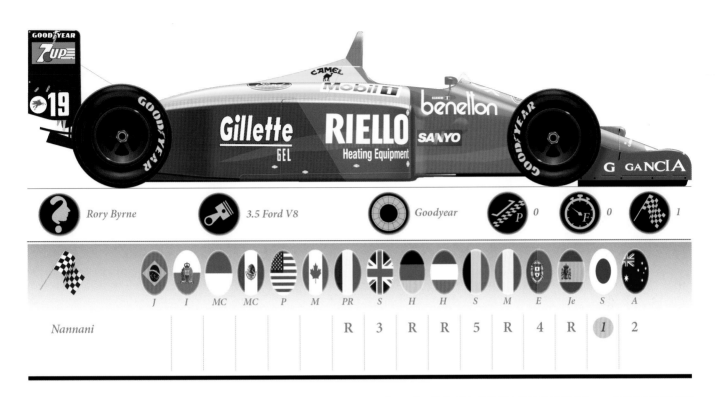

| | Rory Byrne | | 3.5 Ford V8 | | Goodyear | | P 0 | | F 0 | | 1 |

	J	I	MC	MC	P	M	PR	S	H	H	S	M	E	Je	S	A
Nannani							R	3	R	R	5	R	4	R	*1*	2

1989 Williams FW13

Thierry **Boutsen**

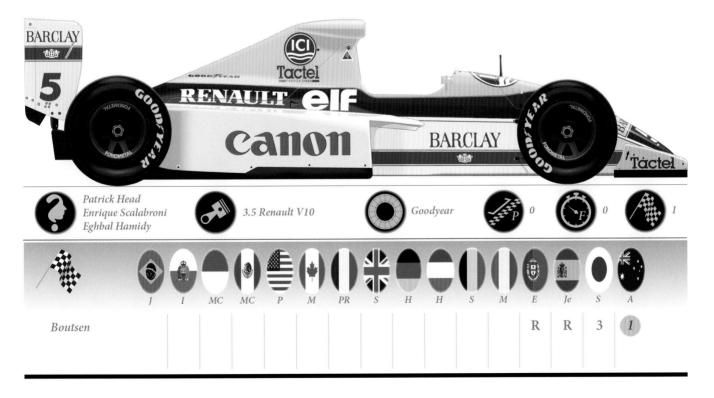

| | Patrick Head Enrique Scalabroni Eghbal Hamidy | | 3.5 Renault V10 | | Goodyear | | P 0 | | F 0 | | 1 |

	J	I	MC	MC	P	M	PR	S	H	H	S	M	E	Je	S	A
Boutsen													R	R	3	*1*

1990-99

The war between Ayrton Senna and Alain Prost continued into the '90s. Michael Schumacher's F1 debut came at the 1991 Belgian Grand Prix with Jordan. He retired on the first lap with clutch failure but had done enough to impress Benetton, whom he stayed with for the rest of the season and the next four years.

Nigel Mansell would finally become World Champion in 1992 with Williams-Renault FW14B and its active suspension, winning eight of the first ten races. The era saw the death of two drivers at the 1994 Imola race, Rolland Ratzenberger crashed in practice and, whilst leading the race, Ayrton Senna crashed at the Tamburello curve, perhaps the biggest shock in F1 history.

Senna's death led to considerable increases in safety standards. The FIA introduced measures to slow cars and improve their safety. Damon Hill would go on to emulate his father, Graham, and win the Drivers' crown in 1996. Two-time World Champion Schumacher switched from Benetton to Ferrari, which would prove to be one of the best partnerships in F1 history and after twenty-two years McLaren changed its body work from red and white to silver.

1990-1999 Seasons race by race.

Year	Argentina	Japan	Australia	Luxembourg	Austria	Malaysia	Belgium	Mexico	Brazil	Monaco	Britain	San Marino	Canada	South Africa	European	Spain	French	Pacific	German	Portugal	Hungary	USA	Italy
1990		S	A				S	MC	I	MC	S	I	M			Je	PR		H	E	H	P	M
1991		S	A				S	MC	I	MC	S	I	M			C	MC		H	E	H	P	M
1992		S	A				S	MC	I	MC	S	I	M	K		C	MC		H	E	H		M
1993		S	A				S		I	MC	S	I	M	K	DP	C	MC		H	E	H		M
1994		S	A				S		I	MC	S	I	M		Je	C	MC	TI	H	E	H		M
1995	BA	S	A				S		I	MC	S	I	M		N	C	MC	TI	H	E	H		M
1996	BA	S	M				S		I	MC	S	I	M		N	C	MC		H	E	H		M
1997	BA	S	M	N	A1		S		I	MC	S	I	M		Je	C	MC		H		H		M
1998	BA	S	M	N	A1		S		I	MC	S	I	M			C	MC		H		H		M
1999		S	M		A1	S	S		I	MC	S	I	M		N	C	MC		H		H		M

Flags (top row): Argentina, Australia, Austria, Belgium, Brazil, Britain, Canada, European, French, German, Hungary, Italy

Flags (bottom row): Japan, Luxembourg, Malaysia, Mexico, Monaco, San Marino, South Africa, Spain, Picific, Portugal, USA

for track abbreviations refer to map on pages 6/7

1990 McLaren MP4/5B

Ayrton
Senna

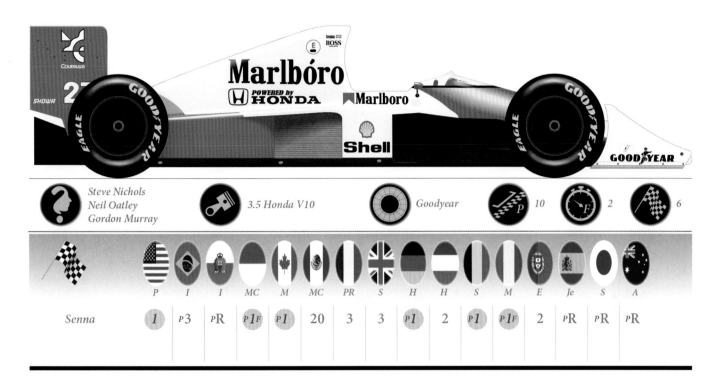

	Steve Nichols Neil Oatley Gordon Murray		3.5 Honda V10		Goodyear		P 10		F 2		6

		P	I	I	MC	M	MC	PR	S	H	H	S	M	E	Je	S	A
Senna		1	P3	PR	P1F	P1	20	3	3	P1	2	P1	P1F	2	PR	PR	PR

1990 Ferrari 641

Alain
Prost

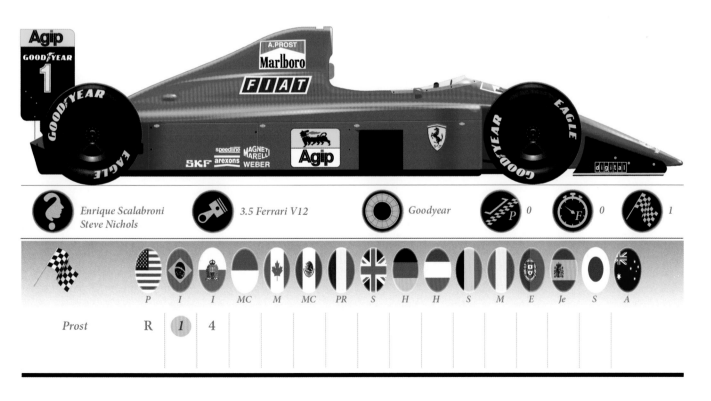

	Enrique Scalabroni Steve Nichols		3.5 Ferrari V12		Goodyear		P 0		F 0		1

		P	I	I	MC	M	MC	PR	S	H	H	S	M	E	Je	S	A
Prost		R	1	4													

1990 Williams FW13B

 Riccardo **Patrese**  Thierry **Boutsen**

Patrick Head
Enrique Scalabroni
Eghbal Hamidy | 3.5 Renault V10 | Goodyear | P 1 | F 5 | 2

	P	I	I	MC	M	MC	PR	S	H	H	S	M	E	Je	S	A
Patrese	9	13	1	R	R	9	6	R	5	4F	R	5	7F	5F	4F	6
Boutsen	3	5	R	4	R	5	R	2	6F	P1	R	R	R	4	5	5

1990 Ferrari 641/2

 Alain **Prost**  Nigel **Mansell**

Enrique Scalabroni
Steve Nichols | 3.5 Ferrari V12 | Goodyear | P 3 | F 5 | 5

	P	I	I	MC	M	MC	PR	S	H	H	S	M	E	Je	S	A
Prost			R	5	1F	1	1	4	R	2F	2	3	1	R	3	
Mansell			R	R	3	2	P18F	PRF	R	17	R	4	P1	2	R	2F

1990 Benetton B190

Nelson
Piquet

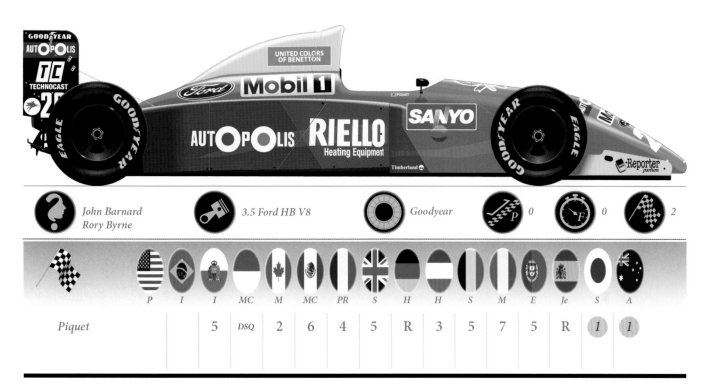

John Barnard Rory Byrne	3.5 Ford HB V8	Goodyear	P 0	F 0	2

	P	I	I	MC	M	MC	PR	S	H	H	S	M	E	Je	S	A
Piquet		5	DSQ	2	6	4	5	R	3	5	7	5	R		*1*	*1*

1991 McLaren MP4/6

 *1st*

Ayrton
Senna

Gerhard
Berger

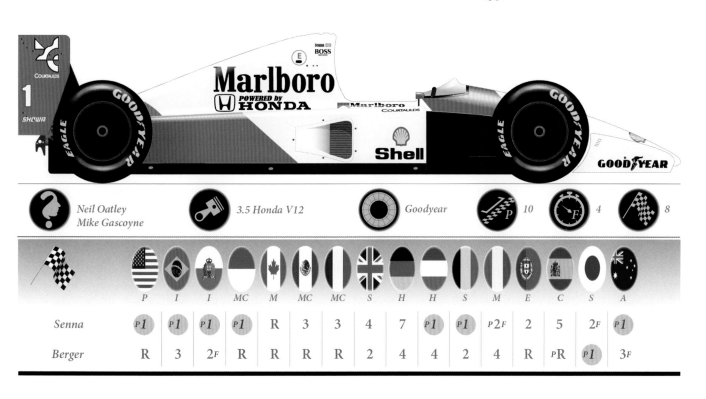

Neil Oatley Mike Gascoyne	3.5 Honda V12	Goodyear	P 10	F 4	8

	P	I	I	MC	M	MC	MC	S	H	H	S	M	E	C	S	A
Senna	P*1*	P*1*	P*1*	P*1*	R	3	3	4	7	P*1*	P*1*	P2F	2	5	2F	P*1*
Berger	R	3	2F	R	R	R	R	2	4	4	2	4	R	PR	P*1*	3F

1991 Benetton B191

Nelson **Piquet**

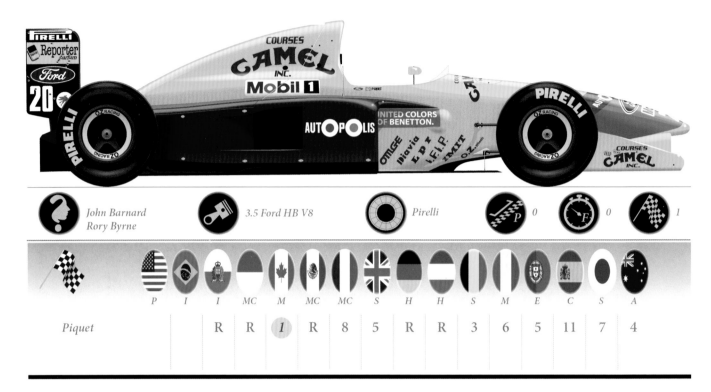

	John Barnard Rory Byrne		3.5 Ford HB V8		Pirelli		P 0		F 0		1

	P	I	I	MC	M	MC	MC	S	H	H	S	M	E	C	S	A
Piquet			R	R	1	R	8	5	R	R	3	6	5	11	7	4

1991 Williams FW14

Riccardo **Patrese** Nigel **Mansell**

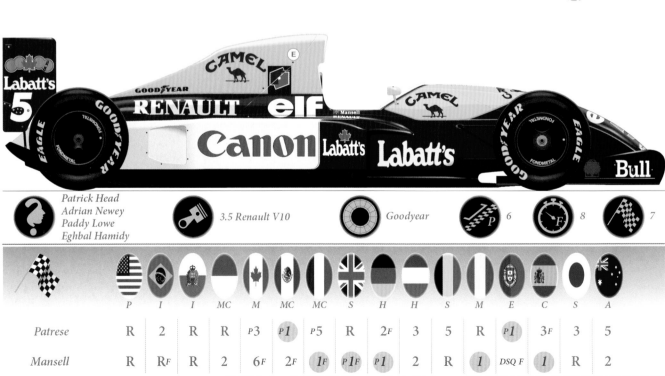

	Patrick Head Adrian Newey Paddy Lowe Eghbal Hamidy		3.5 Renault V10		Goodyear		P 6		F 8		7

	P	I	I	MC	M	MC	MC	S	H	H	S	M	E	C	S	A
Patrese	R	2	R	R	P3	P1	P5	R	2F	3	5	R	P1	3F	3	5
Mansell	R	RF	R	2	6F	2F	1F	P1	P1	2	R	1	DSQ F	1	R	2

1992 Williams FW14B

1st

Nigel **Mansell**   Riccardo **Patrese**

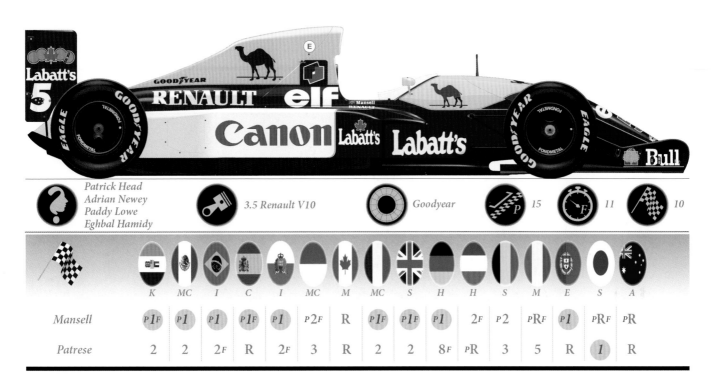

	Designers	Engine	Tyres	P	F	Flag
	Patrick Head Adrian Newey Paddy Lowe Eghbal Hamidy	3.5 Renault V10	Goodyear	15	11	10

	K	MC	I	C	I	MC	M	MC	S	H	H	S	M	E	S	A
Mansell	P1F	P1	P1	P1F	P1	P2F	R	P1F	P1F	P1	2F	P2	PRF	P1	PRF	PR
Patrese	2	2	2F	R	2F	3	R	2	2	8F	PR	3	5	R	1	R

1992 McLaren MP4/7A

Ayrton **Senna**   Gerhard **Berger**

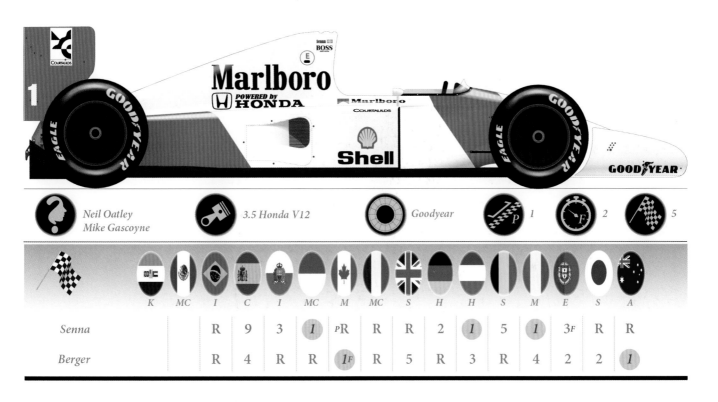

	Designers	Engine	Tyres	P	F	Flag
	Neil Oatley Mike Gascoyne	3.5 Honda V12	Goodyear	1	2	5

	K	MC	I	C	I	MC	M	MC	S	H	H	S	M	E	S	A
Senna			R	9	3	1	PR	R	R	2	1	5	1	3F	R	R
Berger			R	4	R	R	1F	R	5	R	3	R	4	2	2	1

1992 Benetton B192

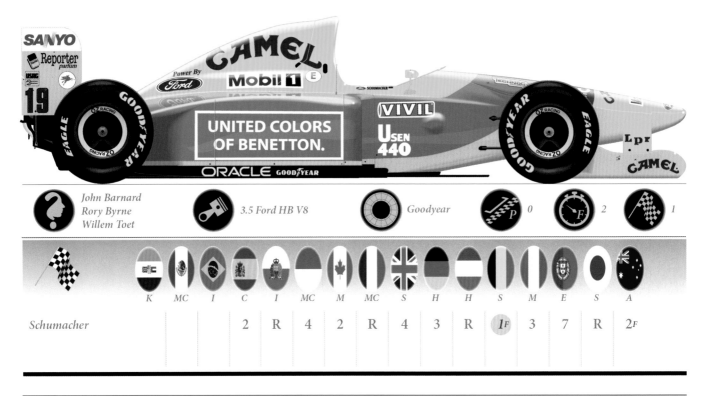

	John Barnard Rory Byrne Willem Toet		3.5 Ford HB V8		Goodyear		P 0		F 2		1

		K	MC	I	C	I	MC	M	MC	S	H	H	S	M	E	S	A
Schumacher			2	R	4	2	R	4	3	R	1F	3	7	R	2F

1993 Williams FW15C

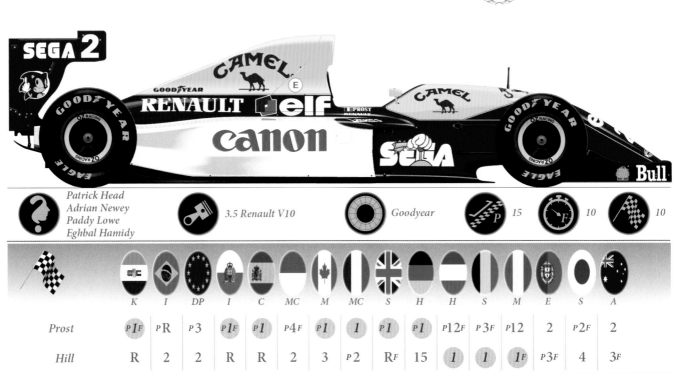

	Patrick Head Adrian Newey Paddy Lowe Eghbal Hamidy		3.5 Renault V10		Goodyear		P 15		F 10		10

	K	I	DP	I	C	MC	M	MC	S	H	H	S	M	E	S	A
Prost	P1F	PR	P3	P1F	P1	P4F	P1	1	P1	P1	P12F	P3F	P12	2	P2F	2
Hill	R	2	2	R	R	2	3	P2	RF	15	1	1	1F	P3F	4	3F

1993 McLaren MP4/8

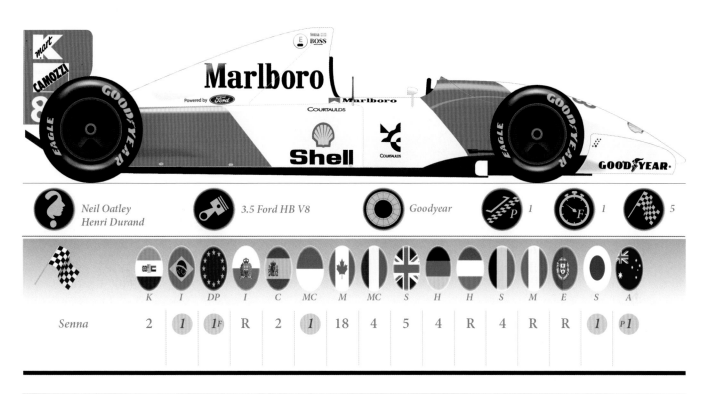

| Neil Oatley Henri Durand | 3.5 Ford HB V8 | Goodyear | P 1 | F 1 | 🏁 5 |

	K	I	DP	I	C	MC	M	MC	S	H	H	S	M	E	S	A
Senna	2	1	1F	R	2	1	18	4	5	4	R	4	R	R	1	P1

1993 Benetton B193B

Michael **Schumacher**

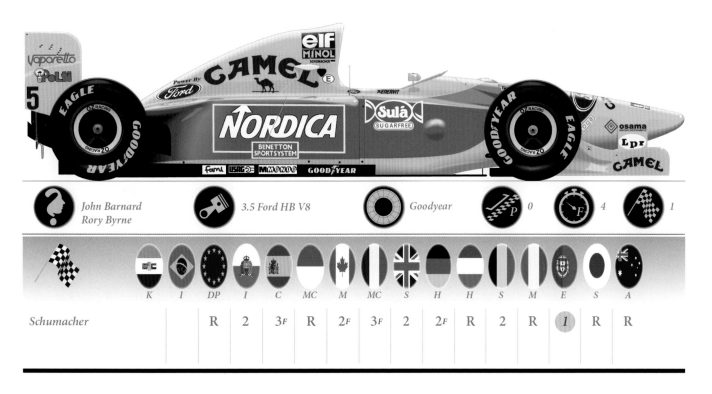

| John Barnard Rory Byrne | 3.5 Ford HB V8 | Goodyear | P 0 | F 4 | 🏁 1 |

	K	I	DP	I	C	MC	M	MC	S	H	H	S	M	E	S	A
Schumacher		R	2	3F	R	2F	3F	2	2F	R	2	R	1	R	R	

1994 Benetton B194

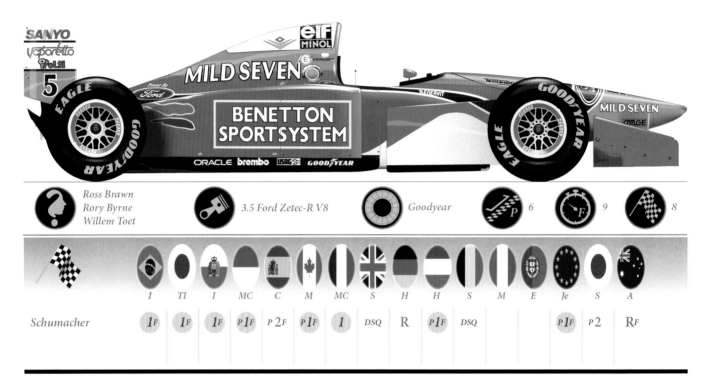

	Ross Brawn Rory Byrne Willem Toet		3.5 Ford Zetec-R V8		Goodyear	P	6	F	9		8

	I	TI	I	MC	C	M	MC	S	H	H	S	M	E	Je	S	A
Schumacher	1F	1F	1F	P1F	P2F	P1F	1	DSQ	R	P1F	DSQ			P1F	P2	RF

1994 Williams FW16

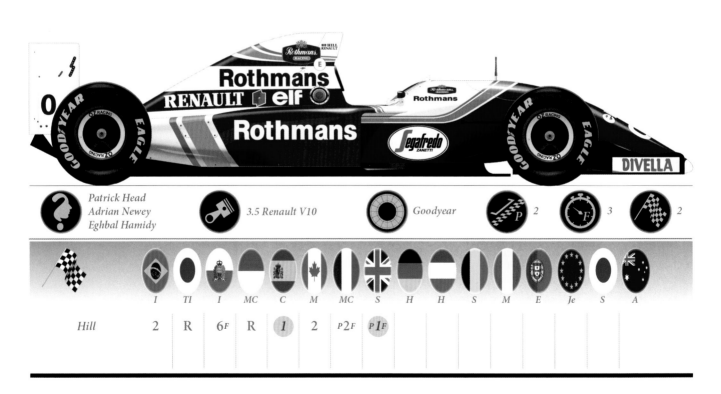

	Patrick Head Adrian Newey Eghbal Hamidy		3.5 Renault V10		Goodyear	P	2	F	3		2

	I	TI	I	MC	C	M	MC	S	H	H	S	M	E	Je	S	A
Hill	2	R	6F	R	1	2	P2F	P1F								

1994 Ferrari 412T1B

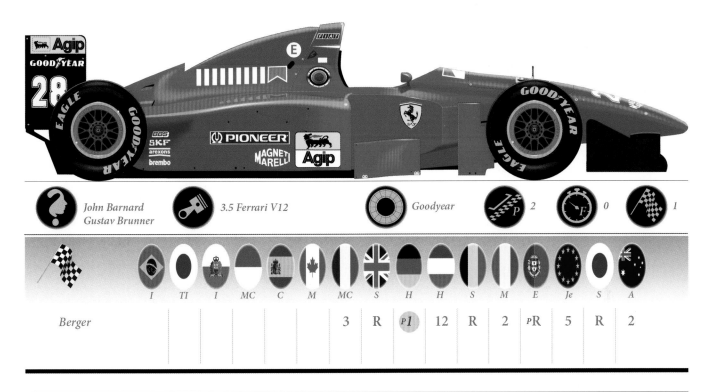

John Barnard Gustav Brunner	3.5 Ferrari V12	Goodyear	P 2	F 0	1

	I	TI	I	MC	C	M	MC	S	H	H	S	M	E	Je	S	A
Berger							3	R	P1	12	R	2	PR	5	R	2

1994 Williams FW16B

1st

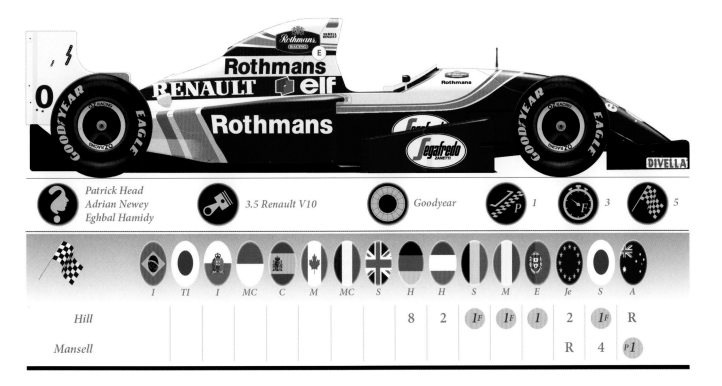

Patrick Head Adrian Newey Eghbal Hamidy	3.5 Renault V10	Goodyear	P 1	F 3	5

	I	TI	I	MC	C	M	MC	S	H	H	S	M	E	Je	S	A
Hill							8	2	1F	1F	1	2	1F	R		
Mansell														R	4	P1

1995 Benetton B195

🏁 1st

Michael **Schumacher**   Johnny **Herbert**

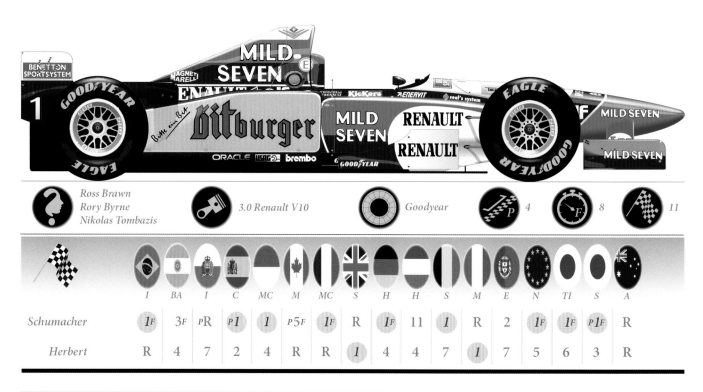

Ross Brawn
Rory Byrne
Nikolas Tombazis

3.0 Renault V10

Goodyear

P 4   F 8   🏁 11

	I	BA	I	C	MC	M	MC	S	H	H	S	M	E	N	TI	S	A
Schumacher	1F	3F	PR	P1	1	P5F	1F	R	1F	11	1	R	2	1F	1F	P1F	R
Herbert	R	4	7	2	4	R	R	1	4	4	7	1	7	5	6	3	R

1995 Williams FW17

Damon **Hill**   David **Coulthard**

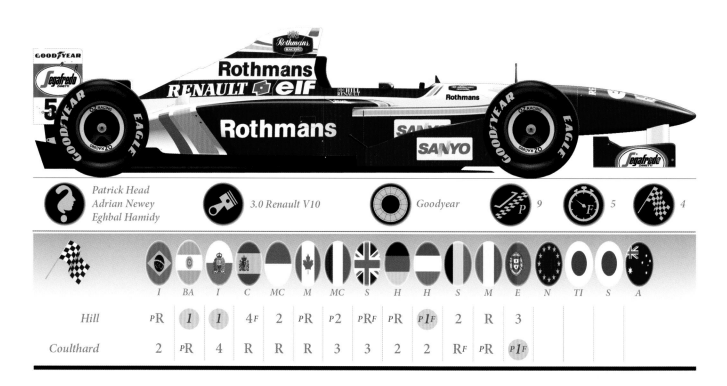

Patrick Head
Adrian Newey
Eghbal Hamidy

3.0 Renault V10

Goodyear

P 9   F 5   🏁 4

	I	BA	I	C	MC	M	MC	S	H	H	S	M	E	N	TI	S	A
Hill	PR	1	1	4F	2	PR	P2	PRF	PR	P1F	2	R	3				
Coulthard	2	PR	4	R	R	R	3	3	2	2	RF	PR	P1F				

1995 Ferrari 412T2

 *Jean* **Alesi**

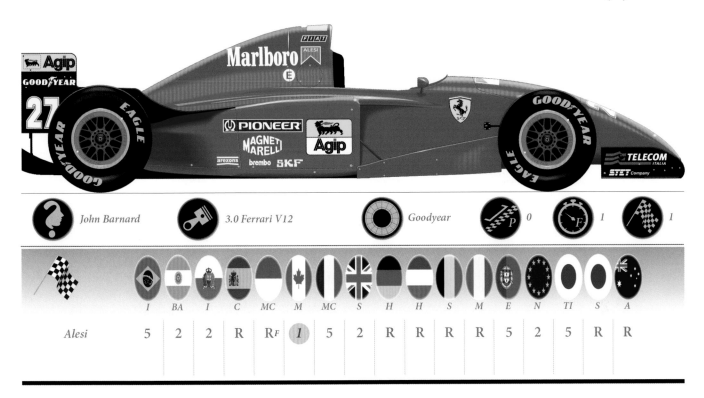

👤 John Barnard	⚙ 3.0 Ferrari V12	◎ Goodyear	🏁 P 0	⏱ F 1	🏁 1

🏁	I	BA	I	C	MC	M	MC	S	H	H	S	M	E	N	TI	S	A
Alesi	5	2	2	R	R F	1	5	2	R	R	R	R	5	2	5	R	R

1995 Williams FW17B

 Damon **Hill**

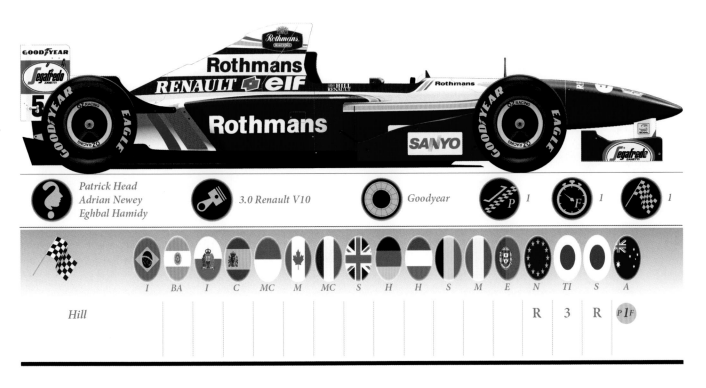

👤 Patrick Head Adrian Newey Eghbal Hamidy	⚙ 3.0 Renault V10	◎ Goodyear	🏁 P 1	⏱ F 1	🏁 1

🏁	I	BA	I	C	MC	M	MC	S	H	H	S	M	E	N	TI	S	A
Hill														R	3	R	P 1 F

1996 Williams FW18

1st

 Damon *Hill*    Jacques *Villeneuve*

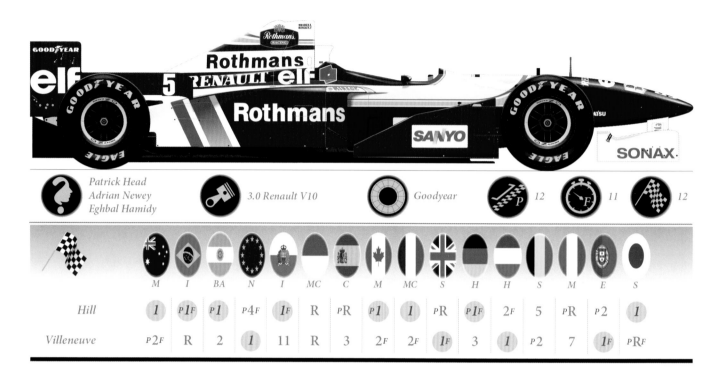

	Patrick Head Adrian Newey Eghbal Hamidy		3.0 Renault V10		Goodyear		P 12		F 11		12

	M	I	BA	N	I	MC	C	M	MC	S	H	H	S	M	E	S
Hill	1	P1F	P1	P4F	1F	R	PR	P1	1	PR	P1F	2F	5	PR	P2	1
Villeneuve	P2F	R	2	1	11	R	3	2F	2F	1F	3	1	P2	7	1F	PRF

1996 Ligier JS43

 Olivier *Panis*

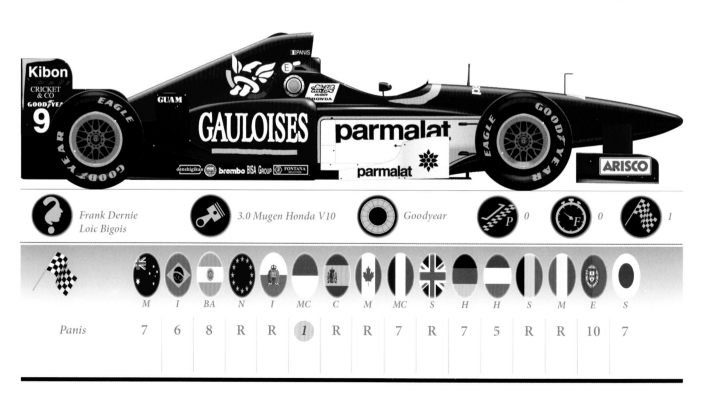

	Frank Dernie Loic Bigois		3.0 Mugen Honda V10		Goodyear		P 0		F 0		1

	M	I	BA	N	I	MC	C	M	MC	S	H	H	S	M	E	S
Panis	7	6	8	R	R	1	R	R	7	R	7	5	R	R	10	7

1996 Ferrari F310

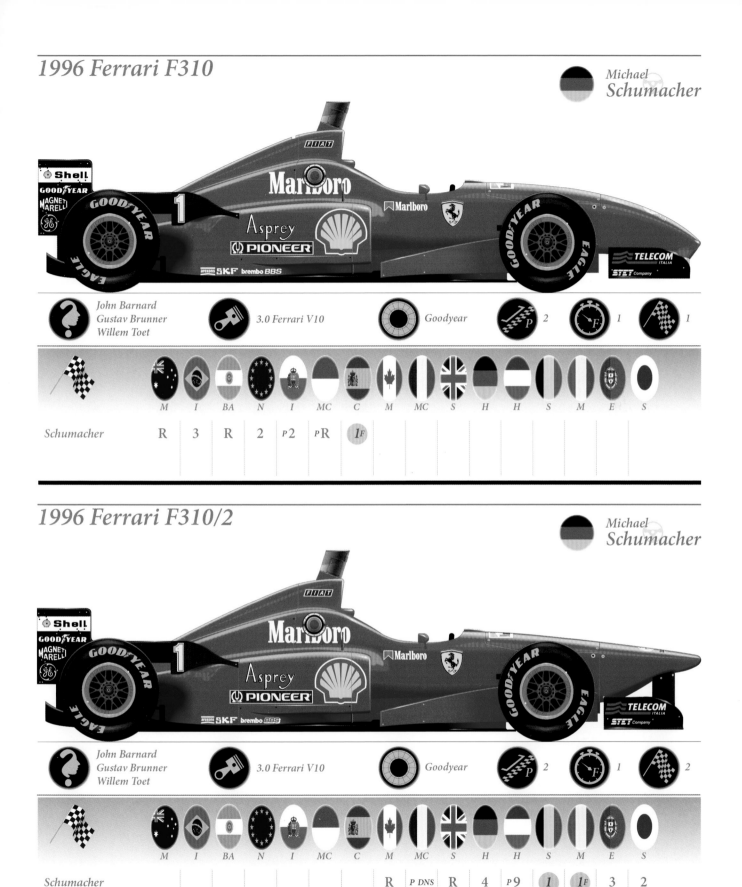

	John Barnard Gustav Brunner Willem Toet		3.0 Ferrari V10		Goodyear		P 2		F 1		1

	M	I	BA	N	I	MC	C	M	MC	S	H	H	S	M	E	S
Schumacher	R	3	R	2	P2	PR	1F									

1996 Ferrari F310/2

	John Barnard Gustav Brunner Willem Toet		3.0 Ferrari V10		Goodyear		P 2		F 1		2

	M	I	BA	N	I	MC	C	M	MC	S	H	H	S	M	E	S
Schumacher								R	P DNS	R	4	P9	1	1F	3	2

1997 McLaren MP4/12

 David **Coulthard**  Mika **Häkkinen**

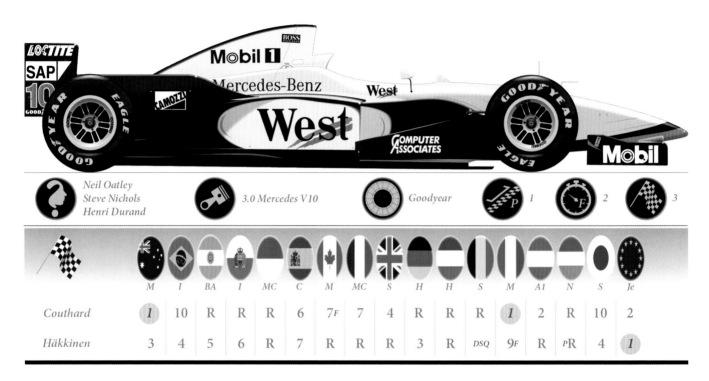

Neil Oatley Steve Nichols Henri Durand	3.0 Mercedes V10	Goodyear	P 1	F 2	3

	M	I	BA	I	MC	C	M	MC	S	H	H	S	M	A1	N	S	Je
Coulthard	1	10	R	R	R	6	7F	7	4	R	R	R	1	2	R	10	2
Häkkinen	3	4	5	6	R	7	R	R	R	3	R	DSQ	9F	R	PR	4	1

1997 Williams FW19

![1st]

 Jacques **Villeneuve**  Heinz-Harald **Frentzen**

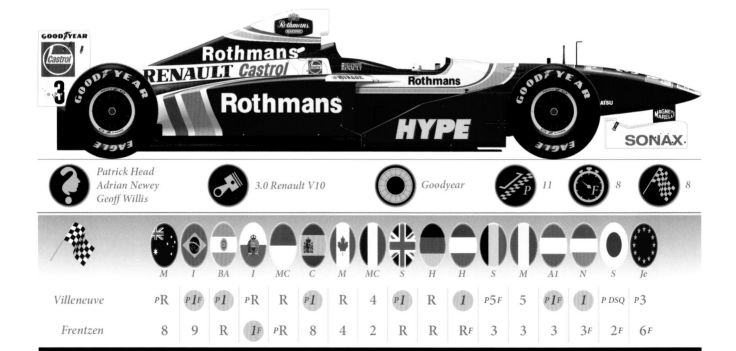

Patrick Head Adrian Newey Geoff Willis	3.0 Renault V10	Goodyear	P 11	F 8	8

	M	I	BA	I	MC	C	M	MC	S	H	H	S	M	A1	N	S	Je
Villeneuve	PR	P1F	P1	PR	R	P1	R	4	P1	R	1	P5F	5	P1F	1	P DSQ	P3
Frentzen	8	9	R	1F	PR	8	4	2	R	R	RF	3	3	3	3F	2F	6F

1997 Ferrari F310B

Michael **Schumacher**

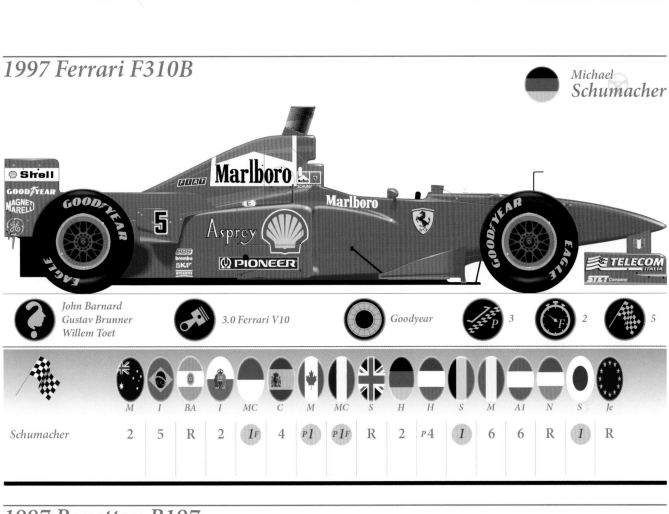

 John Barnard, Gustav Brunner, Willem Toet	3.0 Ferrari V10	Goodyear	P 3	F 2	5

	M	I	BA	I	MC	C	M	MC	S	H	H	S	M	A1	N	S	Je
Schumacher	2	5	R	2	1F	4	P1	P1F	R	2	P4	1	6	6	R	1	R

1997 Benetton B197

Gerhard **Berger**

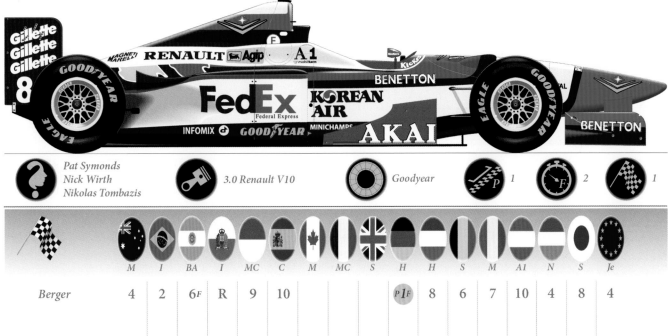

 Pat Symonds, Nick Wirth, Nikolas Tombazis	3.0 Renault V10	Goodyear	P 1	F 2	1

	M	I	BA	I	MC	C	M	MC	S	H	H	S	M	A1	N	S	Je
Berger	4	2	6F	R	9	10				P1F	8	6	7	10	4	8	4

1998 McLaren MP4/13

 Mika **Häkkinen**  David **Coulthard**

1st

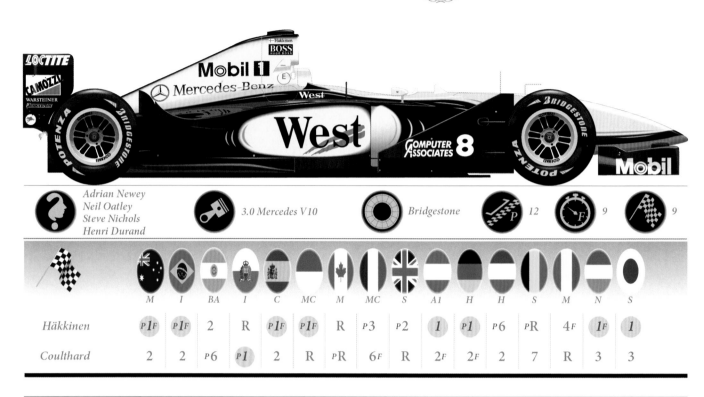

	Adrian Newey, Neil Oatley, Steve Nichols, Henri Durand		3.0 Mercedes V10		Bridgestone		P 12		F 9		9

	M	I	BA	I	C	MC	M	MC	S	A1	H	H	S	M	N	S
Häkkinen	P1F	P1F	2	R	P1F	P1F	R	P3	P2	1	P1	P6	PR	4F	1F	1
Coulthard	2	2	P6	P1	2	R	PR	6F	R	2F	2F	2	7	R	3	3

1998 Ferrari F300

Michael **Schumacher**

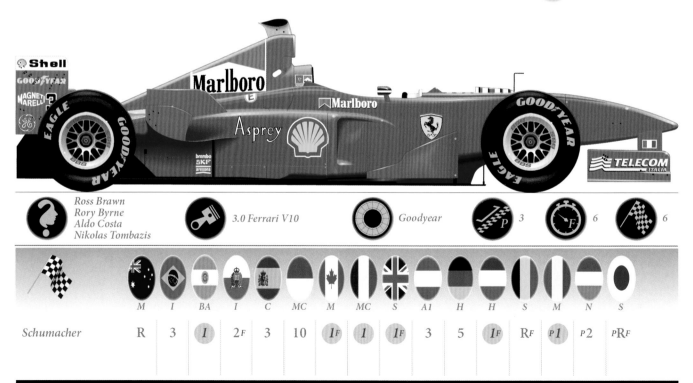

	Ross Brawn, Rory Byrne, Aldo Costa, Nikolas Tombazis		3.0 Ferrari V10		Goodyear		P 3		F 6		6

	M	I	BA	I	C	MC	M	MC	S	A1	H	H	S	M	N	S
Schumacher	R	3	1	2F	3	10	1F	1	1F	3	5	1F	RF	P1	P2	PRF

1998 Jordan 198

Damon
Hill

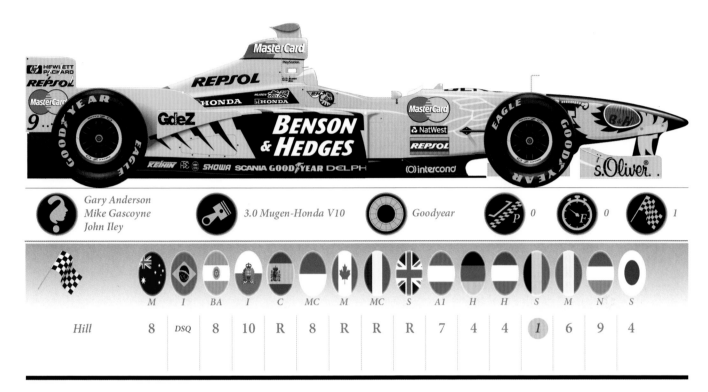

 Gary Anderson Mike Gascoyne John Iley	3.0 Mugen-Honda V10	Goodyear	P 0	F 0	🏁 1

	M	I	BA	I	C	MC	M	MC	S	A1	H	H	S	M	N	S
Hill	8	DSQ	8	10	R	8	R	R	R	7	4	4	1	6	9	4

1999 Ferrari F399

🏁 1st 🏁

 Michael *Schumacher*  Eddie *Irvine*

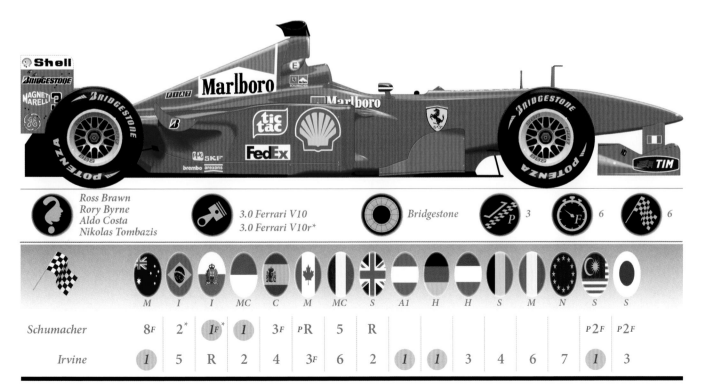

Ross Brawn Rory Byrne Aldo Costa Nikolas Tombazis	3.0 Ferrari V10 3.0 Ferrari V10r*	Bridgestone	P 3	F 6	🏁 6

	M	I	I	MC	C	M	MC	S	A1	H	H	S	M	N	S	S
Schumacher	8F	2*	1F*	1	3F	PR	5	R							P2F	P2F
Irvine	1	5	R	2	4	3F	6	2	1	1	3	4	6	7	1	3

Mika *Häkkinen*

David *Coulthard*

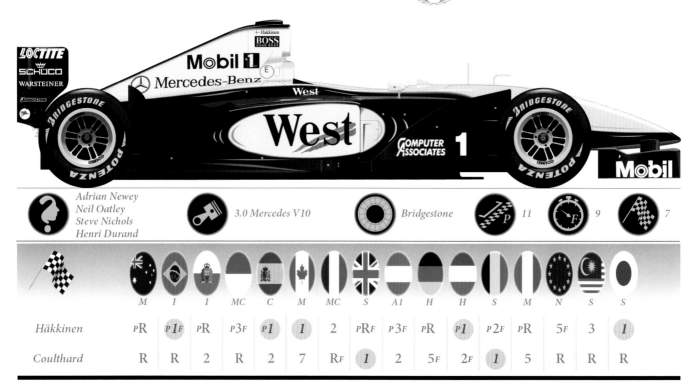

	Adrian Newey Neil Oatley Steve Nichols Henri Durand		3.0 Mercedes V10		Bridgestone		P 11		F 9		7

		M	I	I	MC	C	M	MC	S	A1	H	H	S	M	N	S	S
Häkkinen		PR	P1F	PR	P3F	P1	1	2	PRF	P3F	PR	P1	P2F	PR	5F	3	1
Coulthard		R	R	2	R	2	7	RF	1	2	5F	2F	1	5	R	R	R

Heinz-Harald *Frentzen*

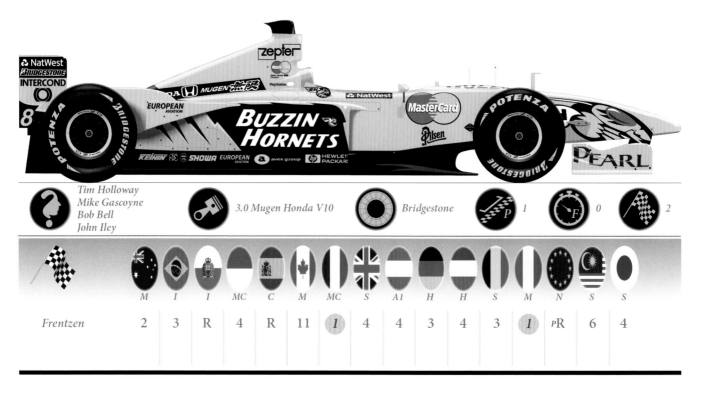

	Tim Holloway Mike Gascoyne Bob Bell John Iley		3.0 Mugen Honda V10		Bridgestone		P 1		F 0		2

		M	I	I	MC	C	M	MC	S	A1	H	H	S	M	N	S	S
Frentzen		2	3	R	4	R	11	1	4	4	3	4	3	1	PR	6	4

1999 Stewart SF3

Johnny **Herbert**

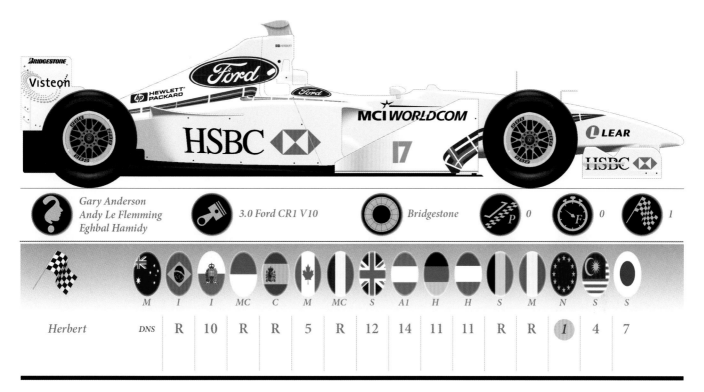

Gary Anderson
Andy Le Flemming
Eghbal Hamidy

3.0 Ford CR1 V10

Bridgestone

P 0

F 0

1

		M	I	I	MC	C	M	MC	S	A1	H	H	S	M	N	S	S
Herbert	DNS	R	10	R	R	5	R	12	14	11	11	R	R	1	4	7

2000-09

The year 2000 saw Michael Schumacher win his third title and the championship for Ferrari. He went on to win the title a further four times in the next four seasons.

At Indianapolis the Michelin-shod teams took to the pit lane at the end of the parade lap on safety grounds following a spate of tyre failures during practice, leaving just six Bridgestone-shod cars to take the start. McLaren Chief Designer Mike Coughlan was found to have received sensitive information from Ferrari chief mechanic Nigel Stepney. The FIA excluded McLaren from the 2007 Constructors' Championship and fined them $100 million.

When Nelson Piquet Jr was fired from Renault in the middle of 2009, he opened up regarding crashing his Renault in the 2008 Singapore Grand Prix, implicating MD Flavio Briatore and Executive Director of Engineering Pat Symonds of engineering the crash so Fernando Alonso could win with the help of the safety car being deployed.

Honda was reborn as Brawn Grand Prix with Jenson Button winning six of the first seven 2009 races, thanks to the double diffusers at the rear of the car which exploited a loophole in the rules. Button and Brawn GP secured the Drivers' Championship and Constructors' Championship titles, the first team to win the Constructors' Championship in their debut season.

2000-2009 Seasons race by race.

Year	Abu Dhabi	Germany	Australia	Hungary	Austria	Italy	Bahrain	Japan	Belgium	Malaysia	Brazil	Monaco	Britain	San Marino	Canada	Singapore	China	Spain	European	Turkey	French	USA
2000		H	M	H	A1	M		S	S	S	I	MC	S	I	M			C	N		MC	I
2001		H	M	H	A1	M		S	S	S	I	MC	S	I	M			C	N		MC	I
2002		H	M	H	A1	M		S	S	S	I	MC	S	I	M			C	N		MC	I
2003		H	M	H	A1	M		S		S	I	MC	S	I	M			C	N		MC	I
2004		H	M	H		M	S	S	S	S	I	MC	S	I	M		S	C	N		MC	I
2005		H	M	H		M	S	S	S	S	I	MC	S	I	M		S	C	N	I	MC	I
2006		H	M	H		M	S	S		S	I	MC	S	I	M		S	C	N	I	MC	I
2007			M	H		M	S	F	S	S	I	MC	S		M		S	C	N	I	MC	I
2008		H	M	H		M	S	F	S	S	I	MC	S		M	MB	S	C	V	I	MC	
2009	Y	N	M	H		M	S	S	S	S	I	MC	S			MB	S	C	V	I		

for track abbreviations refer to map on pages 6/7

2000 Ferrari F1 2000

1st

Michael **Schumacher** Rubens **Barrichello**

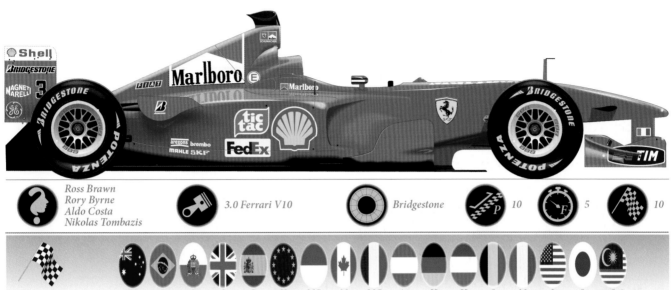

Ross Brawn
Rory Byrne
Aldo Costa
Nikolas Tombazis

3.0 Ferrari V10   Bridgestone   P 10   F 5   🏁 10

	M	I	I	S	C	N	MC	M	MC	A1	H	H	S	M	I	S	S
Schumacher	1	1F	1	3	P5	1F	PR	P1	PR	R	R	P2	2	P1	P1	P1	P1
Barrichello	2F	R	4	PR	3	4	2	2	3	3	1F	4	RF	R	2	4	3

2000 McLaren MP4/15

David **Coulthard**   Mika **Häkkinen**

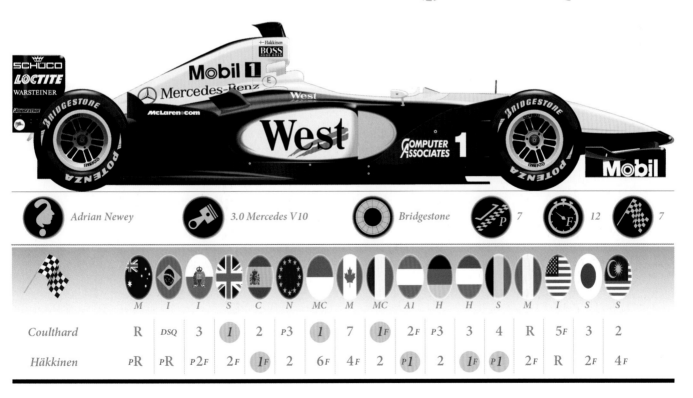

Adrian Newey

3.0 Mercedes V10   Bridgestone   P 7   F 12   🏁 7

	M	I	I	S	C	N	MC	M	MC	A1	H	H	S	M	I	S	S
Coulthard	R	DSQ	3	1	2	P3	1	7	1F	2F	P3	3	4	R	5F	3	2
Häkkinen	PR	PR	P2F	2F	1F	2	6F	4F	2	P1	2	1F	P1	2F	R	2F	4F

2001 Ferrari F2001

1st

Michael
Schumacher

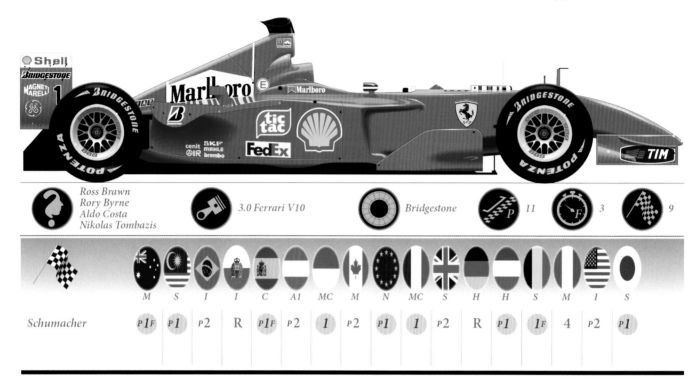

Ross Brawn	
Rory Byrne	
Aldo Costa	3.0 Ferrari V10
Nikolas Tombazis	

Bridgestone · P 11 · F 3 · 9

	M	S	I	I	C	A1	MC	M	N	MC	S	H	H	S	M	I	S
Schumacher	P1F	P1	P2	R	P1F	P2	1	P2	P1	1	P2	R	P1	1F	4	P2	P1

2001 McLaren MP4/16

David
Coulthard

Mika
Häkkinen

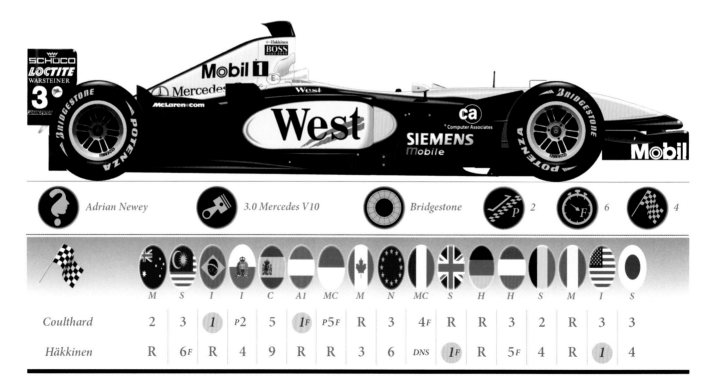

Adrian Newey	3.0 Mercedes V10

Bridgestone · P 2 · F 6 · 4

	M	S	I	I	C	A1	MC	M	N	MC	S	H	H	S	M	I	S
Coulthard	2	3	1	P2	5	1F	P5F	R	3	4F	R	R	3	2	R	3	3
Häkkinen	R	6F	R	4	9	R	R	3	6	DNS	1F	R	5F	4	R	1	4

2001 Williams FW23

 Ralf **Schumacher**  Juan Pablo **Montoya**

 Patrick Head Gavin Fisher Groff Willis	3.0 BMW V10	Michelin	P 4	F 8	4

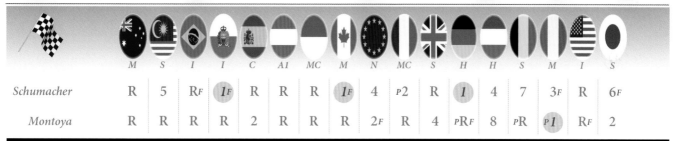

	M	S	I	I	C	A1	MC	M	N	MC	S	H	H	S	M	I	S
Schumacher	R	5	RF	1F	R	R	R	1F	4	P2	R	1	4	7	3F	R	6F
Montoya	R	R	R	R	2	R	R	R	2F	R	4	PRF	8	PR	P1	RF	2

2002 Ferrari F2001B

Michael **Schumacher**

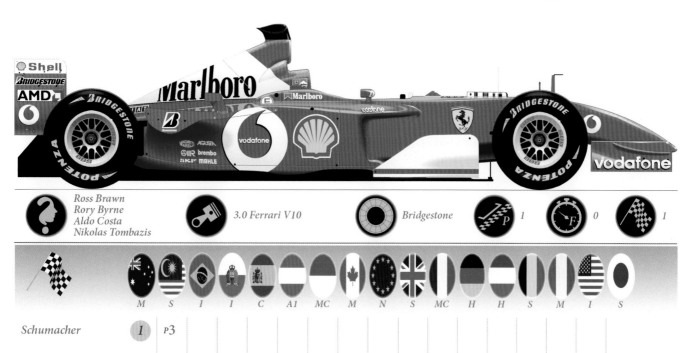

Ross Brawn Rory Byrne Aldo Costa Nikolas Tombazis	3.0 Ferrari V10	Bridgestone	P 1	F 0	1

	M	S	I	I	C	A1	MC	M	N	S	MC	H	H	S	M	I	S
Schumacher	1	P3															

2002 Williams FW24

Ralf *Schumacher*

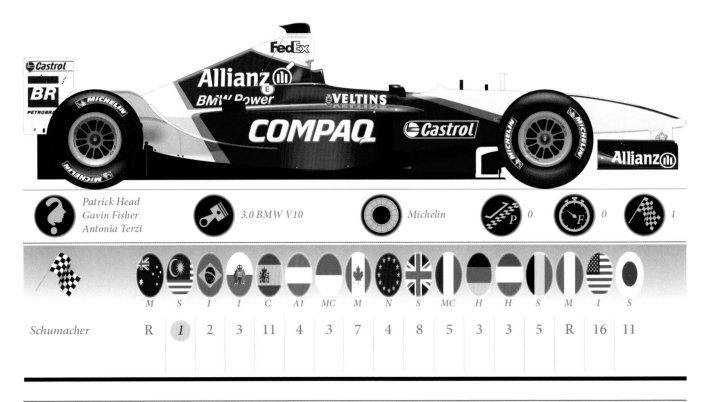

	Patrick Head Gavin Fisher Antonia Terzi		3.0 BMW V10		Michelin		P 0		F 0		1

	M	S	I	I	C	A1	MC	M	N	S	MC	H	H	S	M	I	S
Schumacher	R	1	2	3	11	4	3	7	4	8	5	3	3	5	R	16	11

2002 Ferrari F2002

 **1st**

Michael *Schumacher*   Rubens *Barrichello*

	Ross Brawn Rory Byrne Aldo Costa Nikolas Tombazis		3.0 Ferrari V10		Bridgestone		P 8		F 12		14

	M	S	I	I	C	A1	MC	M	N	S	MC	H	H	S	M	I	S
Schumacher		1	P1	P1F	1F	2	1	2F	1	1	P1F	2F	P1F	2	P2	P1F	
Barrichello		2F	DNS	P2	7F	3	1	2F	DNS	4	P1	2	1F	1F	2		

2002 McLaren MP4/17

David
Coulthard

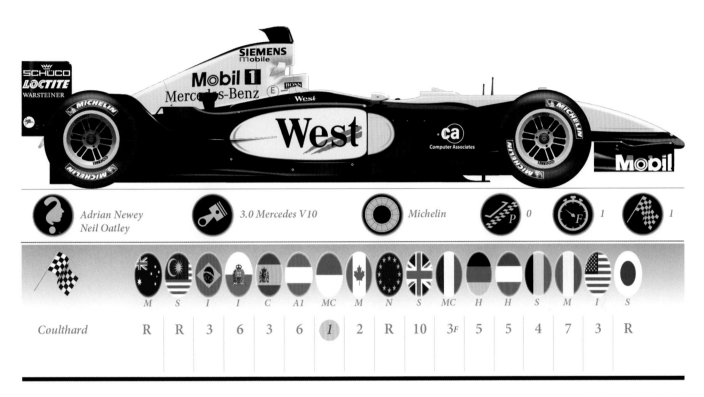

| | Adrian Newey
Neil Oatley | | 3.0 Mercedes V10 | | Michelin | | P 0 | | F 1 | | 1 |

		M	S	I	I	C	A1	MC	M	N	S	MC	H	H	S	M	I	S
Coulthard		R	R	3	6	3	6	*1*	2	R	10	3F	5	5	4	7	3	R

2003 McLaren MP4/17D

David
Coulthard

Kimi
Räikkönen

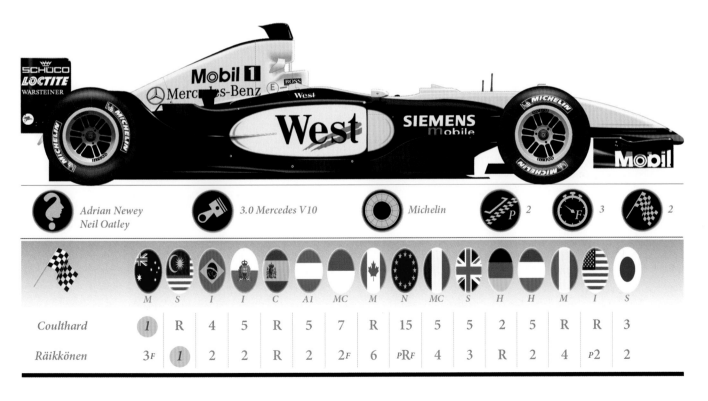

| | Adrian Newey
Neil Oatley | | 3.0 Mercedes V10 | | Michelin | | P 2 | | F 3 | | 2 |

	M	S	I	I	C	A1	MC	M	N	MC	S	H	H	M	I	S
Coulthard	*1*	R	4	5	R	5	7	R	15	5	5	2	5	R	R	3
Räikkönen	3F	*1*	2	2	R	2	2F	6	PRF	4	3	R	2	4	P2	2

2003 Jordan EJ13

Giancarlo
Fisichella

| | | Gary Anderson | | | 3.0 Cosworth V10 | | | Bridgestone | | | P 0 | | | F 0 | | | 1 |
| | | Nicoló Petrucci | | | | | | | | | | | | | | | |

		M	S	I	I	C	A1	MC	M	N	MC	S	H	H	M	I	S
Fisichella		12	R	*1*	15	R	R	10	R	12	R	R	13	R	10	7	R

2003 Ferrari F2002B

Michael
Schumacher

Rubens
Barrichello

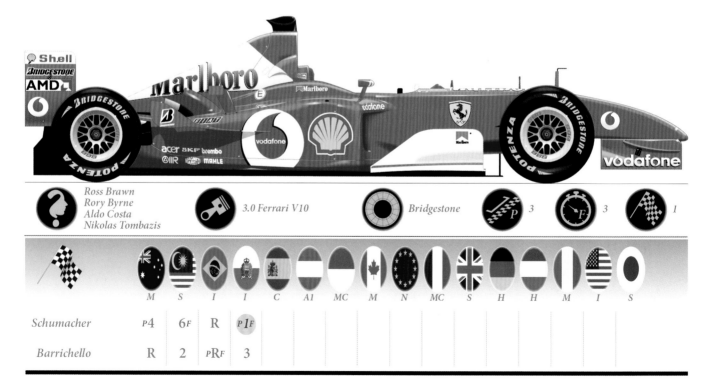

		Ross Brawn			3.0 Ferrari V10			Bridgestone			P 3			F 3			1
		Rory Byrne															
		Aldo Costa															
		Nikolas Tombazis															

		M	S	I	I	C	A1	MC	M	N	MC	S	H	H	M	I	S
Schumacher		P4	6F	R	P1F												
Barrichello		R	2	PRF	3												

2003 Ferrari F2003/GA

1st

 Michael **Schumacher**  Rubens **Barrichello**

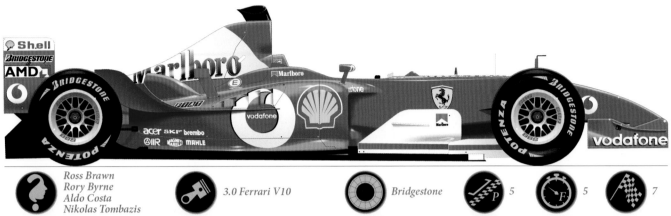

Ross Brawn
Rory Byrne
Aldo Costa
Nikolas Tombazis

3.0 Ferrari V10

Bridgestone

P 5   F 5   7

	M	S	I	I	C	A1	MC	M	N	MC	S	H	H	M	I	S
Schumacher					P1	P1F	3	1	5	3	4	7	8	P1F	1F	8
Barrichello					3F	3	8	5	3	7	P1F	R	R	3	R	P1

2003 Williams FW25

 Juan Pablo **Montoya**  Ralf **Schumacher**

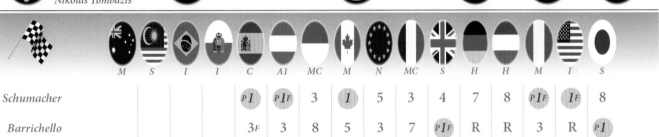

Patrick Head
Gavin Fisher
Antonia Terzi

3.0 BMW V10

Michelin

P 4   F 4   4

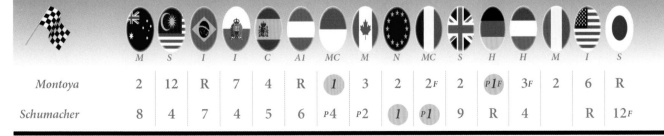

	M	S	I	I	C	A1	MC	M	N	MC	S	H	H	M	I	S
Montoya	2	12	R	7	4	R	1	3	2	2F	2	P1F	3F	2	6	R
Schumacher	8	4	7	4	5	6	P4	P2	1	P1	9	R	4		R	12F

2003 Renault R23B

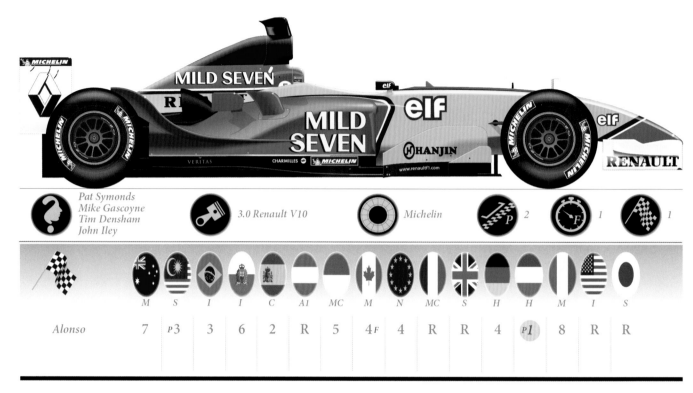

	Pat Symonds Mike Gascoyne Tim Densham John Iley		3.0 Renault V10		Michelin		P 2		F 1		1

	M	S	I	I	C	A1	MC	M	N	MC	S	H	H	M	I	S
Alonso	7	P3	3	6	2	R	5	4F	4	R	R	4	P1	8	R	R

2004 Ferrari F2004

 1st

	Ross Brawn Rory Byrne Aldo Costa John Iley		3.0 Ferrari V10		Bridgestone		P 12		F 14		15

	M	S	S	I	C	MC	N	M	I	MC	S	H	H	S	M	S	S	I
Schumacher	P1F	P1	P1F	1F	P1F	RF	P1F	1	1	1F	1F	P1	P1F	2	2	12F	P1	7
Barrichello	2	4	2	6	2	3	2	2F	P2F	3	3	12	2	3	P1F	P1	RF	P3

2004 Renault R24

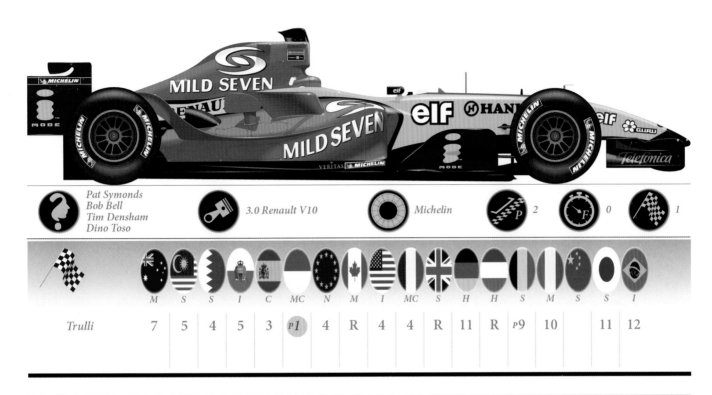

Designer	Engine	Tyres	P	F	Flag
Pat Symonds Bob Bell Tim Densham Dino Toso	3.0 Renault V10	Michelin	2	0	1

	M	S	S	I	C	MC	N	M	I	MC	S	H	H	S	M	S	I
Trulli	7	5	4	5	3	P1	4	R	4	4	R	11	R	P9	10		11	12

2004 McLaren MP4/19B

Kimi *Räikkönen*

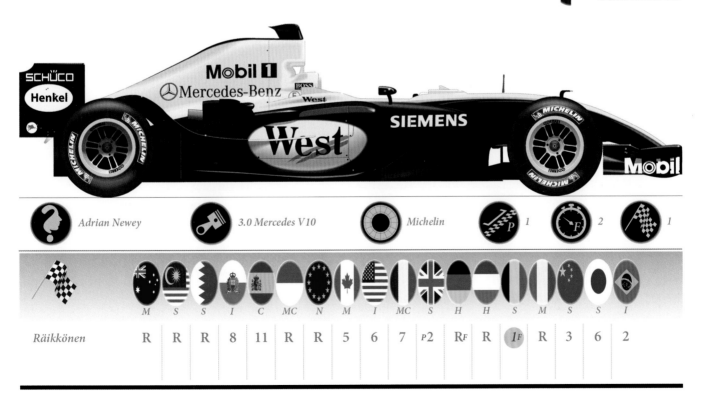

Designer	Engine	Tyres	P	F	Flag
Adrian Newey	3.0 Mercedes V10	Michelin	1	2	1

	M	S	S	I	C	MC	N	M	I	MC	S	H	H	S	M	S	I
Räikkönen	R	R	R	8	11	R	R	5	6	7	P2	RF	R	1F	R	3	6	2

2004 Williams FW26B

Juan Pablo **Montoya**

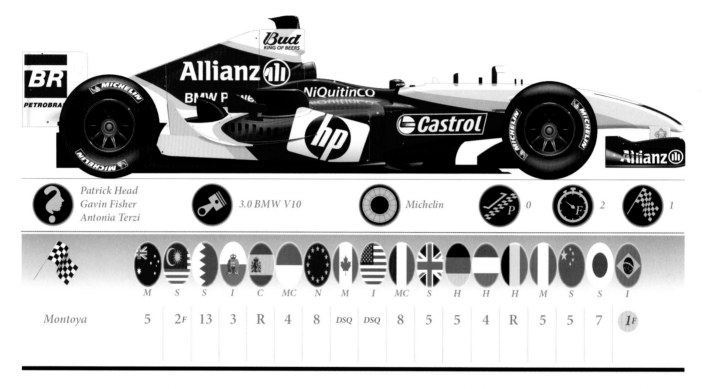

	Patrick Head Gavin Fisher Antonia Terzi	3.0 BMW V10	Michelin	P 0	F 2	🏁 1

	M	S	I	C	MC	N	M	I	MC	S	H	H	H	M	S	I
Montoya	5	2F	13	3	R	4	8	DSQ	DSQ	8	5	5	4	R	5	5	7	1F

2005 Renault R25

 1st

Fernando **Alonso**   Giancarlo **Fisichella**

	Pat Symonds Bob Bell Tim Densham Dino Toso	3.0 Renault V10	Michelin	P 7	F 3	🏁 8

	M	S	S	I	C	MC	N	M	I	MC	S	H	H	I	M	S	I	S	S
Alonso	3F	P1	P1	1	2	4	1F	R	DNS	P1	P2	1	11	2	2	2	P3	3	P1
Fisichella	P1	R	R	R	5F	12	6	R	DNS	6	4	4	9	4	3	R	5	2	4

2005 McLaren MP4/20

Kimi **Räikkönen**    Juan Pablo **Montoya**

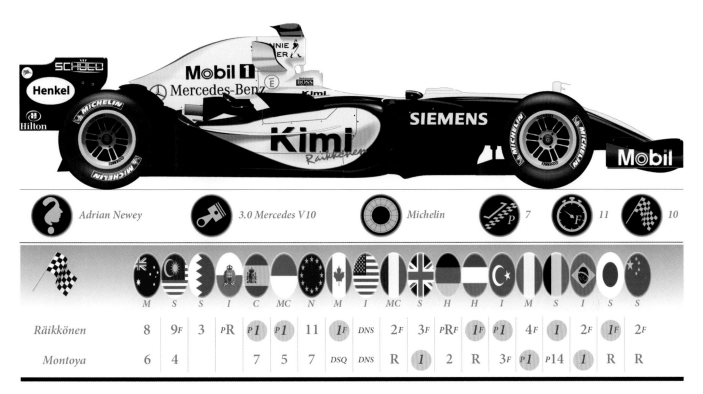

	Adrian Newey		3.0 Mercedes V10		Michelin		P 7		F 11		10

	M	S	S	I	C	MC	N	M	I	MC	S	H	H	I	M	S	I	S	S
Räikkönen	8	9F	3	PR	P1	P1	11	1F	DNS	2F	3F	PRF	1F	P1	4F	1	2F	1F	2F
Montoya	6	4			7	5	7	DSQ	DNS	R	1	2	R	3F	P1	P14	1	R	R

2005 Ferrari F2005

Michael **Schumacher**

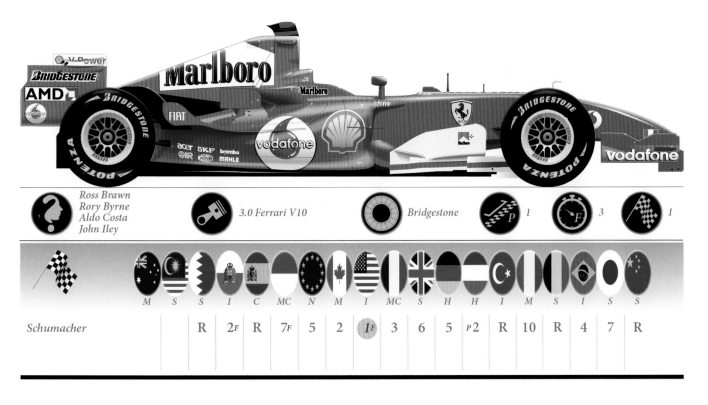

	Ross Brawn, Rory Byrne, Aldo Costa, John Iley		3.0 Ferrari V10		Bridgestone		P 1		F 3		1

	M	S	S	I	C	MC	N	M	I	MC	S	H	H	I	M	S	I	S	S
Schumacher			R	2F	R	7F	5	2	1F	3	6	5	P2	R	10	R	4	7	R

2006 Renault R26

1st

 Fernando **Alonso**  Giancarlo **Fisichella**

 Pat Symonds
Mike Gascoyne
Tim Densham
Dino Toso

 2.4 Renault V8

 Michelin

 P 7 F 5   8

	S	S	M	I	N	C	MC	S	M	I	MC	H	H	I	M	S	S	I
Alonso	1	2F	1	2F	P2	P1	P1	P1F	P1	5	2	5	R	2	R	P2F	1F	2
Fisichella	R	P1	5	8	6	3	6	4	4	3	6	6	R	6	4	3	3	6

2006 Ferrari 248

 Michael **Schumacher**   Felipe **Massa**

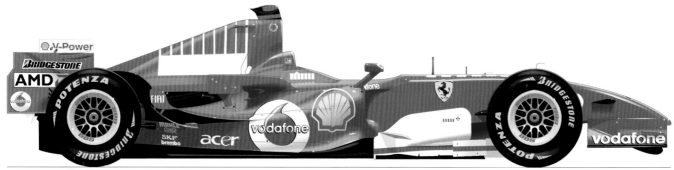

 Ross Brawn
Rory Byrne
Aldo Costa
John Iley

 2.4 Ferrari V8

 Bridgestone

 P 7 F 9   9

	S	S	M	I	N	C	MC	S	M	I	MC	H	H	I	M	S	S	I
Schumacher	P2	6	R	P1	1F	2	5F	2	2	P1F	P1F	1F	8	3F	1	1	R	4F
Massa	9	5	R	4	3	4F	9	5	5	2	3	2	7F	P1	9	R	P2	P1

2006 Honda RA106

Jenson
Button

Geoff Willis Kevin Taylor Simon Lacey	2.4 Honda V8	Michelin	P 1	F 0	1

	S	S	M	I	N	C	MC	S	M	I	MC	H	H	I	M	S	S	I
Button	4	3	P10	7	R	6	11	R	9	R	R	4	1	4	5	4	4	3

2007 Ferrari F2007

 1st

Kimi
Räikkönen

Felipe
Massa

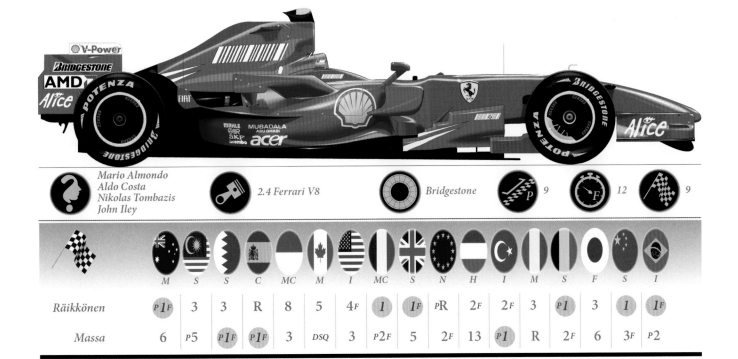

Mario Almondo Aldo Costa Nikolas Tombazis John Iley	2.4 Ferrari V8	Bridgestone	P 9	F 12	9

	M	S	S	C	MC	M	I	MC	S	N	H	I	M	S	F	S	I
Räikkönen	P1F	3	3	R	8	5	4F	1	1F	PR	2F	2F	3	P1	3	1	1F
Massa	6	P5	P1F	P1F	3	DSQ	3	P2F	5	2F	13	P1	R	2F	6	3F	P2

2007 McLaren MP4/22

 Fernando **Alonso**  Lewis **Hamilton**

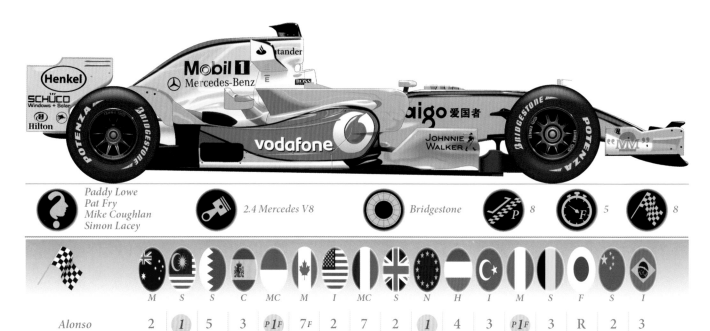

Paddy Lowe
Pat Fry
Mike Coughlan
Simon Lacey

2.4 Mercedes V8 — Bridgestone — P 8 — F 5 — 🏁 8

	M	S	S	C	MC	M	I	MC	S	N	H	I	M	S	F	I
Alonso	2	1	5	3	P1F	7F	2	7	2	1	4	3	P1F	3	R	2	3
Hamilton	3	2F	2	2	2	P1	P1	3	P3	9	P1	5	2	4	P1F	PR	7

2008 McLaren MP4/23

Lewis **Hamilton** Heikki **Kovalainen**

Paddy Lowe
Neil Oatley
Tim Goss

2.4 Mercedes V8 — Bridgestone — P 8 — F 3 — 🏁 6

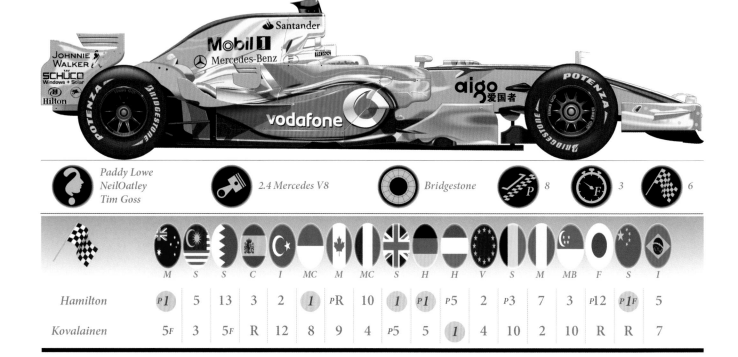

	M	S	S	C	I	MC	M	MC	S	H	H	V	S	M	MB	F	S	I
Hamilton	P1	5	13	3	2	1	PR	10	1	P1	P5	2	P3	7	3	P12	P1F	5
Kovalainen	5F	3	5F	R	12	8	9	4	P5	5	1	4	10	2	10	R	R	7

2008 Ferrari F2008

🏁 1st 🏁

 Kimi **Räikkönen**  Felipe **Massa**

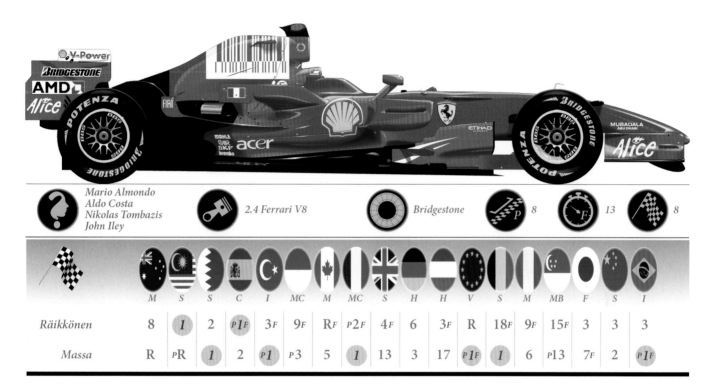

Designer	Engine	Tyres	P	F	Wins
Mario Almondo, Aldo Costa, Nikolas Tombazis, John Iley	2.4 Ferrari V8	Bridgestone	8	13	8

	M	S	S	C	I	MC	M	MC	S	H	H	V	S	M	MB	F	S	I
Räikkönen	8	1	2	P1F	3F	9F	RF	P2F	4F	6	3F	R	18F	9F	15F	3	3	3
Massa	R	PR	1	2	P1	P3	5	1	13	3	17	P1F	1	6	P13	7F	2	P1F

2008 BMW-Sauber F1.08

 Robert **Kubica**

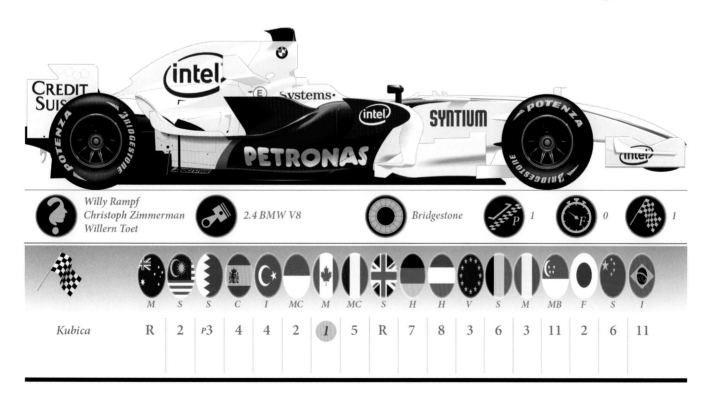

Designer	Engine	Tyres	P	F	Wins
Willy Rampf, Christoph Zimmerman, Willern Toet	2.4 BMW V8	Bridgestone	1	0	1

	M	S	S	C	I	MC	M	MC	S	H	H	V	S	M	MB	F	S	I
Kubica	R	2	P3	4	4	2	1	5	R	7	8	3	6	3	11	2	6	11

2008 Toro Rosso STR3

Sebastian
Vettel

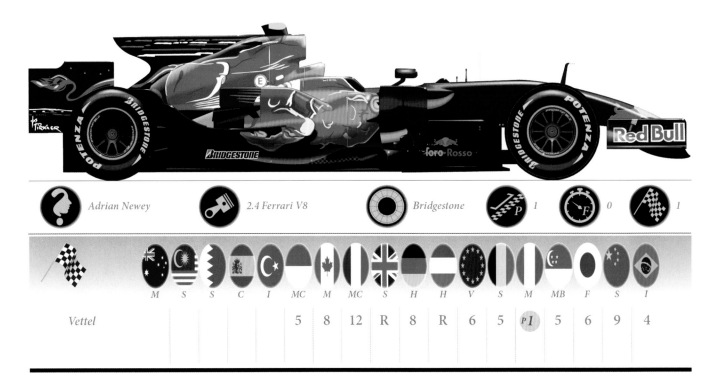

Adrian Newey 2.4 Ferrari V8 Bridgestone P 1 F 0 1

	M	S	S	C	I	MC	M	MC	S	H	H	V	S	M	MB	F	S	I
Vettel						5	8	12	R	8	R	6	5	P1	5	6	9	4

2008 Renault R28

Fernando
Alonso

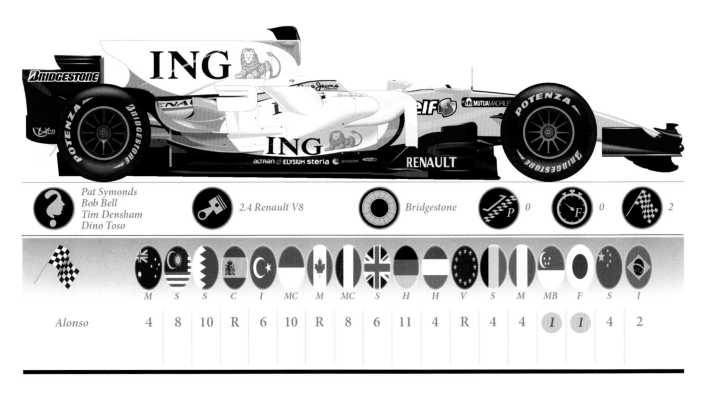

Pat Symonds
Bob Bell
Tim Densham
Dino Toso

2.4 Renault V8 Bridgestone P 0 F 0 2

	M	S	S	C	I	MC	M	MC	S	H	H	V	S	M	MB	F	S	I
Alonso	4	8	10	R	6	10	R	8	6	11	4	R	4	4	1	1	4	2

2009 Brawn BGP001

🏁 1st

 Jenson **Button**
 Rubens **Barrichello**

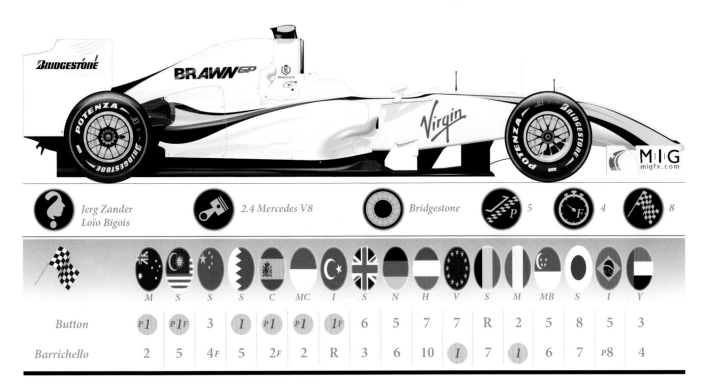

👤 Jerg Zander Loïo Bigois	⚙ 2.4 Mercedes V8	◎ Bridgestone	P 5	F 4	🏁 8

	M	S	S	S	C	MC	I	S	N	H	V	S	M	MB	S	I	Y
Button	P1	P1F	3	1	P1	P1	1F	6	5	7	7	R	2	5	8	5	3
Barrichello	2	5	4F	5	2F	2	R	3	6	10	1	7	1	6	7	P8	4

2009 Red Bull RB5

Sebastian **Vettel**
Mark **Webber**

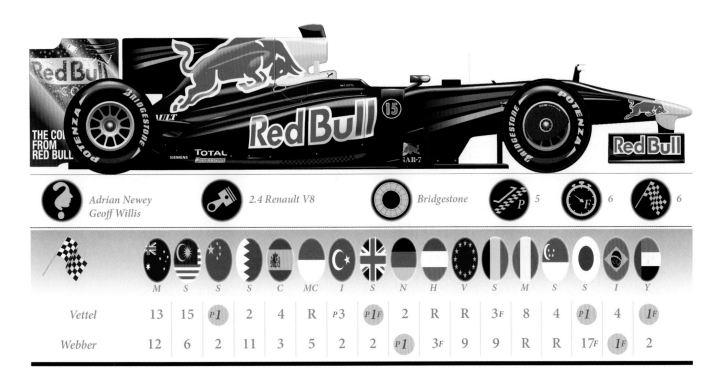

👤 Adrian Newey Geoff Willis	⚙ 2.4 Renault V8	◎ Bridgestone	P 5	F 6	🏁 6

	M	S	S	S	C	MC	I	S	N	H	V	S	M	MB	S	I	Y
Vettel	13	15	P1	2	4	R	P3	P1F	2	R	R	3F	8	4	P1	4	1F
Webber	12	6	2	11	3	5	2	2	P1	3F	9	9	R	R	17F	1F	2

Lewis
Hamilton

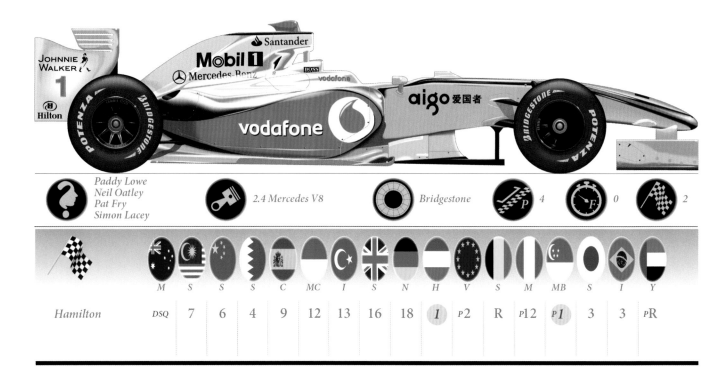

Paddy Lowe	2.4 Mercedes V8	Bridgestone
Neil Oatley		
Pat Fry		
Simon Lacey		

P 4   F 0   2

	M	S	S	S	C	MC	I	S	N	H	V	S	M	MB	S	I	Y
Hamilton	DSQ	7	6	4	9	12	13	16	18	1	P2	R	P12	P1	3	3	PR

2009 Ferrari F60

Kimi
Räikkönen

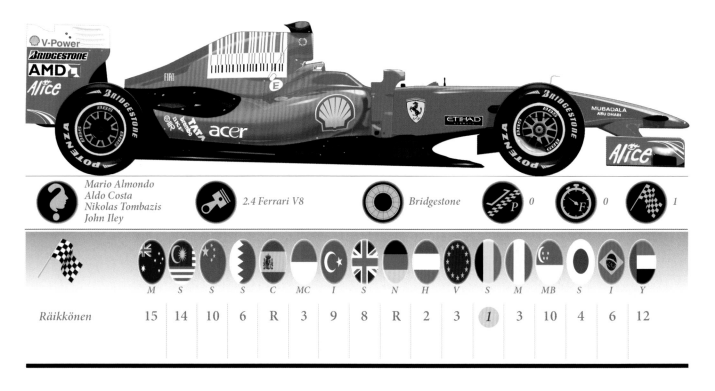

Mario Almondo	2.4 Ferrari V8	Bridgestone
Aldo Costa		
Nikolas Tombazis		
John Iley		

P 0   F 0   1

	M	S	S	S	C	MC	I	S	N	H	V	S	M	MB	S	I	Y
Räikkönen	15	14	10	6	R	3	9	8	R	2	3	1	3	10	4	6	12

2010–19

The 2010s began with four successive titles for Sebastian Vettel and Red Bull. Hailed by many as a true stroke of genius, McLaren's F-Duct system first appeared, the basic idea being that the driver was able to alter the airflow over the rear wing just by moving his hand, thus making the car faster in a straight line.

It was a decade for young drivers making a name for themselves, the youngest being Max Verstappen at just 17 years old. Pastor Maldonado with Williams-Renault winning the Spanish Grand Prix at Barcelona was the most surprising win of 2012. New 1,600cc turbocharged hybrid engines came into force in 2014. Mercedes drivers Lewis Hamilton and Nico Rosberg won all but three of the races, with Hamilton taking the crown. Rosberg took the Drivers' Crown in the final round at the 2016 Abu Dhabi Grand Prix, emulating his father Keke. Five days later, he announced his retirement from the sport. Lewis Hamilton won his sixth Drivers' crown in 2019, bringing him to just one world title away from Michael Schumacher's record of seven.

2010-2019 Seasons race by race.

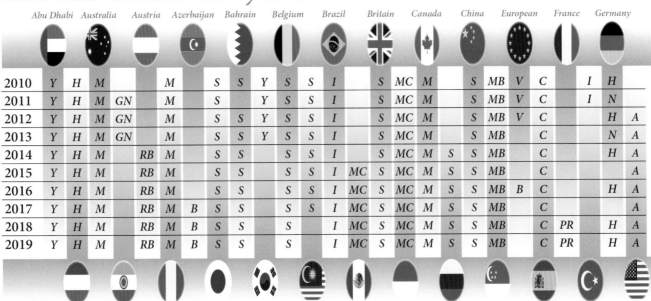

Year	Abu Dhabi	Hungary	Australia	India	Austria	Italy	Azerbaijan	Japan	Bahrain	Korea	Belgium	Malaysia	Brazil	Mexico	Britain	Monaco	Canada	Russia	China	Singapore	European	Spain	France	Turkey	Germany	USA
2010	Y	H	M			M		S	S	Y	S	S	I		S	MC	M		S	MB	V	C		I	H	
2011	Y	H	M	GN		M		S		Y	S	S	I		S	MC	M		S	MB	V	C		I	N	
2012	Y	H	M	GN		M		S	S	Y	S	S	I		S	MC	M		S	MB	V	C			H	A
2013	Y	H	M	GN		M		S	S	Y	S	S	I		S	MC	M		S	MB		C			N	A
2014	Y	H	M		RB	M		S	S		S	S	I		S	MC	M	S	S	MB		C			H	A
2015	Y	H	M		RB	M		S	S		S	S	I	MC	S	MC	M	S	S	MB		C				A
2016	Y	H	M		RB	M		S	S		S	S	I	MC	S	MC	M	S	S	MB	B	C			H	A
2017	Y	H	M		RB	M	B	S	S		S	S	I	MC	S	MC	M	S	S	MB		C				A
2018	Y	H	M		RB	M	B	S	S		S		I	MC	S	MC	M	S	S	MB		C	PR		H	A
2019	Y	H	M		RB	M	B	S	S		S		I	MC	S	MC	M	S	S	MB		C	PR		H	A

for track abbreviations refer to map on pages 6/7

2010 Ferrari F10

Fernando
Alonso

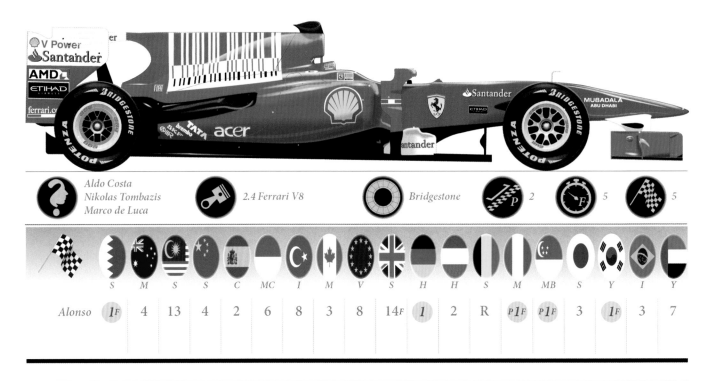

|  Aldo Costa
Nikolas Tombazis
Marco de Luca | 2.4 Ferrari V8 | Bridgestone | P 2 | F 5 | 5 |

	S	M	S	S	C	MC	I	M	V	S	H	H	S	M	MB	S	Y	I	Y
Alonso	1F	4	13	4	2	6	8	3	8	14F	1	2	R	P1F	P1F	3	1F	3	7

2010 McLaren MP4/25

Jenson
Button

Lewis
Hamilton

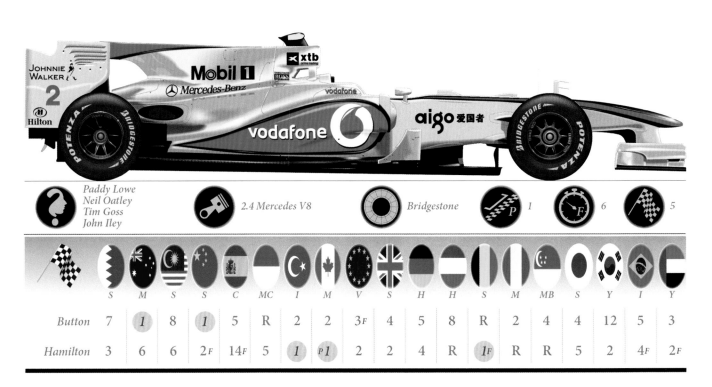

| Paddy Lowe
Neil Oatley
Tim Goss
John Iley | 2.4 Mercedes V8 | Bridgestone | P 1 | F 6 | 5 |

	S	M	S	S	C	MC	I	M	V	S	H	H	S	M	MB	S	Y	I	Y
Button	7	1	8	1	5	R	2	2	3F	4	5	8	R	2	4	4	12	5	3
Hamilton	3	6	6	2F	14F	5	1	P1	2	2	4	R	1F	R	R	5	2	4F	2F

2010 Red Bull RB6

🏁 1st

 Sebastian *Vettel*  Mark *Webber*

 Adrian Newey
Rob Marshall
Peter Prodromou

 2.4 Renault V8

 Bridgestone

 P 15   F 6   9

	S	M	S	S	C	MC	I	M	V	S	H	H	S	M	MB	S	Y	I	Y
Vettel	P4	PR	1	P6	3	2F	R	4	P1	P7	P3F	P3F	15	4	2	P1	PR	1	P1
Webber	8	9F	P2F	8	P1	P1	P3	5	R	1	6	1	P2	6	3	2F	R	2	8

2011 Red Bull RB7

🏁 1st

 Sebastian *Vettel*   Mark *Webber*

 Adrian Newey
Rob Marshall
Peter Prodromou

 2.4 Renault V8

 Pirelli

 P 18   F 10   12

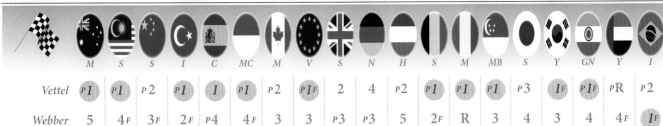

	M	S	S	I	C	MC	M	V	S	N	H	S	M	MB	S	Y	GN	Y	I
Vettel	P1	P1	P2	P1	1	P1	P2	P1F	2	4	P2	P1	P1	P3	1F	P1F	PR	P2	P2
Webber	5	4F	3F	2F	P4	4F	3	3	P3	P3	5	2F	R	3	4	3	4	4F	1F

2011 McLaren MP4/26

Lewis *Hamilton* Jenson *Button*

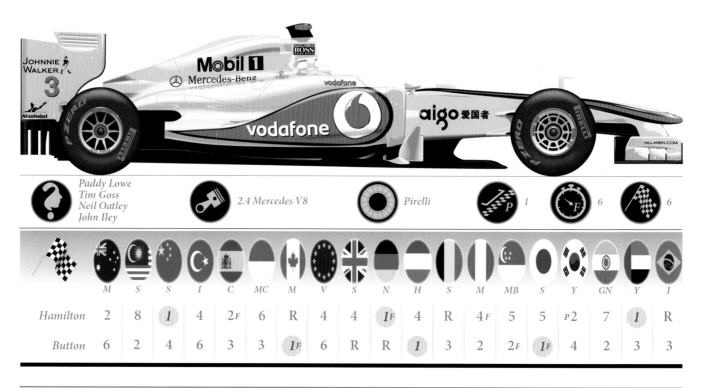

Paddy Lowe
Tim Goss
Neil Oatley
John Iley

2.4 Mercedes V8

Pirelli

P 1

F 6

6

	M	S	S	I	C	MC	M	V	S	N	H	S	M	MB	S	Y	GN	Y	I
Hamilton	2	8	*1*	4	2F	6	R	4	4	*1F*	4	R	4F	5	5	P2	7	*1*	R
Button	6	2	4	6	3	3	*1F*	6	R	R	*1*	3	2	2F	*1F*	4	2	3	3

2011 Ferrari F150

Fernando *Alonso*

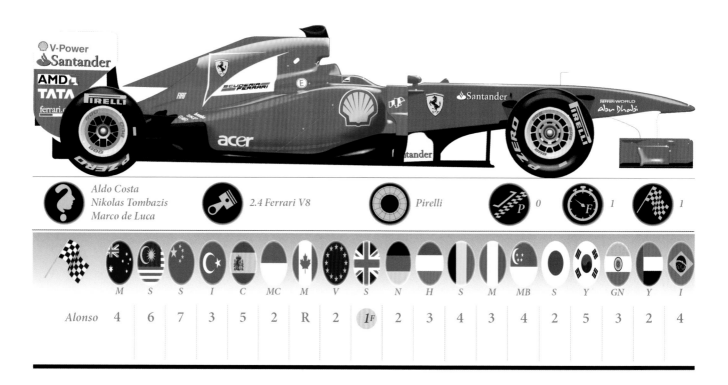

Aldo Costa
Nikolas Tombazis
Marco de Luca

2.4 Ferrari V8

Pirelli

P 0

F 1

1

	M	S	S	I	C	MC	M	V	S	N	H	S	M	MB	S	Y	GN	Y	I
Alonso	4	6	7	3	5	2	R	2	*1F*	2	3	4	3	4	2	5	3	2	4

2012 McLaren MP4/27

🇬🇧 Jenson **Button**   🇬🇧 Lewis **Hamilton**

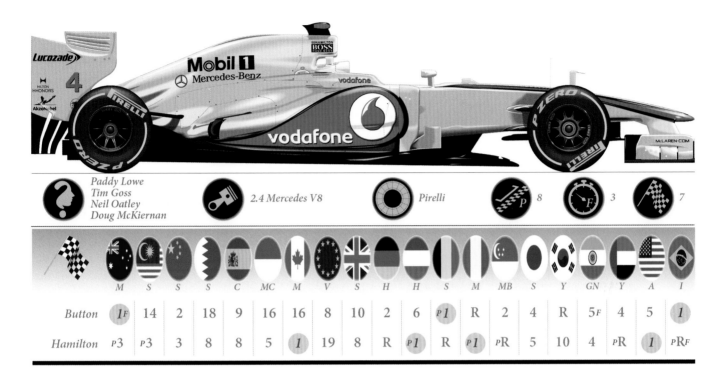

Paddy Lowe, Tim Goss, Neil Oatley, Doug McKiernan	2.4 Mercedes V8 — Pirelli — P 8 — F 3 — 🏁 7

	M	S	S	S	C	MC	M	V	S	H	H	S	M	MB	S	Y	GN	Y	A	I
Button	1F	14	2	18	9	16	16	8	10	2	6	P1	R	2	4	R	5F	4	5	1
Hamilton	P3	P3	3	8	8	5	1	19	8	R	P1	R	P1	PR	5	10	4	PR	1	PRF

2012 Ferrari F2012

🇪🇸 Fernando **Alonso**

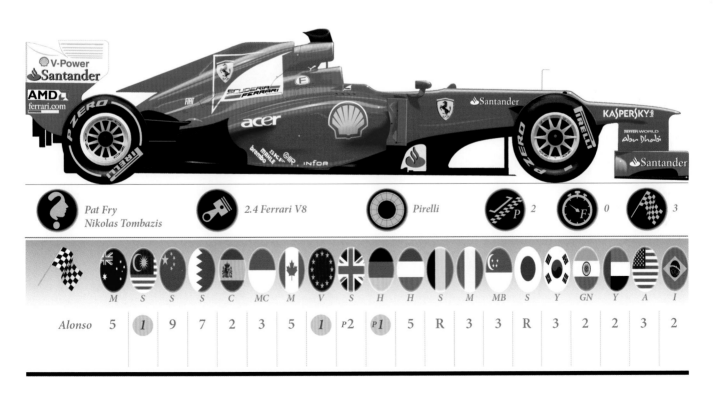

Pat Fry, Nikolas Tombazis	2.4 Ferrari V8 — Pirelli — P 2 — F 0 — 🏁 3

	M	S	S	S	C	MC	M	V	S	H	H	S	M	MB	S	Y	GN	Y	A	I
Alonso	5	1	9	7	2	3	5	1	P2	P1	5	R	3	3	R	3	2	2	3	2

2012 Mercedes F1 W03

Nico **Rosberg**

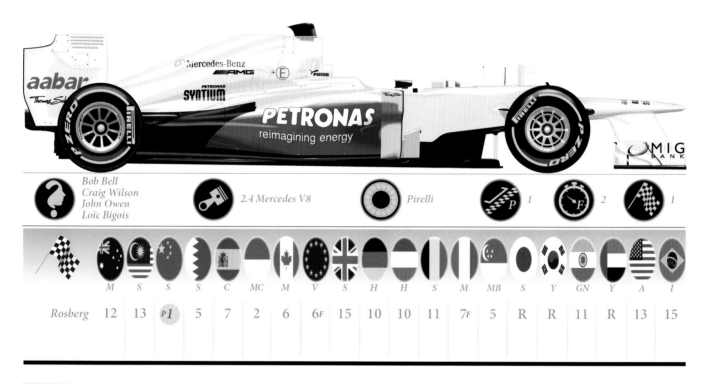

Bob Bell
Craig Wilson
John Owen
Loïc Bigois

2.4 Mercedes V8

Pirelli

P 1   F 2   1

	M	S	S	S	C	MC	M	V	S	H	H	S	M	MB	S	Y	GN	Y	A	I
Rosberg	12	13	P1	5	7	2	6	6F	15	10	10	11	7F	5	R	R	11	R	13	15

2012 Red Bull RB8

 1st

Sebastian **Vettel**

Mark **Webber**

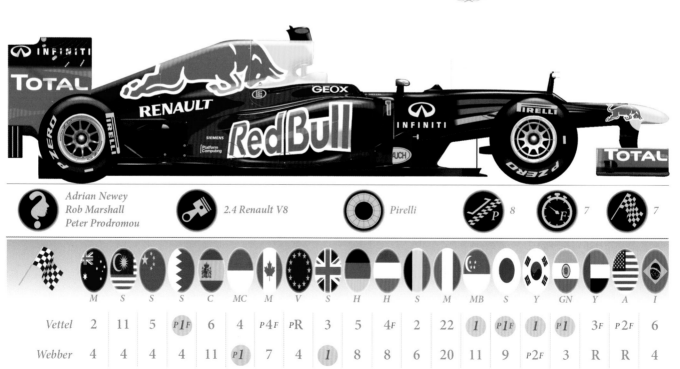

Adrian Newey
Rob Marshall
Peter Prodromou

2.4 Renault V8

Pirelli

P 8   F 7   7

	M	S	S	S	C	MC	M	V	S	H	H	S	M	MB	S	Y	GN	Y	A	I
Vettel	2	11	5	P1F	6	4	P4F	PR	3	5	4F	2	22	1	P1F	1	P1	3F	P2F	6
Webber	4	4	4	4	11	P1	7	4	1	8	8	6	20	11	9	P2F	3	R	R	4

2012 Williams FW34

Pastor
Maldonado

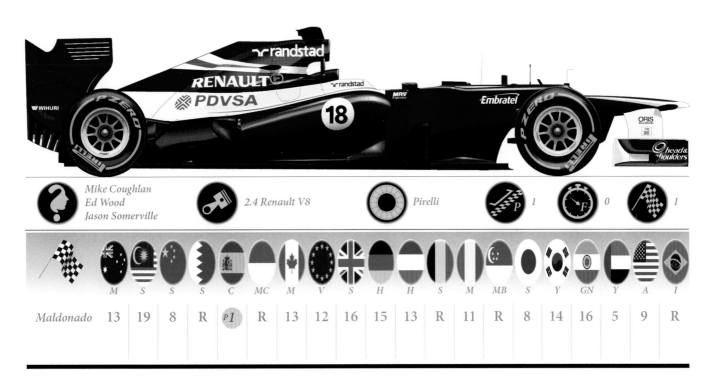

	Mike Coughlan Ed Wood Jason Somerville		2.4 Renault V8		Pirelli		P 1		F 0		1

	M	S	S	S	C	MC	M	V	S	H	H	S	M	MB	S	Y	GN	Y	A	I
Maldonado	13	19	8	R	*P1*	R	13	12	16	15	13	R	11	R	8	14	16	5	9	R

2012 Lotus E20

Kimi
Räikkönen

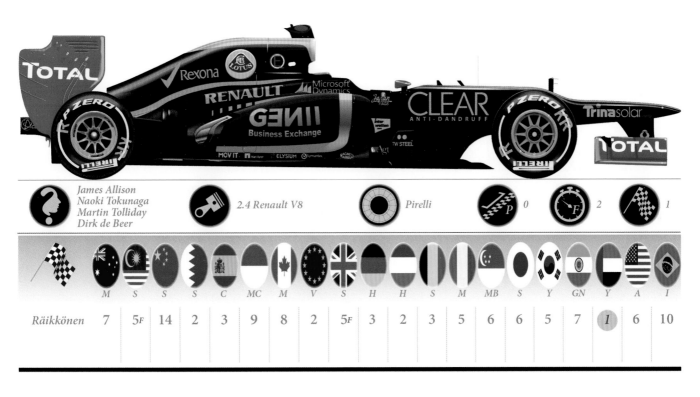

	James Allison Naoki Tokunaga Martin Tolliday Dirk de Beer		2.4 Renault V8		Pirelli		P 0		F 2		1

	M	S	S	S	C	MC	M	V	S	H	H	S	M	MB	S	Y	GN	Y	A	I
Räikkönen	7	5F	14	2	3	9	8	2	5F	3	2	3	5	6	6	5	7	1	6	10

2013 Lotus E21

Kimi
Räikkönen

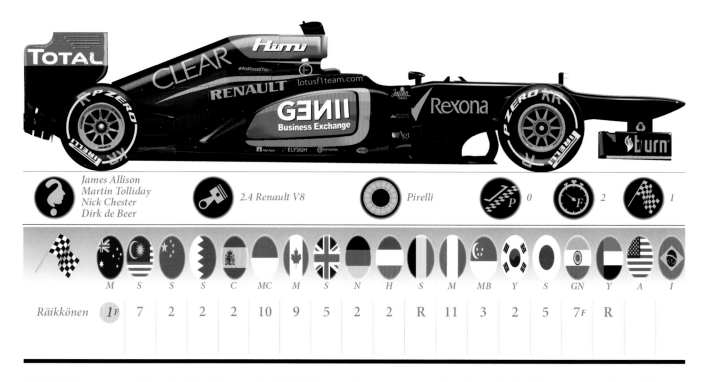

James Allison
Martin Tolliday
Nick Chester
Dirk de Beer

2.4 Renault V8

Pirelli

P 0   F 2   1

	M	S	S	S	C	MC	M	S	N	H	S	M	MB	Y	S	GN	Y	A	I
Räikkönen	1F	7	2	2	2	10	9	5	2	2	R	11	3	2	5	7F	R		

2013 Red Bull RB9

1st

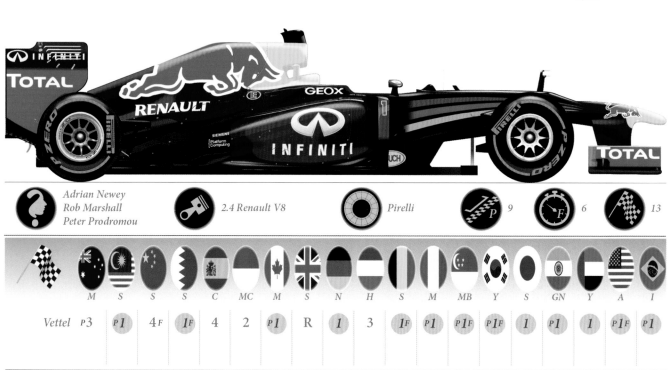

Sebastian
Vettel

Adrian Newey
Rob Marshall
Peter Prodromou

2.4 Renault V8

Pirelli

P 9   F 6   13

	M	S	S	S	C	MC	M	S	N	H	S	M	MB	Y	S	GN	Y	A	I
Vettel	P3	P1	4F	1F	4	2	P1	R	1	3	1F	P1	P1F	P1F	1	P1	1	P1F	P1

2013 Ferrari F138

Fernando *Alonso*

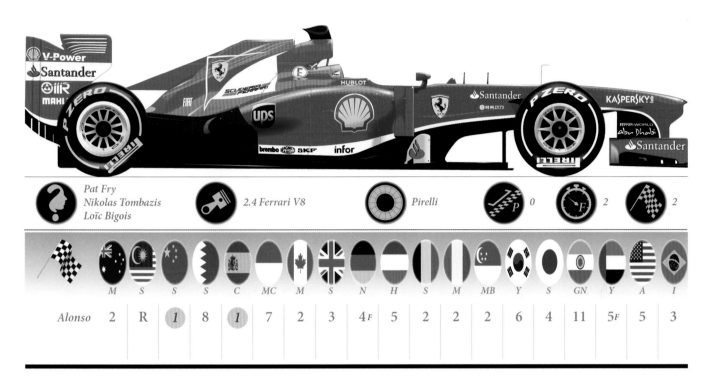

	Pat Fry Nikolas Tombazis Loïc Bigois		2.4 Ferrari V8		Pirelli		P 0		F 2		2

	M	S	S	S	C	MC	M	S	N	H	S	M	MB	Y	S	GN	Y	A	I
Alonso	2	R	1	8	1	7	2	3	4F	5	2	2	2	6	4	11	5F	5	3

2013 Mercedes F1 W04

Nico *Rosberg*   Lewis *Hamilton*

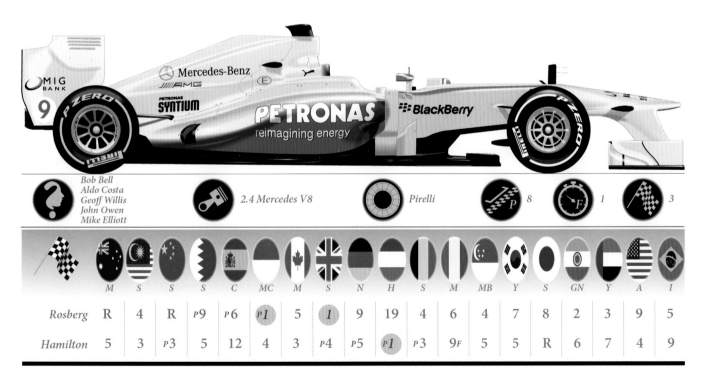

	Bob Bell Aldo Costa Geoff Willis John Owen Mike Elliott		2.4 Mercedes V8		Pirelli		P 8		F 1		3

	M	S	S	S	C	MC	M	S	N	H	S	M	MB	Y	S	GN	Y	A	I
Rosberg	R	4	R	P9	P6	P1	5	1	9	19	4	6	4	7	8	2	3	9	5
Hamilton	5	3	P3	5	12	4	3	P4	P5	P1	P3	9F	5	5	R	6	7	4	9

2014 Mercedes F1 W05 *Hybrid*

1st

Lewis **Hamilton**

Nico **Rosberg**

Paddy Lowe
Aldo Costa
Geoff Willis
John Owen
Mike Elliott

1.6t/c Mercedes V6

Pirelli

P 18

F 12

🏁 16

	M	S	S	S	C	MC	M	RB	S	H	H	S	M	MB	S	S	A	I	Y
Hamilton	PR	P1F	1	P1	P1	2	R	2	1F	3F	3	R	P1F	P1F	1F	P1	1	2F	1
Rosberg	1F	2	P2F	2F	2	P1	P2	1	PR	P1	P4F	P2F	2	R	P2	2	P2	P1	P14

2014 Red Bull RB10

Daniel **Ricciardo**

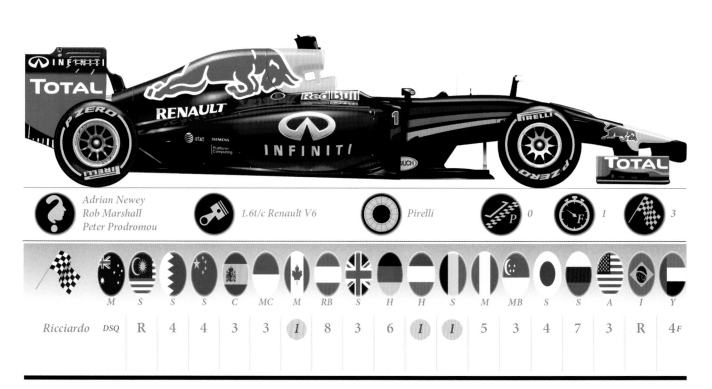

Adrian Newey
Rob Marshall
Peter Prodromou

1.6t/c Renault V6

Pirelli

P 0

F 1

🏁 3

	M	S	S	S	C	MC	M	RB	S	H	H	S	M	MB	S	S	A	I	Y
Ricciardo	DSQ	R	4	4	3	3	1	8	3	6	1	1	5	3	4	7	3	R	4F

2015 Mercedes F1 W06 *Hybrid*

1st

 Lewis **Hamilton**  Nico **Rosberg**

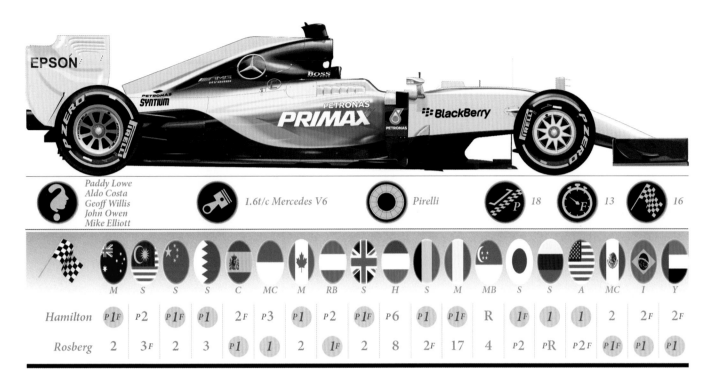

Paddy Lowe
Aldo Costa
Geoff Willis
John Owen
Mike Elliott

1.6t/c Mercedes V6 Pirelli P 18 F 13 16

	M	S	S	S	C	MC	M	RB	S	H	S	M	MB	S	S	A	MC	I	Y
Hamilton	P1F	P2	P1F	P1	2F	P3	P1	P2	P1F	P6	P1	P1F	R	1F	1	1	2	2F	2F
Rosberg	2	3F	2	3	P1	1	2	1F	2	8	2F	17	4	P2	PR	P2F	P1F	P1	P1

2015 Ferrari SF15-T

 Sebastian **Vettel**

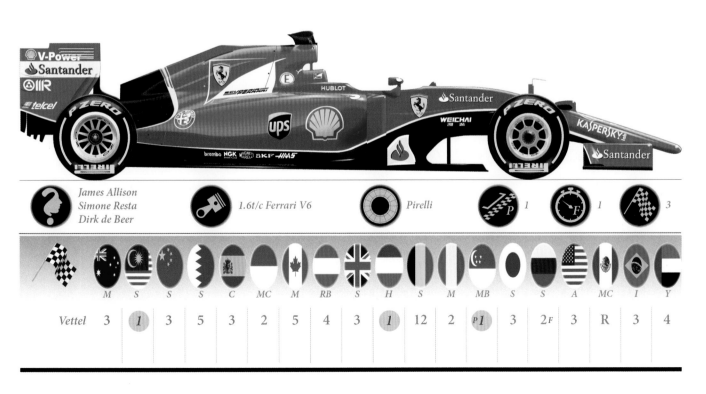

James Allison
Simone Resta
Dirk de Beer

1.6t/c Ferrari V6 Pirelli P 1 F 1 3

	M	S	S	S	C	MC	M	RB	S	H	S	M	MB	S	S	A	MC	I	Y
Vettel	3	1	3	5	3	2	5	4	3	1	12	2	P1	3	2F	3	R	3	4

2016 Mercedes F1 W07 *Hybrid*

1st

 Nico **Rosberg**  Lewis **Hamilton**

Paddy Lowe
Aldo Costa
Geoff Willis
John Owen
Mike Elliott

1.6t/c Mercedes V6 — Pirelli — P 20 — F 9 — 🏁 19

	M	S	S	S	C	MC	M	B	RB	S	H	H	S	M	MB	S	S	A	MC	I	Y
Rosberg	1	1F	P1	P1F	R	7	5F	P1F	4	3F	P2	P4	P1	1	P1	3F	P1	2	2	2	2
Hamilton	P2	P3	7	2	PR	1F	P1	5	P1F	P1	1	1	3F	P2	3	PR	3	P1	P1	P1	P1

2016 Red Bull RB12

 Max **Verstappen**  Daniel **Ricciardo**

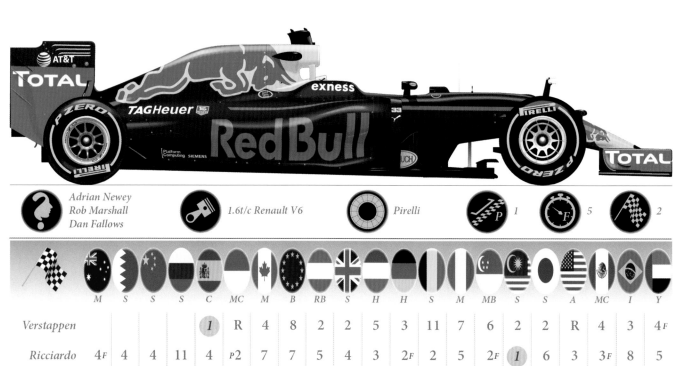

Adrian Newey
Rob Marshall
Dan Fallows

1.6t/c Renault V6 — Pirelli — P 1 — F 5 — 🏁 2

	M	S	S	S	C	MC	M	B	RB	S	H	H	S	M	MB	S	S	A	MC	I	Y
Verstappen					1	R	4	8	2	2	5	3	11	7	6	2	2	R	4	3	4F
Ricciardo	4F	4	4	11	4	P2	7	7	5	4	3	2F	2	5	2F	1	6	3	3F	8	5

2017 Ferrari SF70H

Sebastian *Vettel*

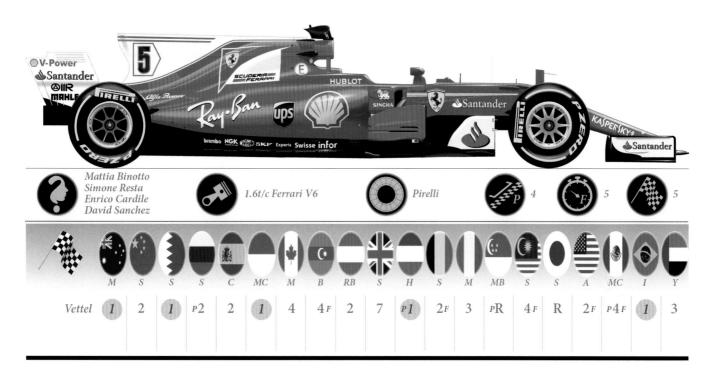

Mattia Binotto Simone Resta Enrico Cardile David Sanchez	1.6t/c Ferrari V6	Pirelli	P 4	F 5	5

	M	S	S	S	C	MC	M	B	RB	S	H	S	M	MB	S	S	A	MC	I	Y
Vettel	1	2	1	P2	2	1	4	4F	2	7	P1	2F	3	PR	4F	R	2F	P4F	1	3

2017 Mercedes AMG F1 W08 EQ Power+

1st

Lewis *Hamilton*   Valtteri *Bottas*

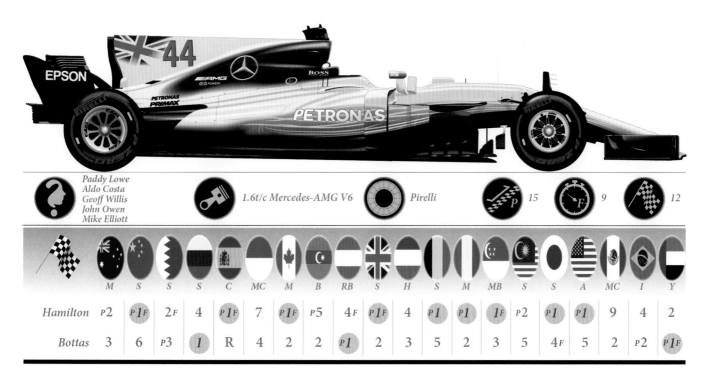

Paddy Lowe Aldo Costa Geoff Willis John Owen Mike Elliott	1.6t/c Mercedes-AMG V6	Pirelli	P 15	F 9	12

	M	S	S	S	C	MC	M	B	RB	S	H	S	M	MB	S	S	A	MC	I	Y
Hamilton	P2	P1F	2F	4	P1F	7	P1F	P5	4F	P1F	4	P1	P1	1F	P2	P1	P1	9	4	2
Bottas	3	6	P3	1	R	4	2	2	P1	2	3	5	2	3	5	4F	5	2	P2	P1F

2017 Red Bull RB13

 Daniel **Ricciardo**  Max **Verstappen**

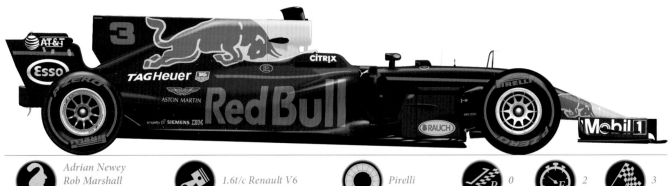

👤 Adrian Newey / Rob Marshall / Dan Fallows   ⚙ 1.6t/c Renault V6   ◉ Pirelli   P 0   F 2   🏁 3

	M	S	S	S	C	MC	M	B	RB	S	H	S	M	MB	S	S	A	MC	I	Y
Ricciardo	R	4	5	R	3	3	3	1	3	5	R	3	4F	2	3	3	R	R	6	R
Verstappen	5	3	R	5	R	5	R	R	R	4	5	R	10	R	1	2	4	1	5F	5

2018 Ferrari SF71H

⬤ Sebastian **Vettel** ✚ Kimi **Räikkönen**

👤 Mattia Binotto / Simone Resta / Enrico Cardile / David Sanchez   ⚙ 1.6t/c Ferrari V6   ◉ Pirelli   P 6   F 3   🏁 5

	M	S	S	B	C	MC	M	PR	RB	S	H	H	S	M	MB	S	S	A	MC	I	Y
Vettel	1	P1	P8	P4	4	2	P1	5	3	1F	PR	2	1	4	3	3	6F				
Räikkönen	3	R	3	2	R	4	6	3	2F	3	3	3	R	P2	5	4	5				

2018 Ferrari SF71H

Sebastian **Vettel** Kimi **Räikkönen**

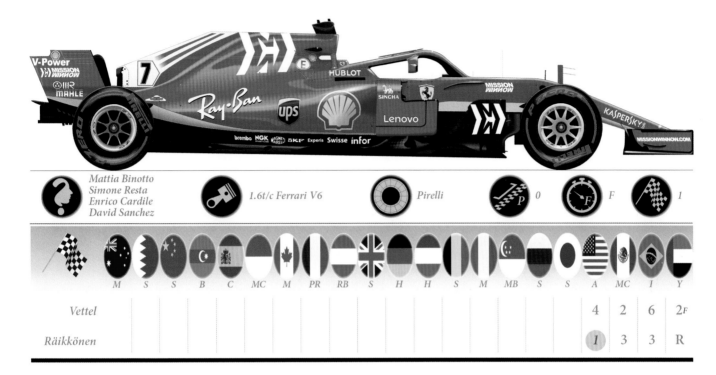

Mattia Binotto Simone Resta Enrico Cardile David Sanchez	1.6t/c Ferrari V6	Pirelli	P 0 F F 1

	M	S	S	B	C	MC	M	PR	RB	S	H	H	S	M	MB	S	S	A	MC	I	Y
Vettel																		4	2	6	2F
Räikkönen																		1	3	3	R

2018 Red Bull RB14

Daniel **Ricciardo** Max **Verstappen**

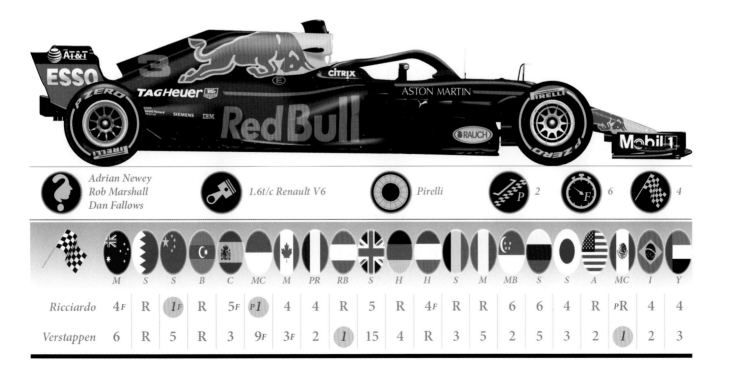

Adrian Newey Rob Marshall Dan Fallows	1.6t/c Renault V6	Pirelli	P 2 F 6 4

	M	S	S	B	C	MC	M	PR	RB	S	H	H	S	M	MB	S	S	A	MC	I	Y
Ricciardo	4F	R	1F	R	5F	P1	4	4	R	5	R	4F	R	R	6	6	4	R	PR	4	4
Verstappen	6	R	5	R	3	9F	3F	2	1	15	4	R	3	5	2	5	3	2	1	2	3

2018 Mercedes AMG F1 W09 EQ Power+

1st

Lewis
Hamilton

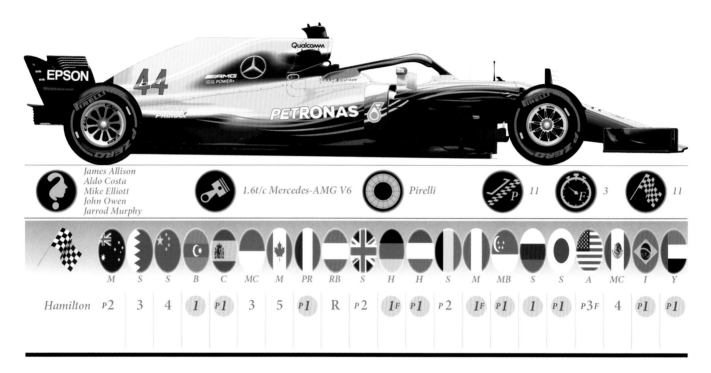

James Allison
Aldo Costa
Mike Elliott
John Owen
Jarrod Murphy

1.6t/c Mercedes-AMG V6   Pirelli   P 11   F 3   11

	M	S	S	B	C	MC	M	PR	RB	S	H	H	S	M	MB	S	S	A	MC	I	Y
Hamilton	P2	3	4	1	P1	3	5	P1	R	P2	1F	P1	P2	1F	P1	1	P1	P3F	4	P1	P1

2019 Mercedes AMG F1 W10 EQ Power+

1st

Lewis
Hamilton

Valtteri
Bottas

James Allison
Aldo Costa
Mike Elliott
John Owen
Jarrod Murphy

1.6t/c Mercedes-AMG V6   Pirelli   P 10   F 9   15

	M	S	S	B	C	MC	M	PR	RB	S	H	H	S	M	MB	S	S	MC	A	I	Y
Hamilton	P2	1	1	2	1F	P1	1	P1	5	1F	P9	1	2	3F	4	1F	3F	1	2	7	P1F
Bottas	1F	2	P2	P1	P2	3	4F	2	3	P2	R	8	3	2	5	2	1	3	P1	RF	4

2019 Red Bull RB15

Max
Verstappen

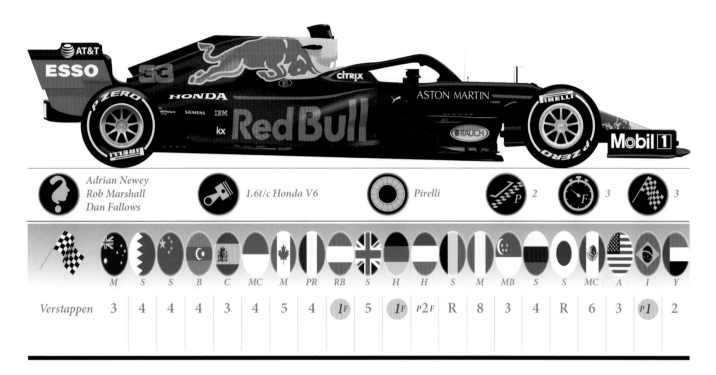

Adrian Newey
Rob Marshall
Dan Fallows — 1.6t/c Honda V6 — Pirelli — P 2 — F 3 — 🏁 3

	M	S	S	B	C	MC	M	PR	RB	S	H	H	S	M	MB	S	S	MC	A	I	Y
Verstappen	3	4	4	4	3	4	5	4	1F	5	1F	P2F	R	8	3	4	R	6	3	P1	2

2019 Ferrari SF90

Charles
Leclerc   Sebastian
Vettel

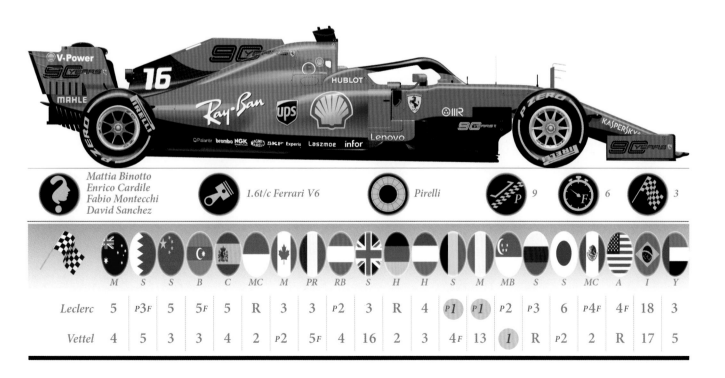

Mattia Binotto
Enrico Cardile
Fabio Montecchi
David Sanchez — 1.6t/c Ferrari V6 — Pirelli — P 9 — F 6 — 🏁 3

	M	S	S	B	C	MC	M	PR	RB	S	H	H	S	M	MB	S	S	MC	A	I	Y
Leclerc	5	P3F	5	5F	5	R	3	3	P2	3	R	4	P1	P1	P2	P3	6	P4F	4F	18	3
Vettel	4	5	3	3	4	2	P2	5F	4	16	2	3	4F	13	1	R	P2	2	R	17	5

2020

2020 marked the 70th anniversary of the F1 championship. It was also the year of the Covid-19 pandemic, which threatened the running of all world sports including the F1 season. In March, the Australian GP was cancelled on the first day of practice much to the dismay of the thousands of fans, followed by the Bahrain and Vietnamese GPs. It wasn't until July that the first race was allowed to be staged in Austria under strict guidelines with no fans in attendance. Valtteri Bottas won the season opener and Mercedes took the first four races. A further sixteen races were planned after a major shake-up of the year's venues. The first upset of the season was Pierre Gasly taking victory at Monza in the AlphaTauri. At Tuscany, Ferrari entered its 1,000 GP but could only manage 8th and 10th positions with Charles Leclerc and Sebastian Vettel respectively. Reigning world champion Lewis Hamilton overtook Michael Schumacher's tally of ninety-one career wins by winning the Portuguese GP, and in the Turkish GP in Istanbul had matched Schumacher's seven world championship titles, with three races remaining. Romain Grosjean crashed out of the Bahrain GP, his car bursting into flames, and ended up in two pieces after splitting the crash barrier. No doubt the halo protection system introduced in 2018 saved his life. Lewis Hamilton was force to miss the 2020 Sakhir GP having tested positive for the Covid-19 virus. There was another surprise when Sergio Perez won, giving him and the Racing Point team their first ever GP win. Again the season was dominated by the 2020 constructor champions Mercedes, driven by Lewis Hamilton and Valtteri Bottas, taking thirteen of the seventeen races between them. Max Verstappen took the honours in the remaining two races including the last race of the 2020 season.

   With the future looking more likely to becoming electric, cars will no doubt continue to evolve and who knows what the cars will look like and what speeds they will reach in the next seventy years.

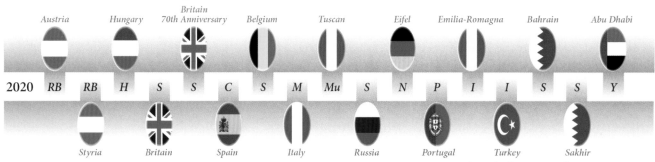

2020 Season race by race.

		Austria	Hungary	Britain 70th Anniversary	Belgium	Tuscan	Eifel	Emilia-Romagna	Bahrain	Abu Dhabi
2020	RB	RB	H	S	S	C	S	M	Mu	S	N	P	I	I	S	S	Y
		Styria	Britain	Spain	Italy	Russia	Portugal	Turkey	Sakhir

for track abbreviations refer to map on pages 6/7

2020 Mercedes-AMG F1 W11 *EQ Performance*

 Lewis **Hamilton**    Valtteri **Bottas**

1st

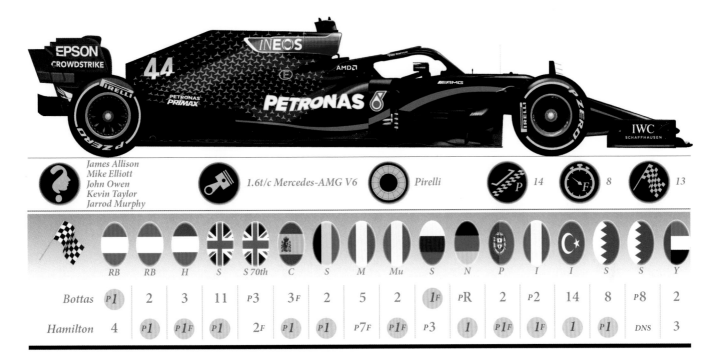

James Allison
Mike Elliott
John Owen
Kevin Taylor
Jarrod Murphy

1.6t/c Mercedes-AMG V6   Pirelli   P 14   F 8   13

	RB	RB	H	S	S 70th	C	S	M	Mu	S	N	P	I	I	S	S	Y
Bottas	P1	2	3	11	P3	3F	2	5	2	1F	PR	2	P2	14	8	P8	2
Hamilton	4	P1	P1F	P1	2F	P1	P1	P7F	P1F	P3	1	P1F	P1F	1	P1	DNS	3

2020 Red Bull RB16

 Max **Verstappen**

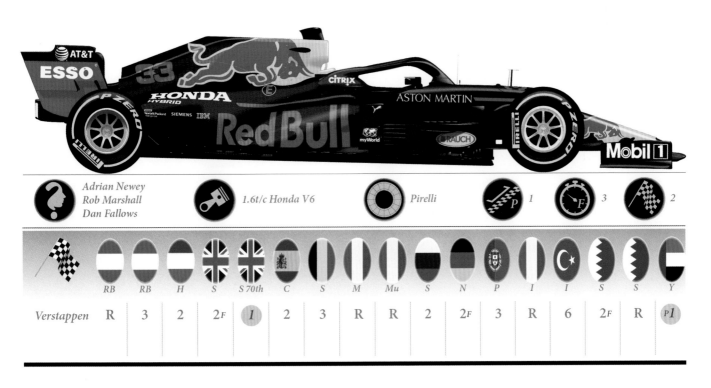

Adrian Newey
Rob Marshall
Dan Fallows

1.6t/c Honda V6   Pirelli   P 1   F 3   2

	RB	RB	H	S	S 70th	C	S	M	Mu	S	N	P	I	I	S	S	Y
Verstappen	R	3	2	2F	1	2	3	R	R	2	2F	3	R	6	2F	R	P1

2020 AlphaTauri AT01

Pierre
Gasly

	Jody Egginton		1.6t/c Honda V6		Pirelli		P 0		F 0		1

		RB	RB	H	S	S 70th	C	S	M	Mu	S	N	P	I	I	S	S	Y
Gasly		7	15	R	7	11	9	8	*1*	R	9	6	5	R	13	6	11	8

2020 Racing Point RP20

Sergio
Perez

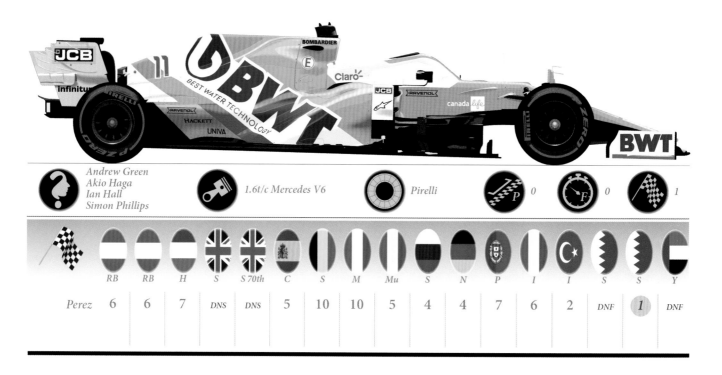

	Andrew Green Akio Haga Ian Hall Simon Phillips		1.6t/c Mercedes V6		Pirelli		P 0		F 0		1

		RB	RB	H	S	S 70th	C	S	M	Mu	S	N	P	I	I	S	S	Y
Perez		6	6	7	DNS	DNS	5	10	10	5	4	4	7	6	2	DNF	*1*	DNF

HELMETS

In the early days of racing, little attention was paid to driver safety, especially head protection. Drivers wore a slim leather cap similar to that worn by fighter pilots. Today, crash helmets have to pass rigorous tests and are not only a vital piece of safety equipment but also the one item that stands drivers apart.

Each driver is instantly recognisable by fans because of their unique helmet design, which over the years has gone from simple designs of stripes and bands to the very busy flashes of colour and sponsorship logos of today.

I have illustrated the winning drivers' helmet designs over the last seventy years. However, for the last decade, as drivers tended to change their helmet designs for every race, I have chosen to illustrate just one helmet for each driver per year unless the design changed dramatically.

1950s

Guiseppe Farina, 1950

Juan Manuel Fangio, 1951

Piero Taruffi, 1952

Alberto Ascari, 1953

José Froilán González, 1954

Juan Manuel Fangio, 1954

Maurice Trintignant, 1955

Stirling Moss, 1955

Luigi Musso, 1956

Tony Brooks, 1957

Mike Hawthorn, 1958

Peter Collins, 1958

Jo Bonnier, 1959

Jack Brabham, 1959

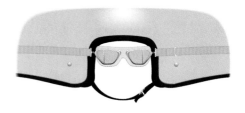

Bruce McLaren, 1959

1960s

Jack Brabham, 1960

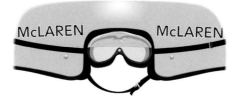

Bruce McLaren, 1960

Giancarlo Baghetti, 1961

Innes Ireland, 1961

Wolfgang Von Trips, 1961

Phil Hill, 1961

Jim Clark, 1962

Graham Hill, 1963

John Surtees, 1963

Lorenzo Bandini, 1964

Dan Gurney, 1964

Richie Ginther, 1965

Jackie Stewart, 1966

Ludovico Scarfiotti, 1966

Denny Hulme, 1967

Pedro Rodriguez, 1967

Jo Siffert, 1968

Jacky Ickx, 1968

1970s

Jochen Rindt, 1969

Jack Brabham, 1970

Jackie Stewart, 1970

Jochen Rindt, 1970

Pedro Rodriguez, 1970

François Cevert, 1971

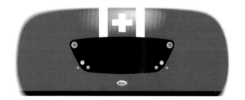

Jo Siffert, 1971

Mario Andretti, 1971

Peter Gethin, 1971

Emerson Fittipaldi, 1972

Jean-Pierre Beltoise, 1972

Jacky Ickx, 1972

Peter Revson, 1973

Ronnie Peterson, 1973

Carlos Reutemann, 1974

Clay Regazzoni, 1974

Denny Hulme, 1974

Niki Lauda, 1974

Carlos Pace, 1975

Jochen Mass, 1975

Vittorio Brambilla, 1975

John Watson, 1976

James Hunt, 1976

Gunnar Nilsson, 1977

Jacques Laffite, 1977

Patrick Depailler, 1978

Gilles Villeneuve, 1978

Mario Andretti, 1978

Jean-Pierre Jabouille, 1979

Alan Jones, 1979

1980s

Jody Scheckter, 1979

Alan Jones, 1980

Nelson Piquet, 1980

Jean-Pierre Jabouille, 1980

Jacques Laffite, 1980

Didier Pironi, 1980

Alain Prost, 1981

Gilles Villeneuve, 1981

John Watson, 1981

Carlos Reutemann, 1982

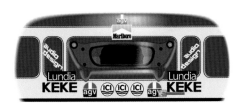

Keke Rosberg, 1982

Niki Lauda, 1982

Patrick Tambay, 1982

Riccardo Patrese, 1982

René Arnoux, 1982

Michele Alboreto, 1983

Niki Lauda, 1984

Nigel Mansell, 1985

Ayrton Senna, 1985

Elio de Angelis, 1985

Gerhard Berger, 1986

Ayrton Senna, 1987

Alain Prost, 1988

Gerhard Berger, 1988

Alessandro Nannini, 1989

Thierry Boutsen, 1989

Nigel Mansell, 1989

Ayrton Senna, 1990

Nelson Piquet, 1990

Thierry Boutsen, 1990

Nigel Mansell, 1992

Riccardo Patrese, 1992

Gerhard Berger, 1992

Alain Prost, 1993

Damon Hill, 1993

Michael Schumacher, 1993

Michael Schumacher, 1994

David Coulthard, 1995

Jean Alesi, 1995

Johnny Herbert, 1995

Damon Hill, 1996

Michael Schumacher, 1996

Olivier Panis, 1996

Heinz-Harald Frentzen, 1997

Jacques Villeneuve, 1997

Damon Hill, 1998

Mika Häkkinen, 1998

Eddie Irvine, 1999

2000s

Michael Schumacher, 2000

Mika Häkkinen, 2001

David Coulthard, 2001

Rubens Barrichello, 2002

Ralf Schumacher, 2002

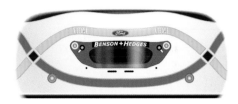

Giancarlo Fisichella, 2003

Juan Pablo Montoya, 2003

Kimi Räikkönen, 2003

Jarno Trulli, 2004

Michael Schumacher, 2004

Fernando Alonso, 2005

Michael Schumacher, 2006

Felipe Massa, 2006

Jenson Button, 2006

Fernando Alonso, 2007

Kimi Räikkönen, 2007

Fernando Alonso, 2008

Lewis Hamilton, 2008

Robert Kubica, 2008

Sebastian Vettel, 2008

Jenson Button, 2009

2010s

Mark Webber, 2009

Fernando Alonso, 2010

Sebastian Vettel, 2010

Jenson Button, 2011

Lewis Hamilton, 2011

Mark Webber, 2012

Lewis Hamilton, 2012

Nico Rosberg, 2012

Pastor Maldonado, 2012

Kimi Räikkönen, 2013

Lewis Hamilton, 2013

Daniel Ricciardo, 2014

Lewis Hamilton, 2014

Sebastian Vettel, 2015

Lewis Hamilton, 2015

Daniel Ricciardo, 2016

Lewis Hamilton, 2016

Max Verstappen, 2016

Nico Rosberg, 2016

Daniel Ricciardo, 2017

Lewis Hamilton, 2017

Max Verstappen, 2017

Sebastian Vettel, 2017

Valtteri Bottas, 2017

Daniel Ricciardo, 2018

Lewis Hamilton, 2018

Kimi Räikkönen, 2018

Max Verstappen, 2018

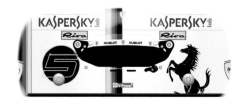

Sebastian Vettel, 2018

Charles Leclerc, 2019

Lewis Hamilton, 2019

Lewis Hamilton, Monaco, 2019

Max Verstappen, 2019

Sebastian Vettel, 2019

Max Verstappen, Austria, 2019

Valtteri Bottas, 2019

2020

Valtteri Bottas, 2020

Lewis Hamilton, 2020

Max Verstappen, 2020

Pierre Gasly, 2020

Sergio Perez, 2020

STICKERS

Not only were the sounds and smells part of the race weekend but as a young fan back in the 1970s I can remember arriving home from the GP and Race of Champions with heaps of stickers, which every team and the JPS ladies would be giving away on a race weekend. As a youngster, my bedroom walls were covered in them. I have included a selection of stickers and advertising logos which for me were a part of the whole racing experience all those years ago, bringing back memories of a bygone age which sadly will never return.

1950s

1960s

1970s

HESKETH RACING

HESKETH

YARDLEY
McLAREN
GRAND PRIX FORMULA 1 TEAM

MOTUL
BRM
FORMULA ONE
CHAMPIONSHIP
TEAM

FINA
Brooke Bond Oxo
Rob Walker
MIKE HAILWOOD

MARTINI
RACING
brabham
ALFA ROMEO

Marlboro World Championship Team
Marlboro
BRM

MAGNETI MARELLI

HEUER

It's
Castrol GTX
for my Ensign
TISSOT

Wolf
Formula One

PENTHOUSE
25

Embassy
RACING
with
Graham Hill

march

SHELL super oil
20w/50

13/14
MAI 1972
MONACO

SKOAL BANDIT
SKOAL BANDIT
RAM GRAND PRIX TEAM
FORMULA ONE WORLD CHAMPIONSHIP

TEXACO
TEXACO
1
TEXACO TEXACO

Grosser Preis von Deutschland
elf Motorenöle rennerprobt
GOOD YEAR
elf
GOOD YEAR
Hockenheim 29. Juli '79

SKOAL BANDIT

fly saudia
SAUDI ARABIAN AIRLINES
Formula One
World Championship Team

GROSSER PREIS VON DEUTSCHLAND
AvD
GOOD YEAR
1. AUGUST 1971 NÜRBURGRING

STP

march

RACING TEAM

65e GRAND PRIX DE FRANCE
CIRCUIT DIJON-PRENOIS
GITANES 26
29-30 JUIN / 1er JUILLET 1979

MONACO
22·23 MAI 1971

Chesterfield
with Brett Lunger

FORMULA ONE
Chesterfield

John Player Team Lotus

NGK SPARK PLUGS

copersucar fittipaldi

fly saudia WILLIAMS
SAUDI ARABIAN AIRLINES
Formula One World Championship Team

ÖSTERREICHRING
ZELTWEG KNITTELFELD

Walter Wolf Racing

SKOAL BANDIT

YARDLEY
TEAM B.R.M.

YARDLEY
TEAM BRM

GOLD LEAF
TEAM LOTUS
WORLD CHAMPIONS 1968-1970

NGK
The spark of genius

Beta UTENSILI
SURTEES

1980s

DENIM
After Shave
1980 F1 World Championship

Grosser Preis von Deutschland
JVC DER ERFINDER DES VHS-VIDEO-SYSTEMS
Hockenheim 8. August '82

CAMPEONATO DEL MUNDO DE FORMULA 1
GRAN PREMIO TIO PEPE DE ESPAÑA
CIRCUITO DE JEREZ

Saudia Leyland
World Champions 1980

GROSSER PREIS VON DEUTSCHLAND
FIATALLIS
HOCKENHEIM 6·7·8 AUGUST '82

84 Championnat du monde
RENAULT elf

SYSTIME
COMPUTER SOLUTIONS

FORMULA 1 IMOLA 88
8° GRAND PRIX SAN MARINO
AUTODROMO DINO FERRARI
C'ERO ANCH'IO CON ANSA marmitte

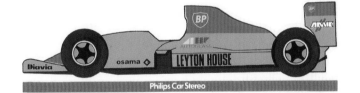

Marlboro

DIJON-PRENOIS

grand prix formule 1 **81**

GRAND PRIX FORMULA 1 **1983**

ZANDVOORT

Marlboro

WORLD CHAMPIONSHIP TEAM

Marlboro British Grand Prix

Britain's round of the FIA World Championship for Drivers

Silverstone

Grand Prix Circuit

JULY 21st 1985

RAC EXPRESS

Marlboro

World Championship Team

Marlboro

Niki Lauda World Champion 1984

Alain Prost Runner - up 1984

McLAREN INTERNATIONAL

80

BRANDS HATCH JULY 13

Marlboro British Grand Prix

FOSTER'S

Adelaide '89

GRAND PRIX

TEAM **COURTAULDS**

World Champions in Technology · Formula One racing with Tyrrell

NORDICA

F1 WORLD CHAMPIONSHIP 1982

LEYTON HOUSE MARCH

GRAND PRIX TEAM

Marlboro

WORLD CHAMPIONSHIP TEAM

Gran Premio d'Italia 1981 Monza

Adelaide Alive 1987

FOSTER'S 1987 AUSTRALIAN FORMULA 1 GRAND PRIX

NOVEMBER 12-15

F1 **Candy**

Toleman TG184

GRAN PREMIO **TIO PEPE** DE ESPANA

CAMPEONATO DEL MUNDO DE FORMULA 1

RENAULT elf FORMULA ONE 1984

Marlboro

DIJON - PRENOIS

grand prix formule 1 **81**

GRAND PRIX FORMULA 1 **1981**

ZANDVOORT

Marlboro

WORLD CHAMPIONSHIP TEAM

TEAM **BARCLAY**

BARCLAY

BARCLAY

ARROWS-BMW

CAMEL

It's fun!

Magny-Cours '95
Red and White Team

Rothmans
Williams RENAULT F1

SG Gigante
GP. PORTUGAL·FORMULA 1

Silverstone
JULY 12th 1992
BRITISH GRAND PRIX

SILVERSTONE **1993** JULY 11th
Canon
BRITISH GRAND PRIX

SUNDAY 10th. JULY 1994

FORMULA 1 WORLD CHAMPIONSHIP TEAM
HITACHI
Castrol
Team Castrol Lotus F1

Benetton
Formula 1
RACING TEAM

WORLD **CHAMPIONSHIP '98**
12th JULY

Team Castrol Lotus F1
HITACHI

WORLD CHAMPION
1
Marlboro
3 TIME 88·90·91
AYRTON · SENNA

Rothmans
Rothmans RACING
Williams RENAULT

MONZA '94 - 65° GRAN PREMIO D'ITALIA
Marlboro
POLE POSITION!

Canon Williams Team

Marlboro
Grand Prix Action
Monaco '97

Beta
24
minardi F1 team

Marlboro Monaco 1992
World Championship Team

1991 FIA FORMULA 1 WORLD CHAMPIONSHIP
HUNGARIAN GP
HONDA WINS
HONDA
F-1 GRAND-PRIX RACING TEAM

TOTAL
Jordan
PEUGEOT F1

F1 Formula 1
GRAND PRIX DE MONACO
25-28 MAI 1995
MILD SEVEN

Simtek
G R A N D   P R I X

BENSON & HEDGES
JORDAN
Honda

G.P. of Belgium '92
Marlboro
Shell
Marlboro
World Championship Team

BMW. WilliamsF1 Team

MILD SEVEN
Benetton Formula 1
RACING TEAM
RENAULT *sport*

TEAM
Rothmans
Williams RENAULT

Williams
Winfield

2000s

2010s

FATAL ACCIDENTS

Driver/Nationality		Track		Date of accident	Fatalities other than driver
Cameron Earl	🇬🇧	MIRA Nuneaton	T	1952 June 18	
Charles de Tornaco	🇧🇪	Modena	P	1953 September 18	
Onofre Marimón	🇦🇷	Nürburgring	P	1954 July 31	
Mario Aalborghetti	🇮🇹	Pau	P	1955 April 11	
Eugenio Castellotti	🇮🇹	Modena	T	1957 March 14	
Luigi Musso	🇮🇹	Reims	R	1958 July 6	
Peter Collins	🇬🇧	Nürburgring	R	1958 August 3	
Stuart Lewis-Evans	🇬🇧	Ain-Diab	R	1958 October 19	
Chris Bristow	🇬🇧	Spa	R	1960 June 19	
Alan Stacey	🇬🇧	Spa	R	1960 June 19	
Giulio Cabianca	🇮🇹	Modena	T	1961 June 15	Eugenio Stefani, Ivo Messori, Gino Arboresi*
Wolfgang von Trips	🇩🇪	Monza	R	1961 September 10	Claudina Polognoli, Giuseppina Lenti, Paolo Perazzone, Albino Albertini, Franz Waldvogel, Laura Zorzi, Luigi Fassi, Luigi Motta, Franca Duguet, Augusto Camillo Valleise, Rinaldo Girod, Roberto Brambilla, Mario Brambilla, Luigi Freschi, Renato Janin. (all Spectators)
Ricardo Rodríguez	🇲🇽	Mexico City	P	1962 November 1	
Carel Godin de Beaufort	🇳🇱	Nürburgring	P	1964 August 2	
John Taylor	🇬🇧	Nürburgring	R	1966 August 7	
Lorenzo Bandini	🇮🇹	Monaco	R	1967 May 7	
Bob Anderson	🇬🇧	Silverstone	T	1967 August 14	
Jo Schlesser	🇫🇷	Rouen	R	1968 July 7	
Gerhard Mitter	🇩🇪	Nürburgring	R	1969 August 1	
Piers Courage	🇬🇧	Zandvoort	R	1970 June 21	
Jochen Rindt	🇦🇹	Monza	Q	1970 September 5	
Jo Siffert	🇨🇭	Brands Hatch	R	1971 October 24	
Roger Williamson	🇬🇧	Zandvoort	R	1973 July 29	
François Cevert	🇫🇷	Watkins Glen	Q	1973 October 6	
Peter Revson	🇺🇸	Kyalami	T	1974 March 22	
Helmut Koinigg	🇦🇹	Watkins Glen	R	1974 October 6	
Mark Donohue	🇺🇸	Österreichring	P	1975 August 17	Manfred Schaller (M)
Tom Pryce	🇬🇧	Kyalami	R	1977 March 5	Frederick Jansen van Vuuren (M)
Brian McGuire	🇦🇺	Brands Hatch	P	1977 August 29	John Thorpe (M)
Ronnie Peterson	🇸🇪	Monza	R	1978 September 10	
Patrick Depailler	🇫🇷	Hockenheim	T	1980 August 1	
Gilles Villeneuve	🇨🇦	Zolder	Q	1982 May 8	
Ricardo Paletti	🇮🇹	Montréal	R	1982 June 13	
Elio de Angelis	🇮🇹	Paul Ricard	T	1986 May 14	
Roland Ratzenberger	🇦🇹	Monza	Q	1994 April 30	
Ayrton Senna	🇧🇷	Monza	R	1994 May 1	
Jules Bianchi	🇫🇷	Suzuka	R	2014 October 5 died 2015 July 17	

*Cabianca crashed through gate onto public road killing the 3 occupants of a passing taxi.

(P) Practice (Q) Qualifying
(R) Race (T) Testing
(F) Firefighter (J) Journalist
(M) Marshal (m) Mechanic
(P) Photographer (S) Spectator

Other Accidents/Fatalities
**Driver survived

1953 January 18 Buenos Aires. Claudio Enrique Rivas (S) Rubén Carrillo (S) Juan Gallo (S) Ítalo Gallo (S) Elvio Ulises Etchegaray (S) Hugo Valdés (S) Juan José Temprano (S) Oscar Argentino Cabret (S) Struck by Giuseppe Farina** 2 Unknown (S) Killed when ambulance entered the circuit.

1958 January 22 Mike Hawthorn killed in high speed crash in Surrey.   1968 April 7 Hockenheim. Jim Clark was killed driving in a wet formula 2 race.

1970 June 2 Goodwood. Bruce Mclaren killed testing McLaren M8D.   1971 July 11 Norisring. Pedro Rodríguez killed in sports car race.

1975 April 27 Montjuïc. Joaquín Morera Benaches (F) Antonio Font Bayarri (J) Mario De Roia (J) Andrés Ruiz Villanova (S) Struck by Rolf Stommelen**

1975 November 29 Graham Hill, Tony Brise, Andy Smallman, Ray Brimble, Tony Alcock and Terry Richards killed in aircraft accident.

1976 August 1 Nürburgring. Niki Lauda** crashed and seriously burnt after being trapped in his Ferrari, weeks later he took 4th place at Monza.

1977 March 18 Carlos Pace was killed in a light aircraft accident.   1977 July 16 David Purley** seriously injured in practice for the British GP.

1977 October 23 Fuji. Kazuhiro Ohashi (P) Kengo Yuasa (M) Struck by Gilles Villeneuve**

1981 May 17 Zolder. Giovanni Amadeo (m) Struck by Carlos Reutemann** in the pits.

1982 August 7 Didier Pironi** seriously injured in practice for the German GP.   1985 July 2 David Purley killed in aerobatic biplane accident.

1987 August 23 Didier Pironi killed in a power boat race off the Isle of Wight.

2000 June 24 Goodwood. Andrew Carpenter (M) Struck by John Dawson-Damer.   2000 September 10 Monza. Paola Gislimberti (M) Hit by flying wheel.

2001 March 4 Albert Park. Graham Beveridge (M) Hit by flying wheel.   2013 June 9 Montréal. Mark Robinson (M) Run over by a recovery vehicle.

ACKNOWLEDGEMENTS

Thanks to: Peter Warr of Lotus for giving me the opportunity to produce my first cutaway of an F1 car, the Lotus 97T. My good friend Bob Draper for his constructive criticism, help and motivation over the years. The late Keith Arney from Brands Hatch for gaining me access to the pits when the F1s were in town. Keith Underwood for allowing me to showcase my artwork in his Brands Hatch shop. Joe Stewart for his enthusiasm, support and positive attitude.

Special thanks to my wife, Pauline, for putting up with me being tucked away every spare moment in my studio for the past four years, evenings and weekends, and for all the typing. Thanks also goes to my family – Michael, Amelia, Calum, Lawrence, Kate and Barney – for their encouragement. Finally, to my grandchildren Emily, Adelynn, Pippa and Penny – your smiles kept me going.

'Unless I'm very much mistaken ... I am very much mistaken.'

Another part of the Grand Prix scene over the last 70 years was Murray Walker, whose commentating was the voice of F1 for as long as I can remember. The news that he had passed away in March 2021 was indeed another sad day in motorsport. Thanks, Murray, for the great memories and your contribution to the first 70 years of F1.

CREDITS

Motorsportmemorial.org for the facts and figures regarding the records of fatalities.

Grand Prix's Winning Colours is not affiliated with or in any way endorsed by Formula 1, the Formula 1 teams, Formula 1 Management, or any other organisation or entity associated with the official Formula 1 governing organisations or their shareholders.